GOVERNING JERUSALEM

GOVERNING JERUSALEM

AGAIN ON THE WORLD'S AGENDA

Ira Sharkansky

WAYNE STATE UNIVERSITY PRESS DETROIT

99 98 97 96 5 4 3 2 1

Library of Congress Cataloging-in-Publication Data

Sharkansky, Ira.
Governing Jerusalem : again on the world's agenda / Ira Sharkansky.
p. cm.
Includes bibliographical references and index.
ISBN 0-8143-2592-0 (alk. paper)
1. Jerusalem—Politics and government. 2. Jerusalem—History.
I. Title.
JS7499.I83J477 1996
956.94'42—dc20 95-41561

For Varda, Tamar, and Mattan

There can be no promotion after Jerusalem.
Sir Ronald Storrs, first British Military Governor of Jerusalem, 1939

It is a city whose very name evokes deep emotions.
Teddy Kollek, Mayor of Jerusalem, 1966–93

Jerusalem is a city of problems, of continuous war.
If there is a moment of quiet, it seems likely to be
the lull before the storm.
Ruth Cheshen, Manager of the Jerusalem Foundation, 1991

Few other questions of our time have so deeply moved
the world conscience and so gravely threatened world peace
as the Zionist usurpation and continued occupation of
Jerusalem and Palestine.
Islamic Council of Europe, 1980

Contents

Preface

Since I joined the Hebrew University in 1975 I knew that I would write about Jerusalem, sooner or later. Local politics had been the subject of my undergraduate and master's theses, and a textbook that I coauthored for American undergraduates. The charms of Jerusalem were prominent among the attractions that brought me to Israel. The city's importance fits the epigram attributed to the late Speaker of the United States House of Representatives, Thomas P. "Tip" O'Neill, that all politics are local politics. However, Jerusalem stretches beyond the meaning that details of neighborhoods and personalities affects who gets what. The importance of Jerusalem in Jewish history makes it a key issue in national policy, even though the city is not the economic center of the country, and may not be the cultural capital. The importance of Jerusalem to others renders its politics international as well as local and national.

The small size of Israel and Jerusalem, and their location at a meeting point of cultures, add to the tensions and excitement of the city. I write these words less than a week after the kidnapping of an Israeli soldier ended with an attack on the house where he was being held captive. That occurred only 5 kilometers (3 miles) from my home, in a Palestinian village that has caused numerous problems for Israeli security forces. Only two days later Israeli and Jordanian officials initialed a peace treaty. That occurred in the Jordanian capital of Amman, 70 kilometers (40 miles) distance. Three thousand years earlier, it was at Rabbat Amon, more or less the same place, where the soldiers of King David were fighting when he looked over his balcony to see Bathsheba bathing on the roof of her house. During the telecast of the treaty ceremony, I went out on my balcony and saw the lights of Amman on the other side of the Jordan Valley. The next night, the Israeli bus company advertised a new service from Jerusalem to Amman for the equivalent of US $4. Cairo is about 400 kilometers (240 miles) to the southeast; Beirut 250 kilometers (150 miles) to the north; and Damascus 230 kilometers (140 miles) to the northeast. The Gaza Strip is 60 kilometers (36 miles) in the direction of Cairo. The West Bank is across the street to the north, east, and south.

Jerusalem's history has seen numerous points of dynamism between long periods of dormancy. The governments of Israel, Jordan, Lebanon, Syria, and Palestinians have been negotiating the disputes among them since 1991. Israeli officials have proclaimed that the status of Jerusalem as the undivided capital of Israel is not on the agenda for negotiations. Yet they have negotiated about negotiating about Jerusalem. They have signed documents containing Palestinian demands to settle their claims with respect to Jerusalem at a later date. And they have annoyed the Palestinians by supporting Jordan's claims with respect to Moslem holy sites in the city. Numerous Christian Churches and Moslem religious authorities have their own agendas for Jerusalem.

The title and subtitle of this book emphasize the interface of municipal and world politics. A construction project to meet neighborhood needs or improve crosstown traffic, or the municipality's response to a family that causes trouble by moving into "someone else's" neighborhood must be planned with an eye to passions and crusades. Israel governs the city as a mission that must justify itself. A strong army with many accomplishments does not overcome the insecurities of Jewish history.

A political scientist should avoid predictions for a setting that seems bound to be fluid. Several of the biblical prophets operated in this city. However, much of what they did was criticize the political and economic elites, rather than predict the future. According to the rabbis, there has been no prophet since Malachi, who prophesied sometime during the period 516–450 B.C.E.

Israel was garrisoned against numerous enemies when I began to collect materials. Teddy Kollek seemed a fixture in the mayor's office, and his comments about Likud ministers in the national government added spice to the local scene. Now there is a Likud mayor and a Labor prime minister. Peace beckons, but there is much to be settled, or perhaps to be avoided in a formal settlement. In mid-October 1994 the whole peace process seemed on the verge of collapse when Israel worried for a week about a soldier kidnapped and then killed by Moslem fundamentalists. Then there was joy after the signing of a peace treaty with Jordan, followed by national rage at a bus bombing in Tel Aviv that killed more than twenty. Rabin's party is by no means assured of victory in the next national elections. A Likud government might deal differently with the issue of Jerusalem. And it is not clear that Rabin and his Labor Party colleagues are inclined to be generous with the Palestinians on the issue of Jerusalem.

This book is being written with an eye to competing claims about the future. Rather than focus on what might happen, I seek to understand the city's governance by focusing on the period since 1967, against events and emotions much older. The emphasis is empirical rather than normative. In two chapters I survey the city's history with an intention to understand the present. In subsequent chapters I describe the institutions of Israeli government that are relevant to the city; the social, economic, and political setting in which governance occurs; and the style and substance of policymaking for Jerusalem. In the final chapter I evaluate the quality of recent governance, describe issues that are prominent on the agendas of one or another interested party, and offer alternate scenarios of what might happen. The influences will come from local and national, as well as regional and global events. Whatever happens, the residents and officials of Jerusalem will continue to cope with issues that are bound to create tensions. Participants and observers might add the materials here to the briefing book that they assemble if serious negotiations on Jerusalem come to the fore.

I began and end the book with aspirations that compete with one another. I have tried to capture the unique traits of Jerusalem and to relate its politics to what has been written about other cities throughout the world. The drama of the peace process draws me to link what I have described to what might occur. Yet I also aspire to write a book that will have some significance even if I miss the mark in scenarios that look toward the future. The great bulk of this book concerns the recent past and the description of patterns that lie behind individual events. They should help the reader understand what transpires, no matter what choices are made about individual issues. History indicates that Jerusalem will survive those who contend for it. The literature of incremental politics, composed in more secure polities, leads us to expect that changes will be marginal. Yet the same literature provides for rare changes that are profound.

Residence in this city of almost twenty years has provided me with close exposure to dramatic events and personalities. The labels of university colleagues, students, contacts in government, friends, and family members are blurred as several individuals fit more than one of those categories. I have developed my ideas and collected data from structured interviews, official documents, scholarly studies, the mass media, and casual conversations. Most of this activity has occurred in Jerusalem, but some has been done in distant countries among individuals interested in the city and passionate about it. An invitation by Efraim Ben-Zadok to contribute a chapter to

Local Communities and the Israeli Polity led me to start assembling materials systematically. Along the way I also contributed articles to *Jerusalem Journal of International Relations, CITIES, The Journal of Conflict Studies,* and *Policy and Politics.* My obligations to individuals and institutions are too many to recall without risking omissions. And some who have helped might not want to be associated with the project. The dedication is for the three Jerusalemites who are closest to me. They have added to my understanding of the city by daily stories of what has happened, and how they have responded.

This book reached final page proofs in November, just one week after the assassination of Prime Minister Yitzhak Rabin. During that week the Israeli media provided one extended discussion, often at an impressive intellectual level, concerned with the various individuals, groups, and social conditions that contributed to the killing, and its implications. Yassir Arafat and other leaders of the Palestinian Authority joined the King of Jordan and the President of Egypt, as well as ranking officials of many other countries in expressing condolences to the Rabin family and the people of Israel.

Hatred against the Israeli government, and especially the prime minister expressed by certain religious and nationalist Jews derived from arrangements made with the Palestinian Authority. Much of the discussion in the period following the killing dealt with the significance of the biblical Land of Israel, how much of that imprecise landscape could be bargained away to those perceived as recent terrorists for the promise of peace, and how Jews should conduct their disputes about these issues. To date the negotiations with the Palestinians had not reached the even more sensitive issues concerned with Jerusalem.

Although it is too early to express serious conclusions about the implications of the assassination for the future of Israel and the Middle East, it appears relevant to several themes of this book, especially those concerned with the vulnerability of Jerusalem to intense passions, and the lack of certainty that anyone should express about to its future.

CHAPTER 1

A Distinctive and Problematic City

Jerusalem is a city like thousands of others, with problems of crowded neighborhoods, inadequate schools, water shortages, competing demands for land use, and a budget that cannot provide for all the needs. Residents of poor neighborhoods complain about the favoritism shown toward the wealthy. Building projects threaten to spoil the skyline, produce more congestion and pollution. Streets created years ago cannot accommodate traffic and parking. Social tensions set Arabs against Jews, and religious against secular Jews.

There is Jerusalem above and Jerusalem below. Jerusalem above refers to the Holy City. Religious Jews believe that the Messiah will come, perhaps today, and cause the city to reappear in its biblical glory. When secular people speak about Jerusalem above, they mean an ideal city that must be better than others architecturally and socially. Jerusalem below refers to the earthly city, with its sounds of traffic, the scurry of cats around the garbage, and the tensions of political competition about emotional issues.

This book focuses on Jerusalem below. Because of the images associated with Jerusalem above, however, as well as the city's place at the focus of international dispute, the earthly city cannot be like other places. Israelis, overseas Jews, and Gentiles expect more from Jerusalem than from other cities. Some only want it to be better than other cities. Others want to take the city from the Jews.

Jerusalem's history has not been peaceful despite the view that its name is a composite of Semitic words for "city" (ir) and "peace" (shalom). Over the course of 3,000 to 4,000 years it has been controlled by Canaanites, Jebusites, Israelites, Assyrians, Egyptians, Babylonians, Persians, Romans, Byzantines, Arabs, Seljuks, Crusaders, Mamluks, Ottomans, British, Jordanians, and Israelis.[1] Transitions from one ruler to the next were usually bloody. By one count the city has been besieged and conquered thirty-seven times.[2] Some conquerors were ousted and returned more than once. The Mongols were "almost conquerors," turned back by the Mamluks in 1260 at Nablus, 25 kilometers to the north.

There is no end to the conflict in sight. Jerusalem has been united under Israeli rule since 1967 but is heavily patrolled by security forces. There are car burnings, stone throwings, knifings, or attempted bombings, most often at the meeting points between Palestinian and Jewish neighborhoods. These are usually the work of Palestinians intent on harming Jews or their property, but there is also violence conducted by individual Jews against Arabs and their property. Palestinians assert that the actions of Israel's security forces are prominent in the city's violence, and outweigh acts of terror committed by individual Palestinians.

JERUSALEM AND OTHER CITIES

Jerusalem shares some of the traits that appear in numerous other cities, and themes in the writing about cities have guided this book. On features that are most important in its governance, however, Jerusalem is an outlier or a counterexample with respect to prominent cities.

The officials of Jerusalem, like those of other cities, deal with policymaking and service delivery. Unlike national authorities, those of cities cannot enjoy the luxury of formulating policy on high and sending it out for some other officials to wrestle with the problems of implementation.

As in other cities, Jerusalem's officials contend with congestion, decaying neighborhoods, complaints about schools, housing, and job opportunities, inequities between neighborhoods, inadequate resources in the public sector, and a lack of authority to deal with local issues.[3] Critics accuse them of avoiding basic problems and of ineffective program implementation.[4]

Local government in Israel resembles European patterns more than those of the United States. The laws provide a minimum of local autonomy. Municipal authorities are primarily concerned with the collection of revenues and delivery of services as defined by national policies and supervised by bureaucrats of national ministries. Within these constraints, local officials may be able to stretch their resources by means of creative financial schemes and quasi-governmental authorities,[5] or by a concerted effort to exploit their cities' special advantages.[6] Local bureaucracies have a greater impact on the services provided by the municipality than local interest groups, political parties, or elected members of the city council. The mayor, though the most prominent figure in the locality, often comes up against forces originating elsewhere.[7]

Jerusalem differs most clearly from other major cities with respect to its economy. The concept of "global cities" has been applied to centers of industry, finance, or commerce typically involved in international networks with other cities, and dominating hinterlands that supply labor, markets, and raw materials.[8] Jerusalem has acquired its status on the world stage despite its economic weakness. Unless one subscribes to the canard, *Protocols of the Elders of Zion,* which anti-Semites created and quoted to justify their view that a cabal of Jews rules the world economically and politically, neither Jerusalem nor Israel is a successful enterprise. The national balance of payments is chronically negative, annual inflation was between 100 and 400 percent during the early 1980s and more recently has been considered modest at 10–20 percent. The city's economy depends on donations sent from overseas, and the budget allocations of a national government concerned to maintain Israel's hold over the city. The workforce is heavily engaged in the provision of government and other public services. Bureaucrats and politicians are more prominent than private capital or business firms.

There is, to be sure, an economic element to the conflict between the city's communities. The city's Jews are significantly better off than the Palestinians, and policies for Jerusalem favor Jews over non-Jews. The Palestinian minority protests against the regime it considers illegitimate by abstaining from political activity within the national or municipal frameworks, and thereby forgoes what might be substantial leverage over economic issues. Jerusalem's population growth has made it more important economically in modern Israel than in all previous regimes back to the city's destruction by the Romans. Individual entrepreneurs apply pressure on local and national officials in order to facilitate their projects. Yet the motive forces of Jerusalem policymaking are more likely to be national and religious than a seeking-after economic advantage.

Related to the weight of religion and nationalism is the importance of the city's history. Without its history, Jerusalem would be a provincial town in the Judean mountains. The city's history clarifies its current separation into Jewish, Palestinian, Moslem, and Christian orbits, and the intensity with which each seeks to remain apart from the others. Contemporary policymakers and commentators argue about what should have been done two thousand years ago when the prime actors were Jews and Romans, or nine hundred years ago between Moslems and Christians, and what might happen now if those lessons are not heeded.

On some dimensions, the case of Jerusalem is one of governing at its most difficult. The city's violence is not random assault and killing but the actions of dedicated individuals who seek to overthrow the regime. In other respects, the very depth of Jerusalem's problems makes some tasks of its governors easier. The appeal of the city to its majority, to the national government and overseas supporters, provides an inflow of resources that allows the municipality to be generous in a country that is penurious. Insofar as the opposing minority has taken itself out of the political system, the resources available for conventional urban services can be distributed to the supportive majority even more than their numbers warrant. This cannot help but add to the outrage of the already disaffected minority. Thus, the financial ease of the local policymakers adds to their problems of physical security.

The severity of social and political tensions that surround the government of Jerusalem not only make it an archetypal city on these dimensions but make it different from other cities with social problems. The basic issues of sovereignty and the legitimacy of the current regime are questioned as in few other places. They render the question "Whose city is it?" more pressing than "Who gets what?" and "How?"

Jews see Jerusalem as the place where David placed the Holy Ark, Solomon built the Temple, and the Jews rebuilt it when they returned from the Babylonian exile. It has served as the focus of Jewish aspirations while under foreign rule for most of the time from 587 B.C.E.[9] For Christians it is the place of Christ's agony. For Moslems, it is the locale of Mohammed's ascent to heaven, and the religious center of an Arab region. Various names and laws of the Almighty are cited in defense of what must and what must not happen in policymaking forums as well as by individuals who seek to kill one another on the city's streets. The spiritual character of the city affects the high proportion of emotion, and the struggles of pragmatists. Were Jerusalem a commercial or political center, elites might be better able to work out a deal and share power.

Conflicting claims of historical rights have been part of Jerusalem's environment, at least since its control by the Persians 2,500 years ago. The Book of Ezra reports the rivalry between Jewish returnees from exile and people of the land who opposed their activities by sending complaints to the imperial capital.[10] About one thousand years later, when Persians were at another of their historical high points and had taken Jerusalem from the Byzantines, the Jews sought imperial authority to rebuild their Temple. At the same time, a delegation of Christians sought to have Jews barred from living in Jerusalem. Christian and Moslem conquerors alternately took over the same holy shrines in the eleventh and twelfth centuries. Roman Catholic and Greek Orthodox priests have shed one another's blood, and provided a reason for the Crimean War by their competition over the Church of the Holy Sepulcher. The British failed to arbitrate between Jews and Arabs, and cast off their mandate to govern what some call the city of peace.

Montreal, Belfast, and several cities in the United States might be compared to Jerusalem, with each demonstrating their own approaches to heterogeneity and conflict. Nicosia and Berlin, along with Jerusalem, have been divided between competing national governments. London, Paris, and Moscow resemble Jerusalem in being the central jewels of their nations, attracting disproportionate investment in public buildings, parks, and monuments. Rome is the world center of a faith whose adherents have been generous with their money and their art. Mecca and Bangkok also attract religious pilgrims. New York resembles Jerusalem among American cities in having the benefit of public sector entrepreneurs who have been creative in producing quasi-governmental organizations that add to the city's resources.

There are problems with each of these candidates for city-to-city comparisons. Mecca is closed to unbelievers, which limits research into local politics. Bangkok's sex industry may now attract more visitors than its religious shrines. New York, London, Paris, and Montreal are economic centers far wealthier than Jerusalem and all of Israel. Rome is not the focus of competitive national movements, each wanting it for their capital city. Belfast and Nicosia lack the appeals and the problems of Jerusalem's holy sites. Such issues must be taken into consideration by anyone who would view Jerusalem in a comparative context.

Several traits of Jerusalem that will be detailed in this book help to set its politics and policymaking apart from other cities.

· Jerusalem has been supported by foreign donors who contribute the equivalent of 15 percent of the city's budget. As will be shown, these donations are different from the moneys given to museums, universities, and other public institutions in more typical cities. During the tenure of Teddy Kollek, the Jerusalem Foundation collected these sums, almost entirely from individuals who did not live in Jerusalem or Israel, for the mayor to allocate pretty much as he wished.

· Jerusalem has been governed by considerations of international relations as much as by municipal administration. Israel's control of the city has been a major item on the country's agenda of foreign policy.

· The city has a history of three to four thousand years, with numerous invasions and changes of regime.

· The city was the target of multinational crusades by Christians in the middle ages; and more recently by competing groups of Moslems and Jews. The struggle for control over Jerusalem hardly resembles that in other cities where social groupings, economic sectors, and national and local officeholders compete over the issue of who should control. In Jerusalem's case it is a fight about national sovereignty, involving military alliances, conventional armies and terror, and possibly the question of giving monopolistic control to one group and throwing the losers out or slaughtering them locally. A "crusade" in Jerusalem is more weighty than that waged by one or another grouping in other cities, although the word might be the same.

· Jerusalem is again at the focus of world attention. Israeli officials say their control of the national capital is not to be negotiated, but their actions belie the assertion. The reading of this book may be viewed as an exercise in preparation for another occasion of tension and perhaps dramatic movement in a long history.

With all its problems, Jerusalem's social frictions are arguably less severe than in New York, Belfast, or numerous swarming cities of the Third World. Social tensions are partly neutralized by groups' mutual disdain and avoidance of one another. Palestinians and Jews, as well as secular and ultra-Orthodox Jews prefer their own neighborhoods, schools, shopping areas, and newspapers. The city is a collection of ghettoes, mostly self-imposed.[11] When violence does occur, it tends to be on the seams between Palestinian and Jewish neighborhoods, where those seeking to provoke or retaliate encounter members of the target group. Palestinians opt out of Israeli politics, and render themselves passive in a democracy where other groups demand and receive benefits. Palestinians' violence has legitimized their marginal status in the eyes of many Israelis.

Jerusalem has other features that mark it off from the prominent traits of other cities. While many urban areas have suffered from excess population growth, Jerusalem continues to encourage the immigration of Jews. And while other metropolitan areas are troubled by tensions between the central city and the suburbs, Israel has expanded Jerusalem's boundaries in order to include new suburbs. The concern is to create a city that is largely Jewish (more than 70 percent of the population), by keeping Jewish suburbs within the Jerusalem municipality. To find metropolitan problems of conflicts between the central city and suburbs in Israel that are more typical of North America or Western Europe, one must look to Tel Aviv and Haifa. Much of Jerusalem's hinterland is Palestinian, but most of the Palestinian hinterland has been excluded from Jerusalem's boundaries.

Jerusalem's restive minority has powerful allies close at hand. Yet Arab governments may have tired of armed struggle, and they sometimes seem tired of Palestinian obstinacy. Many Israelis are also tired of low-level violence and the tension of "no peace, no war." Yet there is no clear indication that the Israeli government or large numbers of Israelis are willing to negotiate away their control over Jerusalem. Neither is it clear that they can achieve a lasting settlement of their disputes with Palestinians or other Arabs without significant concessions about Jerusalem.

The history of conflict as to who should control the city and the intensity of present contenders weigh heavily on those currently in charge. Repeated assertions that Jerusalem will remain the united capital of Israel remind observers that those who make the statement may not be able to assure it, and may not feel confident about the power that they wield. The style of policymaking for Jerusalem is one that reacts to crises, copes, and produces temporary and partial solutions. These may be features of urban policymaking generally, but they are especially prominent in Jerusalem.

An optimistic view is that Jewish history has prepared the current rulers for their tasks. Jews may have learned to cope with unresolved issues better than their competitors for ruling Jerusalem. The city's growth and prosperity under Israeli rule may be built on a shaky foundation. Nevertheless, the record of population growth and construction during the most recent half-century has been more impressive than anything since the era of Herod (37–4 B.C.E.), or Solomon (c. 965–27 B.C.E.).

Describing Israel's governing of Jerusalem is no less complicated than the governing itself. Neither the description nor the governing can avoid contentious perspectives and hostile reactions. Early drafts of this book were termed by different readers as apologies for the Israeli regime and as making dangerous concessions to Palestinian nationalism. Both criticisms seem inevitable for a book that seeks to identify the key problems and characteristics of Israel's governing of Jerusalem, and takes as one starting point of its analysis the partial legitimacy accorded to the Israeli regime in the city.

Political realities advise that the governing of Jerusalem be described in large measure from the Israeli perspective. This is necessary because of the decisions made by the vast majority of Palestinian Jerusalemites to avoid the acceptance of Israeli citizenship (which is required for participation in national elections) and to avoid voting in municipal elections (available to noncitizens who are municipal residents). Also significant are the efforts of Israeli officials to define the city's borders in a way to keep many Palestinians outside those borders. These actions render the Israeli regime in the city almost entirely Jewish. They marginalize Palestinians' perspectives about the regime that they have chosen not to join. Yet it is a margin that weighs heavily on Israeli authorities, and is responsible for numerous actions they have taken, and options they have avoided.

There is a prominent strain of ambivalence in Israeli attitudes towards the Palestinians of Jerusalem. There have been several efforts to provide material benefits to the Palestinian community and to involve Palestinians in the city's politics and administration. To date, Israeli calls on Palestinians to take part in municipal politics have gone largely unheeded. At times Israelis express frustration at the rejection, but at other times they express a recognition that Palestinians have their own national aspirations that cause them to keep their distance from the Israeli regime. There have also been Israeli efforts to assure Jewish dominance of Jerusalem, sometimes in an indelicate fashion or coupled with expressions of dismay at Palestinian rejection of opportunities to participate in the city's management or with expressions of bitterness at Palestinian violence against individual Jews.

Official Israeli postures toward Jerusalem surfaced in two policy issues that were prominent as this book was being prepared. One dealt with a redrawing of the city's borders. They were extended westward in order to increase the Jewish proportion of the city's population. Another concerned the peace negotiations that formally opened in 1991 and were preceded by lengthy bargaining as to the terms of the negotiations. Prominent among the points insisted by Israel was that Jerusalem not be discussed in this round of negotiations and that no Jerusalem residents be among the Palestinian negotiators. These stances were meant to emphasize the Israeli insistence that Jerusalem will remain an Israeli city. For their part,

Palestinians asserted that they could not concede Jerusalem's status as a city solely under Israeli authority. They found a way to have Palestinian Jerusalemites as leading personalities in the peace talks even if they were not initially accorded the status of negotiators. Subsequent movements in these negotiations will be described in the final chapter of this book, along with a review of issues still outstanding, and scenarios as to what might happen.

Not all of the contentious issues involved in this study of Jerusalem governance involve Jews versus Palestinians. There are chronic disputes between religious and secular Jews, and between the Jews of the municipal authority and those of the national government. Local Jews argue among themselves about proposals for constructing new buildings or roads, preserving sites with historic or scenic appeal, and whose homes must be torn down so that progress may go forward. Prominent figures in the Diaspora seek to influence the city that they view as not simply Israeli but the emotional center of all Judaism. There are also arguments between different groups of Christians and Moslems as to who should do what in their holy places.

Israel provides extraordinary resources to Jerusalem in order to make it the showcase of the country. Israel is an explicitly Jewish state, whose policymakers accept the elevated status of the city in Jewish traditions. Jerusalem also benefits in its competition for Israeli resources because of its tenuous status. Most countries of the world do not formally recognize Jerusalem as Israel's capital. Many do not recognize it as a city that is properly Israel's. They adhere formally to decisions of the United Nations from the 1940s that Jerusalem should have an international status and recognize only that cease-fire lines in 1948 and 1967 gave control of Jerusalem to Israel. An unimpressive list of countries maintained their embassies in Jerusalem during 1994: El Salvador, Dominican Republic, Denmark, and Costa Rica. A more impressive list of countries, including the United States, the United Kingdom, and France, maintained consulates in Jerusalem but kept their embassies in what they formally recognized as the Israeli capital of Tel Aviv. The newly independent state of Kirghizistan announced the establishment of an embassy in Jerusalem early in 1993, but skeptics questioned whether the decision could withstand expected pressures from that country's Moslems.[12] The Netherlands put their embassy in Jerusalem and then withdrew to Tel Aviv under international pressure. They presented Mayor Teddy Kollek with a large shipment of tulip bulbs as a consolation.

An element of the ambiguity in Israel's environment is that it is condemned by the United Nations, the United States, and other governments for actions in Jerusalem after 1967, even while the condemnations are softened by implicit recognition of Jerusalem as Israel's capital. Foreign officials come to Jerusalem to meet with their Israeli counterparts, even though their embassies are in Tel Aviv.[13] Israel has been roundly criticized and threatened with economic isolation by the Arab boycott. Like other international pariahs (for instance, South Africa, Taiwan, and Chile) Israel has found friends to provide political, economic, military, and cultural support.[14] The hope in Israel is that its accomplishments in Jerusalem will be viewed positively when the formal status of the city is finally settled, or that more and more countries will accept Israel's claim de facto in the absence of formal arrangements.

Part of Jerusalem's attractions are physical beauty and pleasant climate. It sits on ridges of the Judean Mountains at about 800 meters (2,600 feet) above sea level, with weather that is moderate by North American and European standards. The average maximum temperature is 29 degrees Celsius (84 Fahrenheit) in the warmest of the summer months, and the average minimum is 4 degrees Celsius (39 Fahrenheit) in the coldest of the winter months. Average humidity ranges from 54 to 67 percent in the summer. There are about 80 days per year with rain in the period October through May, with an average 820 millimeters (32 inches) of rain per year. Mountain winds and a lack of heavy industry keep most indicators of air pollution substantially below the measurements for Tel Aviv and Haifa.[15] On clear nights the lights of Amman, some 70 kilometers (40 miles) across the Jordan Rift, can be seen from the city's eastern hills. It is about the same distance to the coast, and Tel Aviv's lights can be seen from the western hills. Jerusalem's crime rates are lower than in Israel as a whole.[16] Almost all of Jerusalem's buildings are faced by native stone, which reflect the morning and afternoon sun in pink and gold. Figure 1.1 is a schematic map of Israel that shows the small size of the country and the short distances from Jerusalem to the capitals of neighboring states.

The Old City sits pretty much where it has since the Israelite period. It is approximately one square kilometer, surrounded by the walls built by Suleiman the Magnificent in the beginning of Ottoman (Turkish) rule in 1537–41. The major streets within the walls were laid out by the Romans.[17] The Old City contains sites holy to

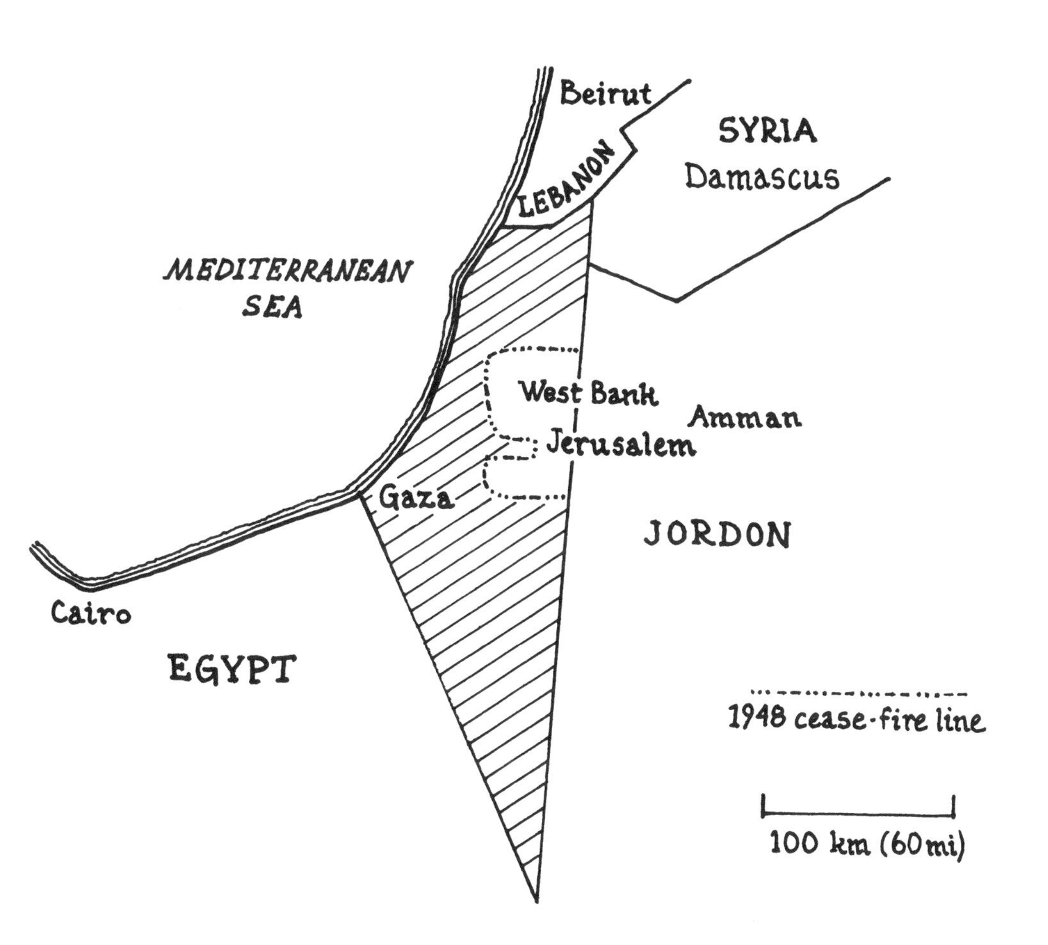

Figure 1.1
Israel

Jews, Christians, and Moslems, as well as the homes of some 27,200 residents (18,200 in the Moslem Quarter, 4,600 in the Christian Quarter, 2,200 in the Armenian Quarter, and 2,200 in the Jewish Quarter). Until the middle of the last century, all of Jerusalem was within the walls, and the gates were closed against Bedouin raiders each night. The irregular boundaries of the present municipality extend some 16 kilometers (10 miles) from north to south, and 8 kilometers (5 miles) east to west. Jerusalem's total population was estimated at 556,500 in 1994. Jews make up 72 percent of the population, Moslems 25 percent, and Christians 3 percent. As will be explained in later chapters, the municipal boundaries are significant in producing the large Jewish majority.

Cultural diversity adds to the charms as well as the problems of Jerusalem. It has long been on a border between east and west. Under the Greeks, Romans, and Crusaders it was in the far east of western regimes. Under the Babylonians and Persians, it was on the western edge of eastern empires. Modern Jerusalem includes one of the world's major fault lines between west and east, separating the Jews from the Arabs. A minor fault line of this kind runs through the Jewish community, and sets off Jews who came from Asia and North Africa from those with roots in Europe. Middle- and upper-income secular Jews live a western European lifestyle and flavor their Hebrew with English, French, Spanish, German, Hungarian, Czech, Romanian, or Russian. They are never more than a short ride from the exotic east. When Jewish-Arab tensions are not high they wander and shop among the bazaars and restaurants of the Old City or the Arab commercial area just outside of the Damascus Gate. If they want a reminder of their shtetl heritage, they can go to the ultra-Orthodox Jewish neighborhoods of Mea She'arim or Mahane Yehuda.

Jerusalem's social indicators show a closing of the socioeconomic gaps between western and eastern Jews (Ashkenazim and Sephardim) along with a mixture of those heritages that occurs in about 20 percent of Jewish marriages.[18] Yet there remain working-class neighborhoods where the residents and the synagogues retain the cultures brought in the 1940s and 1950s from Yemen, Iran, Iraq, Kurdistan, and Morocco. More recent immigrations from Ethiopia and republics of the former Soviet Union contribute to the city's mosaic and its problems.

POLITICS AND EMOTIONS

Readers familiar with the Israeli-Arab conflict know the arguments and the passions about Jerusalem. Hyperbole is a fixed element of the Jerusalem scene.

According to a publication of the Islamic Council of Europe: "the Zionist usurpation and continued occupation of Jerusalem and Palestine . . . has perpetuated untold human misery and unleashed a seemingly unending reign of terror in a land held sacred by Moslems, Christians and Jews alike. As a result, more than a million men, women and children have been hounded out of their homes and forced to become refugees, while merciless Zionist persecution goes on throughout the length and breadth of their homeland."[19]

Arab propagandists have sought to reshape history in order to give Palestinians a monopoly claim to Jerusalem, and to minimize the legitimacy of a Jewish claim.

> The native inhabitants, Christian and pagan, were descended from the original Carmel Man of Palestine, and from the Semitic Arab tribes of Amorites, Canaanites, and others who had entered the land from Arabia in migratory waves . . . the Hebrews of the Old Testament were a limited group, [whose] rule in Jerusalem as a city-state was of short duration. . . . The invasions by Hittites, Hyksos, Hurrians, Persians, Greeks, and Romans were generally more extensive and lasted longer. . . . Despite Israeli propaganda, there are in fact no important Jewish monuments of religious significance in Jerusalem. It is true that there is a Jewish ritual of mourning at the Wailing Wall, but this in fact is a portion of the wall of the Haram Esh-Sharif, and is actually Muslim property.[20]

Jews are no less expansive. The 1967 victory has been described as, "an act of God, providential, irreversible, final."[21] "We could see the Western Wall, through an archway. . . . It was like new life . . . I could see them, men who were too tired to stand up any more, sitting by the Wall, clutching it, kissing the stones and crying. We all of us cried. That was what we had been fighting for."[22] Some Jews assert the greater justice of their own claim on the city. "Jerusalem has a far more powerful corporate meaning for Judaism than for Christianity and Islam. Christians have Rome and Muslims have Mecca, but Jews have only Jerusalem."[23]

Jews emphasize that the Jordanians did not honor their 1948 commitments with respect to Jewish access to their holy sites and claim that Arab Jerusalemites live better under Israeli rule than they did under Jordanian rule. Israel has renovated the Old City with new sanitary water and underground sewer systems, provided additional school rooms and library resources in Arabic, and improved medical facilities in Arab neighborhoods outside the Old City. Israelis claim that they have increased the literacy rates of East Jerusalemites and offer more political liberty and press freedom, with more liberal voter qualifications than under the Jordanians. Some disparage the demand of Palestinians for a national capital in Jerusalem by noting that Palestinians never ruled the city. They assert that Palestinian nationalism developed from within the larger Arab community only in recent decades. They note that it was a Kurd, Salah al-Din, who took the city from the Crusaders in 1187, and that subsequent rulers came from Baghdad, Cairo, Constantinople, London, and Amman.

Some Israelis are ambivalent about their control of a city that is sacred to others as well as themselves. The novelist Amos Oz walked through the Old City soon after the battle that took it from the Jordanians and was not as hopeful as he wanted to be. "With all my soul, I desired to feel in Jerusalem as a man who has dispossessed his enemies and returned to the patrimony of his ancestors. . . . Were it not for the people. I saw enmity and rebelliousness, sycophancy, amazement, fear, insult and trickery. I passed through the streets of East Jerusalem like a man breaking into some forbidden place. Depression filled my soul."[24]

Intensity and drama are not the entire story of Jerusalem. Most of what happens is prosaic. The municipal council debates the budget, proposals for new construction, and social programs. Committees in charge of theaters and museums schedule events to attract audiences of various ages and tastes. Politically active individuals and groups seek favorable coverage from the local and national media. The mayor and municipal department heads pursue funds or project approvals from ministries of the national government. Individuals pursue their livelihoods and raise their families, overlook the landmarks that attract tourists, and complain when special events cause traffic jams.

PRINCIPAL THEMES

Several themes run through the following chapters. The formulation of them here reflects what is distinctive in the governing of Jerusalem, as well as what might help to explain its governance by demonstrating its differences from other prominent cities.

One theme is the prominence of professional bureaucrats and elected officials in Jerusalem's development. Major actors are national and local authorities, and the institutions that are responsible to them or to other public bodies. Less prominent are citizen groups, private entrepreneurs, and business firms. A second theme appears in the efforts of local authorities to find significant autonomy of action, despite a formal structure that favors control by the central government. A third theme deals with policy strategies of accommodation or domination with respect to population groups that have been pursued by the regimes in Jerusalem since ancient times. A fourth theme concerns the impact of international relations and Israel's foreign policy on Jerusalem's local administration. A fifth theme reflects the multiple pressures focused on Jerusalem. They produce a style of decision-making for Jerusalem that is concerned with coping. Jerusalem's officials react to crises with imperfect and temporary actions, as opposed to decisions that can deal with a problem fully, and remove it once and for all times from the city's agenda. Coping is also prominent at the national level of Israel, and may be a trait of Jewish political culture as well as being a characteristic of governing under conditions that are especially difficult.

The Public Nature of Jerusalem's Development

Jerusalem differs from other world cities in not being an arena that attracts private entrepreneurs. Historically, the centers of the country's commerce have been along the coast, near the ports and the land routes to other major cities in the region. The headquarters of the country's banks are in Tel Aviv. Most major industries are found in an area from the Haifa metropolitan area in the north to the Tel Aviv metropolitan area in the south.

Even in its economic centers, major actors in Israel tend to be public rather than private. Israel ranks among the western democracies with the highest proportion of economic resources controlled by the government. The nation's preoccupation with security assures a large role for the government in the nation's finance, as does the Zionist concern to build a strong state, and the socialism that has its roots in Zionist ideology and Jewish culture. Companies or other organizations affiliated with the government, the Labor Federation (Histadrut), or international Jewish organizations represent substantial portions of the country's industry, finance, agriculture, and public transportation. Privatization has attracted a following in Israel as elsewhere, but so far has not altered the dominance of the economy by public organizations.[25]

The economy of Jerusalem features government ministries, educational institutions, and hospitals supported by tax revenues, and aid from overseas governments or private individuals. The most prominent actors in recent public controversies have been the mayor; the minister of interior; the head of the Jerusalem Development Authority, who is responsible to national ministries and the municipality; the prime minister and other ministers who have spoken out about the issue of Jerusalem in Israel's international negotiations.

Local Autonomy in the Context of Formal Centralization

The theme of local autonomy in the context of conditions that favor the central government touches upon two contrasting lines of argument in the literature about cities. On the one hand are those authors who emphasize the impotence of local policymakers. For them, the city is at the mercy of a political economy that maximizes the benefits of regional or national interests, where crucial decisions are more likely to come from superior levels of government or the executive suites of economic enterprises.[26]

Other scholars take exception to the dismal perspective on local authorities.[27] They describe creative uses of local finance or quasi-governmental authorities.[28] Entrepreneurial executives of local authorities have creditable records of social programming, physical construction, and economic development.[29] Some scholars find that the pessimism about local self-government is more pronounced in the United States than elsewhere, and conclude that it reflects cultural expectations of municipal autonomy and a limited concern for national management.[30]

Some of Jerusalem's traits seem to render the city especially vulnerable to extra-local policymakers. The formal structure subordinates the city to national ministries, and the city is important to Christianity and Islam, Palestinian nationalists, overseas Jews, and international organizations. National officials have expressed a need to intervene in the city's administration in order to assure that it is governed in a manner to justify continued Israeli control.[31]

In practice, the same traits that would appear to heighten central government control over Jerusalem add to local officials' autonomy. The international concern for Jerusalem has provided the municipality some room for maneuver in dealing with the national government. Jerusalem's importance as a spiritual center exceeds its economic importance, and its governance has been more dependent on politics than economics. While Teddy Kollek served as mayor from 1966 to 1993 he was creative in attracting donors from overseas. Partly because of the money he raised, he had some success in resisting policy initiatives from national officeholders.[32]

Accommodation versus Domination

Cultural diversity has long been recognized as an urban trait, and policy strategies that pursue the accommodation or domination of minorities have been apparent in urban regimes from ancient times. Religious and ethnic tensions are the most pressing of Jerusalem's problems. Migrations from one or another empire or cultural homeland have created a heterogeneous population. The spiritual nature of the city has contributed to its residents being identified according to their religion. During the most recent century, the development of Arab and Palestinian nationalism has produced ethnic alliances between many of the city's Moslems and Christians in opposition to the Jews.

A strategy of accommodation has been marked by efforts to keep the peace by providing concessions on sensitive issues to restive populations. It was pursued at least part of the time during the periods ruled by Persians, Greeks, Romans, Moslems, British, and Israelis. A contrasting strategy of domination was most prominent in the Crusader and Jordanian periods, and appeared in Greek and Roman periods. It was marked by a concern to repress severely or even exclude segments from the city population.

The concepts of policy strategy, accommodation, and domination are problematic, especially in the context of numerous regimes over a span of 2,500 years. "Strategy" implies a plan of action explicitly chosen to achieve certain goals that lends itself to being implemented in a systematic fashion.[33] It is widely recognized that even modern, sophisticated governments have trouble defining their problems clearly, selecting goals and policies, and administering them systematically.[34] Developing countries have more serious problems.[35] Loosely articulated feudal or imperial governments, of the types that governed Jerusalem until modern times, fell far from the standard of centrally defined policies that were strictly observed in remote provinces.[36]

The comparison of policy strategies from one period to another is complicated further by great changes in the expectations and performance of government. The major divide separates the current regime from all that preceded it. Earlier governments were concerned largely with raising revenue and keeping order. The agenda of social programming was minimum, if it existed at all.

What residents obtained by way of education, health services, housing, and income security they acquired by their own efforts, from family, or their religious community. The religious communities regulated their members, judged disputes, and punished wayward behavior. At various times the regime set the boundaries for each community's self-government, intervened in the cases that interested it, and dealt with disputes between members of different communities. There are still prominent traces of service provision, courts, and discipline in Jerusalem's Moslem, Christian, and Jewish communities. In the current regime, there are also secular courts, as well as programs of national or local authorities to provide a range of social services comparable to those of Western Europe and North America.

In Jerusalem's history, a strategy of accommodation has been only relatively more accommodating than a strategy of domination. The city has never had an egalitarian, pluralist regime where all citizens and communities are equal. Those regimes that have followed a strategy of accommodation have sought to keep the peace in the contentious city by providing benefits to various communities. Each has provided more benefits to one or another of the city's communities than to others. Even the present regime, which may be the most explicitly accommodating in the city's history, offers its benefits to non-Jews in the context of Israeli policy that Jerusalem have a substantial Jewish majority and be the capital of a Jewish state.

The labels of accommodation or domination suggest sharp contrasts in policy, whereas political scientists are alert to finer gradations along a spectrum between two extremes.[37] Figure 1.2 arrays regime traits from extremes of accommodation to domination. It takes account of access to politics and governing; shares of policy benefits and personal opportunity ("who gets what?"); an ideology that favors egalitarianism or the attribution of formal privileges; and the degree of legitimacy attributed to the regime. At the extreme of accommodation is a pluralist democracy with equalities of political access, policy benefits, and personal opportunities; and widely viewed as legitimate. At the extreme of domination is a regime that benefits some groups and excludes others, and may even expel whole communities from its area. The minimum degree of accommodation indicated by the dotted line is "D-a," that is, a nondemocratic polity that provides out-of-favor groups concessions on sensitive issues in order to co-opt their tolerance of the regime. In the city's long history it may only be the Israeli regime that has

Figure 1.2
Key Points on the Spectrum between Accommodation and Domination

Accommodation

A. Pluralist democracy with an ideology and a practice of providing equality of political access, policy benefits, and personal opportunities; and a widely shared perception that the regime is legitimate

B. Legal forms of democracy but with inequalities of political access, policy benefits, or personal opportunities; and population segments who feel themselves deprived by a regime that, in their eyes, is not fully legitimate

C. Legal forms of democracy but with provisions that favor certain groups of the population with respect to political access, policy benefits, or personal opportunities; and population segments who perceive that the regime is illegitimate

D. Nondemocratic structure that is explicit in ranking population groups with respect to their political access and/or policy benefits and personal opportunities without reference to the traits or behaviors of individuals, to the extent that members of some groups are assured access, benefits and opportunities, while members of other groups are limited or denied them

a. Preferential structure as described above, with out-of-favor groups provided concessions on sensitive issues in order to co-opt their tolerance of the regime

b. Preferential structure as described above, with out-of-favor groups severely limited in their policy benefits and personal opportunities or denied them altogether

E. A legal structure that expels entire groups, together with an ideology that provides one group a monopoly of political control

Domination

achieved a policy strategy more accommodating than that. However, opponents of the present regime might not be so generous in their ranking.[38]

International Relations in the Municipal Context

International relations and municipal administration are seldom taught together in political science courses. This reflects the domestic nature of most local government, secure within national boundaries and the concern of one national regime. Where local issues come up against international relations, it is likely to be in the context of cross-national economic competition or linkages between cities that strive for dominance in industry, finance, or commerce. Here Jerusalem is different. The city is not much of a factor in international commerce or finance. However, themes of international relations appear in the following conditions that are never far from the local agenda.

1. Issues associated with the city are prominent among Israel's international problems.

2. The issue of national sovereignty with respect to Jerusalem, as well as the city's boundaries are not widely recognized among the governments of the world.

3. There is communal conflict and occasional violence among Moslems, Christians, and Jews, as well as between religious and secular Jews and different Christian sects. Each group of local antagonists is able to call upon foreign support. Partly on account of what it viewed as Jerusalem's undefined status, the Vatican refused until the end of 1993 to conclude formal diplomatic relations with Israel. Most Moslem countries have viewed Jerusalem as a major problem and until recently have avoided any overt dealings with Israel.

4. As long as the Cold War lasted, issues involving Jerusalem could widen beyond the Middle East to involve the great powers.

5. The city's prominence in United Nations resolutions provides a testing point, so far not promising, for the capacity of international organizations to deal with issues of international dispute.

Jerusalem is not internationalized in a practical sense. Israel is not generally viewed as "weak and half-civilized," an expression used to describe the nominal sovereign of the internationalized city of Tangier in the mid-1950s.[39] Unlike the port of Tangier that sat astride the Straits of Gibraltar, Jerusalem has few economic attractions to encourage internationalization. Its holy places are important symbolically, and they have been involved in the run-up to more than one war. In the secularism that currently prevails among the world's great powers, Jerusalem's holy places seem unlikely to provoke a crusade by countries capable of determining its destiny, at least in the absence of an outright despoliation. Israel has been able to treat Jerusalem as its capital de facto. Yet the issue of "whose city is it?" appears only slightly beneath the surface and contributes to the style of policymaking. Jerusalem's own history cautions that the authorities who currently govern it, whether they be officials of the municipality or Israel's national government, do not control it in the full sense of that term.

The negotiations that began in late 1991 may become one of the great events in Jerusalem's history. Israel has sought to avoid or postpone deliberations on Jerusalem. For Arab delegations and especially the Palestinians, the city's status is a topic that requires negotiations sooner rather than later. It is hard to imagine that the negotiations will not affect the city and its communities. A best case analysis is that Jerusalem and Israel will have a period of peace as a result of the bargains that are struck. For a worst case analysis, Jews need only read the Book of Jeremiah, or Josephus's *The Jewish War*.

Coping

The theme of coping appears in the context of multiple pressures on Jerusalem policymakers and what seems to be the impossibility of solving the city's problems once and for all times.

There is no simple formulation for the "Jerusalem problem." Its components are the control of a city that has been subject to religious and ethnic contention for millennia; the definition of city boundaries, which are linked to the percentages of one or another group in the population, and the issue of which group should control the city; measures taken or avoided that might add to the benefits provided to one or another of the city's population groups; and the linkage of these elements to the security enjoyed by Israel in its conception as a Jewish state.

Coping implies something less than *solutions*.[40] Terms like *adapting, managing, dealing with,* and *satisficing* appear in discussions of coping.[41] These imply decisions that are "good enough," even if they are not what any of the participants really want. Psychologists define coping as responses to stress, and have grouped coping behaviors in ways that are suggestive politically. Formulations for what some term "active" and "passive" coping are similar to what others call "hardiness" and "helplessness." These concepts have their parallels in policymaking, where the terms *engagement* and *avoidance* are appropriate. Engagement (active coping) responds to stress with control, challenge, commitment, creativity, objective information seeking, the definition and ranking of goals, organization, and discipline. It includes salvaging something from a difficult situation; keeping a process going in the expectation of greater opportunities or holding off great losses; surveying options and recruiting support; maintaining the integrity and political assets of oneself and one's organization; changing expectations in the face of conditions that are not likely to change in the short range; ranking priorities in order to achieve the more important at the expense of the less important. Avoidance (passive coping) responds to stress with a lack of control, hopelessness, confusion, rigidity, distortion, disorganization, randomness, disorder, distress, depression, anxiety, withdrawal, flight, or submission. It exhibits pointless emoting that involves loss of control and direction for oneself and potential allies; quixotic choice of options in an effort to *do something!* without taking account of likely costs and benefits; and frittering away resources in efforts that do not produce significant accomplishments.[42]

Michael Walzer's study of the biblical exodus theme in numerous political movements, including Zionism's encounter with Arab nationalism, contrasts pragmatism versus messianicism in the original biblical story and in subsequent history. His depiction is appropriate to different approaches to coping: one that seeks to move slowly, pragmatically, postponing gratification and preparing one's people for conditions that are inevitable (engagement coping), and another (avoidance coping) that seeks to "force the future" all at once, with brave but foolhardy challenges to a stressful condition that are likely to involve severe costs.[43] Critics chastise the Israeli establishment for its failure to plan and formulate policy rationally and to solve its problems. Another view is that coping reflects an acquired cultural capacity of Israeli Jews to deal at least partially with vexing problems.[44]

THE END OF AN ERA?

A book on Jerusalem must deal with history. Events important for the modern city occurred in millennia past, even while the present is largely a product of the period since the Six-Day War of 1967. Teddy Kollek became mayor in 1966 and served until he lost an election in November 1993. It may be a misnomer to refer to this period as the Kollek era. The mayor struggled to influence what happened in the city against national officials who were often more powerful than he, and he could not overlook international events that affected Jerusalem. Yet he was the most prominent if not always the most powerful actor in the city. He deserves being identified with a period of growth that rivaled, and by some measures exceeded, what occurred in ancient periods identified with Solomon or Herod. Kollek won impressively at the polls through the election of 1988, dominated city politics, and was creative in developing institutions that enabled him to finance building and programming outside the frameworks of the municipal and national budgets. In the run-up to the 1993 election, he alternately announced his retirement and then gave into Labor Party colleagues that he run once again in order to save Jerusalem for the party. Kollek's age (eighty-two) and personal frailties were prominent issues in the campaign. It was not a glorious end to a great career.

The change in city hall occurred only two months after the signing of an accord between the Israeli government and the Palestinian Liberation Organization (PLO). The accord was consistent with Israeli policy to avoid or postpone negotiations about Jerusalem. However, the accord seems likely to affect Jerusalem sooner or later. Until now, Palestinian politics in the city have been conducted at a distance from the formal procedures of the municipality. Most Palestinians have boycotted city elections. The community's leadership, organizations, and activity has been partly illegal and underground. Palestinian politics has not been exposed for systematic inquiry as in the cases of ethnic politics in more conventional cities where leaders compete openly for a place in local government and a share of public resources. Palestinian avoidance of Jerusalem politics continued even after the signing of the Israeli-PLO accord, as Palestinian leaders dithered about supporting Kollek in the November elections. The widespread Palestinian avoidance of the polls contributed to his defeat. The next book on governing Jerusalem should include more extensive treatment of the substantial Palestinian community. As yet, however, it is not possible to write that book.

As in other cities, the governing of Jerusalem is the product of individuals and organizations. Their decisions reflect both their own desires and compromises, as well as the influence of some conditions that originate outside of the locality, and events that occurred long ago. It is helpful to think of *micro* and *macro* influences on public policy.[45] Micro influences include the people and institutions in current politics. The macro influences are everything else: geographic conditions and the details of topography that shape urban development; historical events and cultural traits that affect current perspectives; national policies that set the parameters for local action; economic conditions that influence residents' demands for services and the resources that are collected by local and national taxes; plus political demands and constraints that originate in international forums. The remaining chapters of this book survey both micro and macro factors in the Jerusalem context to answer questions that are widely asked about cities:

- What are the critical issues?
- What policies are being pursued?
- Who governs? How?
- Who gets what? or Who benefits and who suffers from the policies that are pursued?

· What are the influences that shape the policy actions of governmental institutions? or Why does governing occur the way it does? and

· How successful are the policies?

This neat listing of questions does not foretell a simple rendering of clear answers. Jerusalem is dynamic and fluid. It is on the world's agenda, whether or not Israeli officials want it there. Disputes among the authorities with responsibility for Jerusalem lead to policies that, at least to some extent, contradict one another. Efforts to strengthen the Jewish presence in Jerusalem, for example, hamper efforts to keep the peace among Jews, Moslem and Christian clerics, and Palestinian nationalists, or to persuade international observers that the Israeli regime is sufficiently enlightened to be entrusted with the perpetual care of the Holy City.

An urban scholar might ask, "Why consider the governance of a city that is so different from others?" First, this study of Jerusalem may lead others to question whether widely shared views about the economic motors of urban development do, in fact, describe all important cities. Jerusalem demonstrates a prominence of spiritual values of long germination, the realpolitik of state interest, and the stubborn refusal of a disaffected minority to parley its numerical importance in a conventional political quest for material benefits.[46] Secondly, the Jerusalem case reveals national policymaking for issues of the highest priority, along with the aspirations and pressures of city and even neighborhood politics. It shows how national and local policymakers are forced to deal with each other despite a formal structure that gives a near monopoly of policymaking to national figures. A third reason for taking a close look at governing in Jerusalem is the extreme nature of the problems facing city officials. How Jerusalemites respond to the problematic of their city will contribute to some general points about governing under conditions of extreme constraint. The final and ultimate reason for considering Jerusalem is its history, and its proven capacity to stimulate dreams and crusades. Jerusalem deserves a place in the literature of urban political science, partly because it is so different from other cities.

Yet another reason for studying Jerusalem has nothing to do with issues of political science concerned with cities. Jerusalem is on the agenda of the international media, and is likely to reach the top of that agenda as Israeli-Palestinian conflicts or accords focus on the city. With the signing of an agreement between Israel and the PLO in September 1993, Israelis and Palestinians took a step to alter their relationship from one of enemies to that of adversaries. The issue of

Jerusalem was postponed to later stages of negotiations, and some Israelis may hope that their control over the city is never lessened. Palestinians, for their part, assert that they can never be satisfied with a city that is wholly under Israeli control. The following chapters should help the international audience understand the issues at stake when the city becomes a subject of negotiations. Or alternatively, they may clarify why Israeli officials will seek to keep the city off the bargaining table.

The avowed focus of this book is empirical rather than normative or prescriptive. It seeks to describe the governance of Jerusalem, and convey an understanding of why things occur as they do. It is not oblivious to the passions that surround the city. It is also sensitive to the competing versions of justice held by those concerned about Jerusalem. Especially where passions are intense, it is appropriate to offer an orderly and dispassionate analysis of questions like those to be addressed. Those who would determine the city's future according to their own vision could then know which values they are maximizing, and which they are likely to forego.

Chapter 2 describes Jerusalem's geopolitical setting. It asks how a city of such importance came to be located on Jerusalem's site and persist as a topic of world concern. It reviews major features of ancient Israelite history in order to clarify the spiritual importance of the city in Jewish tradition. Related to that review is a survey of conditions that troubled ancient Israelites and parallel conditions that are part of the modern setting. These conditions are integral to the insecurity of Israel and Jerusalem. Their deep roots in Jewish history also may have something to do with the capacity to cope shown by the present generation of the city's policymakers.

Chapter 3 continues the review of historical episodes that have an impact on contemporary Jerusalem. It shows the residues apparent from Roman, Crusader, Moslem, and British rulers. Most important for the contemporary period are substantial Jewish immigrations that began in the latter part of the nineteenth century, the transition from Turkish to British rule during World War I, Israel's War of Independence in 1948, a period of divided Jordanian and Israeli rule from 1948 to 1967, the Six-Day War, and postwar developments and tensions. Both chapters 2 and 3 document the policy strategies of accommodation and domination that have appeared in various Jerusalem regimes from ancient times to the present.

Chapter 4 describes the governmental structure that helps to shape policymaking for Jerusalem. It portrays the themes of local versus national authorities and the prominence of public bodies in

Jerusalem's development. The formal rules in Jerusalem and other Israeli cities favor centralization. The mayor, city council, and municipal departments depend on decisions made in national ministries. The nature of Israeli politics provide local authorities with some working autonomy within the formal rules. From 1966 until 1993, Teddy Kollek's personality and political style, as well as the resources raised from foreign donors and investors, provided him with independent resources and leverage, and allowed physical developments that may surpass those of any previous regime.

Chapter 5 describes the social, economic, and political traits of Jerusalem that complicate local administration and present problems of national and international dimensions. Religion and ethnicity are associated with variations in occupation, family traits, living standards, and political perspective. There are chronic tensions among Jews, Christians, and Moslems, as well as between religious and secular Jews. The city's economy has long been problematic. It lacks an independent base of natural resources or industry, and is not well located with respect to markets, sources of supply, and international ports. The city depends on substantial outlays from the central government and continues the historical pattern of receiving financial support from overseas.

Chapter 6 describes key elements of policymaking that reflect materials presented in earlier chapters. The symbolic importance of Jerusalem renders prosaic issues intense. Especially problematic are those that rub the tender feelings of Moslems, Christians, religious and antireligious Jews, and nationalist Palestinians or Jews. The details of chapter 6 illustrate the major themes of the book: how local officials run their city, despite pressures from national authorities and formal procedures that favor national ministries; the prominence of public officials as opposed to private entrepreneurs in city affairs; efforts by some ranking policymakers to accommodate the communities that are jealous in guarding their interests, alongside demands that domination would be a more suitable strategy; and what appears to be a pervasive need to cope with one crisis or another, as the suspicions and demands of one community or another keep Jerusalem in national and international spotlights and hinder a comprehensive treatment of underlying problems. The competition between national and local figures precludes any simple and authoritative definition of Israel's policy for Jerusalem. Nevertheless, chapter 6 concludes by inferring a summary of the policy goals recently pursued in Jerusalem on the basis of prominent episodes, as well as the statements and actions of key officials.

Chapter 7 offers a summary view of politics and policymaking in Jerusalem at the end of the Kollek era, roughly a quarter-century after Israeli assumption of control over the city in 1967. It also deals with the tricky issues of evaluating Jerusalem under the Israeli regime. It asks:

- How do the benefits of the city's residents compare with those of other Israelis?
- How do various groups within Jerusalem benefit or suffer from existing policies?
- How may Jerusalem's current condition be judged in the context of its long history, and periods of progress and decline?
- How does policymaking for Jerusalem measure up to norms of assessing the city's problems and needs rationally, and implementing policies that are effective and efficient in dealing with those problems?
- Have the national government and the municipality achieved their policy goals for Jerusalem?
- Is Jerusalem secure? and
- Are there solutions for the problems of Jerusalem?

Chapter 7 returns to the theme of policymaking by way of coping amidst difficult problems, as well as the themes of accommodation and domination, the pursuit of local autonomy amidst conditions that favor control by the central government, and the infusion of international relations into Jerusalem's local administration. It arrays the perspectives about Jerusalem likely to be expressed in the peace process; the options on the agenda of Palestinians and other claimants; pressures on various sides of each issue; and alternative scenarios of local, national, regional, and global factors that might affect the outcomes. It also portrays the problems likely to be faced by any authority having the responsibility to govern Jerusalem into the next century. Finally, it asks if the governing of Jerusalem offers lessons useful for understanding other polities that suffer from severe constraints.

No actors are portrayed in this book as heroes or villains. Perhaps there are none in a setting that is so intensely contentious, whose policymakers use the political tools of persuasion and force to deal with one another and their adversaries. A reader is urged to adopt the author's sense of skepticism with respect to the claims of actual and aspiring policymakers, as well as a historical perspective. The focus on governance since 1967 is only a moment in a long history of much anguish and numerous changes of regime.

Hyperbole, frustration, failure, and foibles may be inevitable in a city that is beset by so many conflicting claims and so much nervous energy. What some will see as a foible will be to others tragedy or severe injustice, and a cause for yet another crusade. Irretrievable personal loss and death, tears and blood, as well as songs of joy are part of Jerusalem now, just as they have been for those who have been governors and subjects in millennia past.

CHAPTER 2

Geopolitics and Spiritual Attachments

How did a city of Jerusalem's importance come to be located where it is? And how has it maintained its status despite sharp variations in its fortunes? These are central questions in any study of Jerusalem. The answers help to explain the charms of the city, the political emotions that attach to it, and details of its development in the distant past and the present.

There are several facets to the character of Jerusalem, and they have changed from one period to another. The city has been important spiritually since David made it his capital about 1000 B.C.E. At times it has been important strategically, as the capital of an Israelite kingdom or modern Israel. At other times, Jerusalem has been a sleepy provincial town, with crumbling monuments and a small population.

In the united kingdom of David and Solomon (c. 1000–927 B.C.E.), as well as in the later kingdoms of Judah, the Hasmoneans, and the reign of Herod (927–586; 167–4 B.C.E.), Jerusalem was the center of the government, the cult, and the nation's economy. During almost the entire period from the destruction of the Temple by the Romans in 70 C.E. until the latter part of the nineteenth century, Jerusalem was notable for the contrasts of poverty and filth with its glorious past. Except for a brief period under the Crusaders, Jerusalem was not a political capital during its long dormancy. Even when it was the Crusaders' capital, it was inferior economically to other Crusader cities. Before and after the Crusader period, Moslem rulers occasionally tended to the city walls and the Haram al-Sharif (Temple Mount), but mostly they allowed the city to decay.

The city began its spurt into modernity with Jewish immigration in the latter part of the nineteenth century. It began another period of dramatic growth after its reunification in the 1967 war. However, age-old limitations traceable to the city's geography show their influence in comparisons with the stronger economies of Tel Aviv and Haifa.

This chapter details the ancient period of Jerusalem that includes its origins in Jewish tradition. The next chapter carries the historical survey from the Roman period to the present. Both chapters seek to explain the roots of various communities' attachments to the city, as well as to describe the strategies of accommodation or domination as pursued in each major era of the city's history.

Readers might consider the relevance of this material for other multicultural communities. It is tempting to conclude from these chapters that a policy of accommodation is more successful in managing conflict than a policy of domination. Those regimes that have been completely dominating (the Crusader and Jordanian) have been the shortest in the city's history. Against this simple observation, several items are prominent. In Jerusalem's case, no regime has been so accommodating as to be genuinely egalitarian. The policy pursued within the city has been only one of the factors responsible for a regime being able to maintain control of the city, and policy seems to have been less important than economic wealth and military power. This does not deprive a policy of accommodation of moral appeal in its own right, as a way of providing substantial satisfactions to all communities in a locale affected by cultural rivalries.

ANCIENT GEOPOLITICS

Scholars quarrel about the reliability of the history depicted in the Hebrew Bible.[1] Yet the ancient text is suggestive, at least, about the attractions of Jerusalem's site and the character of its development. According to the Bible, Jerusalem's original importance derived from geography and the tribal structure of the Israelites.

The kingdom said to be created by Saul, perhaps about 1020 B.C.E., was based among the northern tribes of Israel. Saul's area seems to have reached from near the modern town of Metullah on the Lebanese border in the north to an area north of Jerusalem, without including the city. It included a region across the Jordan almost to Amman, but did not reach the coastal plain controlled by the Philistines.[2] David was from the Judean city of Bethlehem, south of Jerusalem. After his falling out with Saul, he spent a number of years roaming the south, perhaps a leader of outlaws: "every one that was in distress, and every one that was in debt, and everyone that was discontented."[3] David had himself crowned king in the

Judean city of Hebron, some 25 kilometers south of Jerusalem. After Saul's death, David overcame Saul's son in a civil war.

Jerusalem beckoned as an area that had never succumbed to the Israelites, between the northern tribes that had been loyal to Saul and David's southern tribe of Judah. It was an enclave that David would want to occupy in order to create a united country. As an intertribal area, Jerusalem could be chosen as David's capital without giving offense to the tribes of either region. Jerusalem had the additional appeal of being defensible. It was built on a ridge extending northeast to southwest, surrounded on three sides by steep ravines.

As at subsequent stages in its history, the site desired by one party was occupied by another. It was a Jebusite city when David wanted to move in, and he had to overcome its natural defenses. The Bible does not report clearly how it was done. Some commentators expand on a few of the words in the Second Book of Samuel and infer that David or his men climbed up into the city through a water tunnel, and began fighting from within the walls.[4]

David's city was outside the walls known to the present generation of tourists. Archaeologists have exposed and partly reconstructed it on a small ridge outside the southeastern corner of the Old City. According to the biblical report, David began the expansion of his city when he purchased a threshing floor on a plateau to the north of his ridge.[5] Solomon built his Temple on what became the Temple Mount for Jews, the Haram al-Sharif for Moslems, and the site of a Christian church and the headquarters of the Templars during the Crusader kingdom.

David's city and the larger city that developed alongside of it are defended on two sides by the Kidron and Hinnom Valleys, which run north-south and east-west respectively and meet at a low point below the southeast corner of Jerusalem. These valleys directed Jerusalem's development to the more level areas to the north. Because of the easier terrain, the city's northern edge also required its most elaborate defenses of walls, towers, and moats. The floors of the Kidron and Hinnom Valleys remain devoid of settlement to this day. The city spread beyond the walls to the north and west during the nineteenth century and skipped over the Kidron and Hinnom Valleys to the east and south.

The heartland of David's kingdom was similar to that of modern Israel. His city was roughly midway on a chain of mountains that dominate the interior of the country. The ridges of the mountains offered the best route between Hebron and Bethlehem in the south, through Jerusalem to Shechem (Nablus) in the north. Jerusalem was also on a saddle 100–200 meters lower than the hills to the north and the south. Thus it was alongside an east-west transit through the mountains.

The availability of easily workable limestone added to the attractions of the site. Stone has remained the construction material of choice. Its use for modern construction was written into the building code by the British and continued by the Israelis. New buildings have stone facing on a concrete structure but have the aesthetics of earlier buildings with solid stone walls.

The Judean hills provided wool, hides, milk, and olive oil. Once the Temple was established, Jerusalem became a magnet for visitors and payments from overseas communities. Pilgrimages and religious sites supported by foreign donors continued when the Temple of the Jews was replaced by Christian and Moslem shrines. Tourism and monetary transfers from overseas are still mainstays of the Jerusalem economy.

Water has always been a problem. The city sits on a natural border between a region of sufficient rainfall to the west and virtually no rainfall in the Judean desert to the east. There are no rivers or lakes in the vicinity. One major spring was located just outside of David's city and was the subject of ancient engineering to bring its waters inside the city walls for access during siege. Over the years, this and other sources were supplemented by pools and cisterns to store rainwater, aqueducts from sources near Hebron, and carriers who hauled water by cart, animal, or human pack from other springs. Water shortages in Jerusalem were a military problem as recently as Israel's War of Independence in 1948, when Arabs cut the pipelines running to the city. The residents suffered severe rationing. Those living in older homes with cisterns were more fortunate than others.[6]

BIBLICAL JERUSALEM

The authors of the Hebrew Bible produced the spiritual aura that continues to surround Jerusalem. Jewish traditions and ritual celebrate national history, with a central concern for the relationship between God and his people. Jerusalem plays a key role in Jewish memory and aspirations.

A reader who relies on the Hebrew Bible for the early history of Jerusalem is not on solid ground. It is the only extant source for the period of David and Solomon and the major source for the later period of divided monarchies. Some scholars conclude that sections dealing with Jerusalem were compiled and edited by priests who served in Jerusalem in the sixth or fifth centuries B.C.E. (400–500 years after Solomon's death). By one view, the glorification of Jerusalem that developed in Judaic doctrine may owe something to the competition between these biblical compilers and other religious leaders whose base was in the northern kingdom of Israel. By another view, the glorification of David and Solomon's city was meant to provide symbols of national unity for a people then rent by military defeat, the destruction of Jerusalem, and exile to Babylon.[7]

The Bible credits David's son, Solomon, with turning Jerusalem into a world center of opulence and wisdom. He undertook the building of the Temple, which David had put off in deference to the counsel of the prophet Nathan. Solomon constructed his royal palace adjacent to the Temple and took on priestly functions in the religious ritual. The First Book of Kings describes an imperial court more elaborate than David's in its administrative structure. There is an idealized description of great wealth and domestic harmony: "Solomon ruled over all the kingdoms from the river Euphrates to Philistia and as far as the frontier of Egypt; they paid tribute and were subject to him all his life . . . All through his reign Judah and Israel continued at peace, every man under his own vine and fig-tree, from Dan to Beersheba."[8] The Bible reports that the Queen of Sheba was favorably impressed with Solomon's wisdom, the wealth of his court, and the happy condition of his wives.[9] Ethiopian traditions embroider a love affair onto this story and claim that the royal line that reached to Haile Salassie began with the Queen's visit to Jerusalem.

Along with the idealized description of Solomon's Jerusalem, there are also indications of policy failure and popular unrest. The full picture suggests that Solomon may have been clever, but not wise. The grandeur of his projects indebted him to foreign suppliers of material and labor and produced heavy levies of taxation that led to unrest during his reign and later to the rebellion of the north and the division of the united kingdom. The good life at court may have left insufficient resources to maintain the empire created by David. Solomon had to surrender some Galilean towns to pay debts to Hiram of Tyre.[10] Damascus to the northeast and Edom to the southeast asserted their independence, and Edom actually threatened Solomon's heartland.[11] Some scholars write about the personalized nature of the united kingdom and the failure of David or Solomon to institutionalize it in a way that it could benefit from the continuing support of Israelites from all tribes and regions.[12]

The conquest of the northern kingdom of Israel by Assyria in 722 B.C.E. produced an exile of some northerners to other parts of the Assyrian empire and a migration of others into the southern kingdom of Judah. Jerusalem's population may have reached 24,000 as a result of this migration, perhaps its greatest size prior to the Hasmonean or Roman periods.

Few Judean kings who ruled in Jerusalem were models of virtue. The Books of Kings tell one story after another of incompetence, cruelty, and idolatry. Manasseh served a long period of forty-six years (696–642 B.C.E.) but may have owed his success to appeasing the Assyrians by putting their idols in the Temple and repressing Judeans who sought to rebel against the Assyrians. This is an early example of a regime that was not accommodating even toward its own citizens. Manasseh earned one of the sharpest biblical condemnations directed against the Judean kings: "Manasseh shed so much innocent blood that he filled Jerusalem full to the brim."[13]

Perhaps the entire Israelite enterprise never amounted to much in a material sense. The Jewish homeland was poor and marginal. The description recorded in the Book of Numbers of a land "flowing with milk and honey"[14] was a judgment made by spies who had come from the desert. The Judaic heartland was in the mountains, away from more powerful people along the coast. It lacked an abundance of water and rich soils. It never developed the agricultural wealth or the large populations associated with the Nile River of Egypt or the Tigris and Euphrates Rivers of the eastern empires. It also lagged behind other empires in the sophistication of its governmental structure and administrative controls. "The country was always a cultural backwater, impoverished artistically as well as economically."[15]

The Land of Israel was a crossroads for other powers but not the homeland of a major empire. It was on a land bridge between Asia Minor, Mesopotamia, Africa, and Arabia, "a meeting place between continents and civilizations."[16] It was the corridor by which Egypt attacked Assyria, Babylon, and Persia, and by which Egypt was invaded by those powers. It was on the route that the Phoenicians used in trading with Africa, Arabia, and India via the Red Sea. Caravans crossed the land from Mesopotamia to Egypt, and from Arabia to Asia Minor. The Israelites were mostly set-upon by others and concerned to protect what they had. Usually they paid tribute to one imperial capital or another. Occasionally they sought to play off one empire against another. This led to national disaster on more than one occasion.

One writer expresses the marginal character of the Promised Land by describing Babylon's destruction of Jerusalem as a routine maneuver to punish rebellious peoples on the borders of its empire.[17] From the perspective of the Jews, that routine act was the greatest of historical catastrophes. Another writer states that Alexander the Great "incidentally wrest[ed] Judea . . . away from Persia" as part of his eastern conquests.[18] For the Jews, the Hellenization of Jerusalem after Alexander's conquest was a period of profound historical significance and a national trauma.

Despite its chronic weakness, Jerusalem was a symbol of hope. Their meager numbers, poor economy, and dependence on great powers may have contributed to the Israelites' development of the cultural and spiritual traits that produced the Hebrew Bible and its glorification of Jerusalem. Why they among all the small and weak peoples of history produced such material is something that is beyond this book's field of inquiry.

The prophet Isaiah emphasized the desolation left by the Assyrians in the northern kingdom after 722 and saw Zion (Jerusalem) as the salvation of God's people. "Your country is desolate, your cities lie in ashes. Strangers devour your land before your eyes . . . Only Zion is left, like a watchman's shelter in a vineyard . . . In days to come the mountain of the Lord's house shall be set over all other mountains . . . All the nations shall come streaming to it . . . out of Jerusalem comes the word of the Lord."[19] A New Testament view of the Holy City as it would be renewed is similar to the vision of Isaiah: "I saw the Holy City, new Jerusalem, coming down out of heaven from God, made ready like a bride adorned for her husband."[20]

Assyria weakened by the end of the seventh century, B.C.E., but the geopolitical setting of Judah remained unenviable. It became subject to the competition between Egyptian and Babylonian regimes. "Assyria's crash was not to bring peace to Judah . . . the Babylonians . . . and the Egyptians . . . both had their eye on erstwhile Assyrian holdings west of the Euphrates. And between the upper and nether millstones of their rival ambitions Judah was caught and crushed."[21]

The Egyptians killed the Judean king Josiah, took his successor prisoner, and placed their own candidate on the Judean throne. For much of the next ten fateful years, that king (Jehoiakim) would lead a pro-Egyptian party in the court of Jerusalem. The choice between

Babylon and Egypt was difficult. Egypt was significantly closer than Babylon. Its troops could reach Jerusalem after a march of fifteen days, while those of Babylon were seventy-five days' distance.[22]

The prophet Jeremiah cursed Jehoiakim and his court for exploiting the people economically and introducing pagan observances to the Holy City. Jeremiah also perceived that Babylon was the coming power and that Judah had better align itself with the winner. His prophecy of what Babylon would do to Jerusalem if it did not pay tribute to that power (perhaps written after Babylon's conquest) ranks among the goriest sections of the Hebrew Bible. "Says the Lord . . . I will make Jerusalem heaps, a lair of jackals . . . . the cities of Judah a desolation, without an inhabitant."[23] Jerusalem will be "an astonishment, and a hissing; every one that passeth thereby shall be astonished and hiss because of all the plagues thereof . . . [the city's residents will] eat the flesh of their sons."[24] Babylon's troops destroyed Jerusalem in 586 B.C.E.

Years later, after Jerusalem had been rebuilt and then destroyed again by the Romans, and the Jews were forbidden to enter the city, Jewish pilgrims would gather on the hills overlooking the site of the Temple and weep as they recited the Book of Lamentations. By Rabbinical tradition, Lamentations was written by Jeremiah after the city's destruction by the Babylonians. The first verse of that book expresses the importance of the lost city: "How solitary lies the city, once so full of people! Once great among nations, now become a widow; once queen among provinces, now put to forced labor!"[25]

The 137th Psalm was written from the perspective of the exiles in Babylon who yearned for Jerusalem. It has been read over the years in numerous other Diaspora communities. "By the rivers of Babylon we sat down and wept when we remembered Zion. . . . Our captors called on us to be merry: 'Sing us one of the songs of Zion.' How could we sing the Lord's song in a foreign land? If I forget you, O Jerusalem, let my right hand wither away; let my tongue cling to the roof of my mouth if I do not remember you, if I do not set Jerusalem above my highest joy."

Fifty years after the Babylonian exile, Persia had become the dominant power in the east. According to biblical materials, Persian rule of Jerusalem was accommodating with respect to the Jews who had been exiled to Babylon and to some extent with respect to their rivals in the area of Jerusalem (described as "people of the land," who may have been Samaritans). In 537 B.C.E. Emperor Cyrus decreed that exiles might return to Jerusalem and rebuild their Temple.

Some years later the imperial court sent the Jews Ezra and Nehemiah to promote the rebuilding of Jerusalem and to govern Judea. As reported in the Hebrew Bible, the people of the land complained in the imperial capital about the policies pursued for the sake of the returnees. The regime was accommodating to those who complained, at least to the extent that their claims interrupted the city's reconstruction.[26]

The Judea created under the Persians was little more than Jerusalem and a small hinterland. The Persians did not give the Jews control over the Negev to the south or Samaria to the north. The province of Judea extended outward from the city for about 30 kilometers.[27] Perhaps 10,000 Jews lived in Jerusalem, with about 25,000–100,000 in all of Judea.[28] The Books of Ezra and Nehemiah provide examples from this time of competition involving Jerusalem. Nehemiah mentioned an Arab among those who challenged the Jews for rebelling against the king. Nehemiah's response identifies him as an early proponent of domination as opposed to accommodation. "The God of heaven will give us success. We, his servants, are making a start with the rebuilding. You [the Arabs] have no stake, or claim, or traditional right in Jerusalem."[29] Despite the problems with outsiders, the achievements of the postexile period were considerable. Jerusalem was rebuilt. A Temple was constructed, even though it was viewed by the prophet Haggai as a pale shadow of that destroyed by the Babylonians.[30] The prophet Zechariah proclaimed "the words of the Lord of Hosts . . . once again he will make Jerusalem the city of his choice."[31]

The next change in world order came in 332 B.C.E. with the defeat of the Persians by Alexander the Great. Greek language, styles of education, athletics, theater, and local government attracted many Jews, as did the abstract thought that was more typically Greek than Jewish.[32] Like the Persians before them and the Romans after them, the Greek rulers of Judea were accommodating, during part of their reign at least. They allowed the Judeans, along with other peoples they had conquered, to live according to their ancient laws.

The Chanukah story (placed about 167 B.C.E.) of a revolt against tyranny suggests that the Greek regime became dominating toward the Jews. According to Jewish tradition, Antiochus IV Epiphanes forbade circumcision and Sabbath observances and ordered the sacrifice of swine in the Holy Temple. A revisionist historian concludes that Antiochus's decrees may have come in response to a revolt already under way by Jews who felt that the Greeks were not sufficiently accommodating.[33] According to material in 1 Maccabees, the revolt was by Jews who were zealous in their faith against Hellenized Jews as much as it was against the Greek regime per se. "Some of the people built a gymnasium in Jerusalem, in the heathen fashion, and submitted to uncircumcision, and disowned the holy agreement . . . and became the slaves of wrongdoing."[34] Mattathias Maccabee saw a Jew who went to offer sacrifice at a Greek altar "and was filled with zeal, and his heart was stirred, and he was very properly roused to anger, and ran up and slaughtered him upon the altar. At the same time he killed the king's officer who was trying to compel them to sacrifice, and he tore down the altar."[35]

It is difficult to judge the ancient record without taking account of disputes between those Jews who argue that any interference in Jewish autonomy is intolerable and those Jews who value cosmopolitan culture and welcome outside help against their own zealots. Modern Jews with different political and religious persuasions have shaped the story of the revolt and the celebration of Chanukah to their own views. Some have emphasized the heroic nationalism of those who resisted foreign rule. Others have stressed those aspects of the story that justify violence only under severe provocation.[36]

The attractions of Greek culture appear in the record of the Hasmonean dynasty established by the Maccabees. Although their regime was established as a protest against Hellenism, the Hasmoneans adopted Greek names and other cultural traits and pursued Greek-style political intrigues at court.[37] These intrigues brought the Romans to Jerusalem, first as patrons of one side in a court dispute and then as rulers.

The Roman regime, like that of the Greeks, brought prosperity, cosmopolitan culture, and an appreciation of internal autonomy among some Jews in Jerusalem. The Romans were initially accommodating to the Jews. They allowed the Jews internal autonomy in religious and social matters and permitted Diaspora Jews to send contributions to the Temple in Jerusalem. By the Roman period, there were substantial Jewish communities around the Mediterranean and in Mesopotamia. Within Jerusalem itself, Roman officials brought sacrifices to the Temple to be offered by Jewish priests.

As in the Greek period so in the Roman period: some Jews felt that foreign rule was intolerable. Jews today still quarrel about the issue. Some claim that Jewish revolts of 66 C.E. and 132 were justified responses to Roman domination, while others say that the revolts were the work of Jewish extremists who rebelled against a regime that was enlightened in many respects. Administration was by no means perfect during the Roman period. There are reports of Roman soldiers who insulted Jewish sensitivities (for instance, baring their bottoms in the vicinity of the Temple) when their commanding officers were pursuing a policy of accommodation.[38] The riots and repression that followed such incidents made the regimes seem anything but accommodating.

The Roman period provided the setting for several crucial events in Jerusalem's history: the physical developments of Herod, the crucifixion of Jesus, Jewish revolts against foreign rulers, and the city's destruction. The story of Jesus produced the New Testament, and one Jewish revolt stimulated the work of Josephus. Both the New Testament and Josephus's writings are rich but problematic sources for describing Jerusalem at the onset of the Common Era.[39]

The reign of Herod represented both the prosperity and the suffering during Rome's ascendance over the Jews. Herod ruled as a Jewish king from 37 to 4 B.C.E. He rebuilt Jerusalem's walls and undertook a major reconstruction of the Temple. He contributed to synagogues, libraries, educational, and charitable institutions in the Diaspora.[40] He may have wanted to solidify his position in the eyes of his subjects. He was appointed by the Romans, and he was not really Jewish in the eyes of some subjects. Perhaps he wanted to make Jerusalem an international showcase and expand the region that he controlled. He may also have had messianic aspirations. According to Josephus, Herod departed from the tradition among earlier Israelite kings and had himself celebrated as a god.[41]

During the Herodian period, construction activity on the Temple, palaces, and other public buildings was a major feature of the economy. The work may have employed as many as eighteen thousand workers in a total Jerusalem population of thirty thousand. As projects were finished, others were begun in order to provide a living for workers who otherwise might have been a cause of unrest.[42]

Local regulations were designed to protect the environment of the Temple. Tanneries were restricted to an area at least fifty cubits east of the city, where prevailing winds would carry their smell to the desert. Potters were not allowed in the city on account of their smoke. Work in bronze and iron were forbidden during the lesser days of the feasts (when other work was allowed) in order to minimize the noise. The commotion and stench associated with Temple sacrifices had to be tolerated on account of their ritual importance. By what may be an exaggerated account, Josephus reports that 255,000 birds and animals were killed in the Temple during a Passover celebration. The bloodletting explains the considerable outlays from the Temple treasury made for water and drainage lines.[43]

There is a continuing controversy about the testimony of Josephus concerning the revolt of 66 C.E. He wrote in the preface to *The Jewish War:* "I shall contrast the brutality of the [Jewish] party chiefs towards their countrymen with the clemency of the Romans towards aliens, and the persistence with which Titus showed his anxiety to save the City [Jerusalem] and the Sanctuary by inviting the insurgents to come to terms."[44]

Josephus described how the zealots appealed to the lower classes of Jews by burning the public records of their debts. He wrote how one group of rebels ravaged a Jewish settlement at Ein Ged (Ein Gedi) in order to gather provisions for their fortress on Masada. These are the same Jews who have come to be revered for their heroic stand, and their choice of suicide over falling into Roman hands. Josephus called them fanatics, assassins, and bandits who murdered their own wives and children.[45]

Such views must be seen alongside Josephus's personal interests to appear both as a proud Jew and as a loyal Roman, against the background of having changed sides in the rebellion.[46] He was born as Joseph ben Mattathias. After his change of loyalties he adopted the name of the Roman emperor and became Flavius Josephus. The Romans circulated Josephus' works among Jewish communities in Palestine and elsewhere in their empire,[47] presumably to facilitate the acceptance of Roman rule by the Jews. The Romans provided Josephus with a pension of revenues earned from land taken from Judeans.[48] Modern Israelis debate the issue of whether Josephus was a traitor or a pragmatist who sought to protect his people from a poorly conceived revolt.

Controversy about the Bar Kokhba rebellion of 132–35 was brought into contemporary disputes by the late Yehoshafat Harkabi. He emphasized the dangers of fanatic nationalism and the faulty strategy of the Jewish rebels and warned modern Israelis against admiring Bar Kokhba.[49] According to Harkabi, Bar Kokhba failed to take account of the prevailing peace in the Roman Empire, the capacity of the Empire to focus massive resources in putting down the rebellion, and the Romans' concern not to let a rebellion against the Empire go unpunished. The result of his revolt was the almost complete destruction of the Judaic community in Jerusalem and its environs. Emperor Hadrian pursued a policy of explicit domination in Jerusalem. He renamed the city Aelia Capitolina and forbade the entry of circumcised persons under penalty of death. For Harkabi, writing in the 1980s, before dealing with the PLO was acceptable to most Israelis, modern unrealists are the nationalist and religious extremists who would decide by themselves that the West Bank must be Israel's possession. He wrote that such extremism could bring intervention by the great powers of Europe and North America, and the end of Israel.

The Roman period produced both the end of the ancient Jewish country and the development of rabbinical institutions that were to provide Jewish communities with their leadership for centuries of dispersion. The story of Rabbi Yohanan Ben Zakkai portrays the sad state of Jewish politics and represents Jewish survival and vitality via political accommodation with non-Jewish secular authorities. Ben Zakkai's departure from a besieged Jerusalem during the revolt of 66–73 was anything but heroic. He was taken away in a coffin in order to deceive the Jewish zealots who killed those attempting to desert the besieged city. Later he established a rabbinical academy that adjusted the rites of Judaism to the destruction of the Temple.

Figure 2.1 provides a chronology of major events having political significance for Jerusalem. It serves for the biblical period covered in this chapter and for later periods to be covered in chapter 3.

THE RETURN OF ANCIENT PROBLEMS

Jerusalem's importance in the biblical period does more than clarify the city's spiritual appeal. It also points to some traits of modern Jerusalem and Israel that seem to have returned after a lapse of two millennia. Some of Israel's problems are a repeat of the difficult situation faced by the regimes of the ancient Israelites in essentially the same locale. They illustrate the tenuous hold that Israelis have on their country and its capital city. The long period when Jews did not have even a tenuous hold on Jerusalem or Israel adds to the fervor with which Israelis look upon Zion.

Modern parallels with ancient conditions must be offered with a recognition of the numerous changes in detail that occurred over the course of Israel's ancient history and of debates among historians as to what was myth and reality in the Bible and other ancient sources. It is appropriate to focus on economic, social, and political *conditions*, defined in general terms, that persisted from one ancient era to another and are recognized by a wide variety of scholars.[50]

Conditions associated with the ancient and modern periods include economic and military weakness; dependence on great powers; a mixed population of Jews and non-Jews; conflicts between

Figure 2.1
Landmarks in Jerusalem's History

c. 2000 B.C.E. First settlement

c. 1390 Amarna letters included a call for help to Egypt from its loyal vassals in Jerusalem.

c. 1200 Israelite tribes appeared in the Promised Land.

c. 1020–1000 Saul emerged as Israel's first king. His regime was modest, without the royal accoutrement of substantial buildings or a permanent cadre of officials, and did not control Jerusalem.

c. 1000 David captured Jerusalem from the Jebusites, brought the Ark of the Lord, and made the city his capital between the two major regions of Israel and Judah.

965–927 Reign of Solomon. His most prominent addition to David's kingdom was the Temple in Jerusalem. He is identified with large levies of wealth and conscripted labor. Substantial opposition to these levies developed, especially in the northern regions.

927 Division of the united kingdom between Israel in the north and Judah in the south. The following two hundred years were marked by numerous violent changes of regime in Israel, somewhat lesser instability in Judah, and periods of cooperation and warfare between the two kingdoms.

722 Assyria conquered and destroyed the northern kingdom of Israel after Israel sought to rebel against its position as a vassal to Assyria.

586 Babylon destroyed Jerusalem and the Temple, and exiled a portion of the Judean elite. This marked the end of what is variously called the First Temple, the First Kingdom, or the First Commonwealth.

537 Emperor Cyrus II of Persia, which had succeeded Babylon as the major power, permitted exiles to return from Babylon to Jerusalem.

330 Alexander the Great defeated Darius III of Persia, beginning the period of Greek rule.

167 Maccabees revolted, captured, and purified the Temple, giving rise to the celebration of Chanukah and the onset of the Hasmonean dynasty.

63 Judea became a Roman client, and later (after the reign of Herod that lasted from 37 to 4 B.C.E.), a Roman province.

66–73 C.E. First Jewish Revolt led to the fall of Jerusalem, the destruction of the Temple (70), and Masada (73).

132–35 The Roman Emperor Hadrian suppressed the Bar Kokhba Rebellion, marking an important stage toward the end of the ancient country of the Jews. Hadrian, renamed Jerusalem Aelia Capitolina, began the creation of a Roman city, and forbade entry to circumcised persons.

324 Emperor Constantine converted to Christianity. His mother, Helena, visited Jerusalem, claimed to locate the site of Christ's crucifixion and burial, and initiated construction of the Church of the Holy Sepulcher. Jerusalem entered the period of Byzantine rule.

614 Persian invaders took Jerusalem, providing to the Jews short-lived hopes of rebuilding the Temple.

638 Jerusalem came under the rule of Moslems with its capture by Omar.

1099 Crusaders captured Jerusalem.

1187 Saladin (Salah al-Din) recaptured Jerusalem for the Moslems.

1253 Beginning of Mamluk rule.

1537 Beginning of Ottoman rule. Suleiman the Magnificent built the walls that have remained until the present.

1831–39 Egyptian interruption of Ottoman rule, onset of European interest in Jerusalem, and the city's modernization.

1850s Construction outside the city walls of the Schneller Orphanage, the Russian Compound, and the Jewish residential neighborhood Mishkenot Sha'ananim.

1870s Immigration created a Jewish majority in Jerusalem.

1917 British took Jerusalem from the Turks.

1948 Israeli War of Independence, resulting in the division of the city between Israeli and Jordanian sectors.

1967 Six-Day War, producing the reunification of Jerusalem.

Jews of different perspectives and between Jews and non-Jews; substantial Diasporas outside the Promised Land; and a prophetic tradition, or a severe criticism of the regime by respected figures.

The land said to be promised to the Jews by God was attractive to other peoples insofar as it lay on the routes that they used for commerce, conquest, and defense. At a number of times an Israelite state may have been able to develop, or thrive, only because greater powers were temporarily weakened.

One of the Israelites' problems in maintaining a strong state was their lack of unity. A number of modern writers stress the tribal origins of the people and see this as a continuing source of tension in ancient periods.[51] A north-south division was especially prominent. It appeared in the struggle between Saul and David, rebellions against David, and the split between Israel and Judah after the death of Solomon.

The criticism that several prophets directed against the harsh treatment of the poor indicates the existence of socioeconomic tensions among the Jews. Government authorities, landowners, and creditors pressed the poor with their demands for taxes and the repayment of debts.[52] There were also controversies about doctrine and ritual. Pious Jews who emphasized the detailed application of religious ordinances were criticized by other pious Jews who demanded righteousness and justice. The prophet Hosea said that the Lord "desire[s] mercy, and not sacrifice, And the knowledge of God rather than burnt offerings."[53]

By the time of the Second Temple (after 537 B.C.E.) there seems to have been a pluralism of faith and practice that reflected immigrations, mixed marriages, and regional groups that adopted Judaism voluntarily or by force at various times and to various degrees of completeness.[54] At least by the third century B.C.E. there were also Jews who were attracted to the cultures of the regional powers, especially the Greeks and the Romans.

Tensions among the ancient Jews were associated with an inability to resist foreign invasion or with the temptations of foreign assistance. The sons of Queen Salome Alexander contributed to the end of Hasmonean independence when they asked the Romans to select one of them as the next king of the Jews. Later in the Roman period, bloody conflicts between cosmopolitan and zealous Jews facilitated the conquest of the country, the destruction of the Temple and Jerusalem, and the loss of whatever independence Judea had enjoyed.

Tensions between Jews and non-Jews were a prominent feature of Israelite history. Passages in the Book of Joshua describe the conquest of the Land by the Israelites. Other passages of Joshua and Judges indicate that substantial pockets of non-Israelites remained.[55] Reports of censuses taken by David and Solomon indicate proportions of Jews and non-Jews similar to those in modern Israel.[56] The marriages of Solomon and other Israelite kings with non-Israelites and the worship of idols practiced by the kings may have reflected the monarchs' efforts to cement their heterogeneous country.[57]

To be sure, there is much about modern Israel that differs from the ancient country of the Jews. Modern Israel is a democracy with an elected government. Political change has been orderly, without the killings that marked the ruling families of biblical Israelites. The vast majority of the modern population is urban rather than rural. Agriculture and industry are sophisticated. Workers are well organized, and the state is an active provider of social services. Modern Israel has been stronger militarily than its immediate neighbors. Israel's mastery of weapon technology has given it an important edge over armies with several times its manpower. The great powers of today are not Israel's neighbors. These differences provide modern Israel with more room for maneuver in international politics than its predecessor. One can only speculate about the subsequent course of history if the prophet Jeremiah could have threatened ancient Babylon and Egypt with nuclear weapons.

Attitudes and political behaviors differ from those of ancient times. The nature of political debate in modern Israel reflects the details of contemporary problems, along with an awareness of Jewish history. National leaders and many citizens know what they do not want to repeat. The record of Jewish zealotry, civil wars, false messiahs, statelessness, and the Holocaust may lessen the hope for heavenly intervention in Israel's behalf, and lessen the tendency of Jews to elevate the temperature of policy debates by claiming to speak in God's name.

Despite these differences between ancient and modern Israel, a number of conditions have returned from ancient times to render the country insecure. As in ancient times, many of Israel's problems derive either directly or indirectly from its location.[58] The place is again important strategically. The proximity to the Suez Canal and oil and the claim that Israel is "Arab land" assure that the country is a constant topic of international politicking. It is the site of holy places for people more powerful than the Jews. The Archbishop of York expressed his sense of affinity with the place in the middle of the nineteenth century: "This country of Palestine belongs to you and me, it is essentially ours. . . . It was given to the father of Israel . . . that land has been given unto us. It is the land from which comes news of our redemption. It is the land to which we turn as the fountain of all our hopes; it is the land to which we look with as true a patriotism as we do to this dear old England."[59]

Great powers have dominated the environment of modern Israel, albeit in a different context and with different techniques than the great powers that dominated the ancient country. The concept of "independence" must be applied to modern Israel with qualifications. Like the ancient country, modern Israel does not have the size, the population, or the wealth to determine its own destiny. The new country's numerous wars and its cumbersome relations with non-Jewish residents and neighbors reflect different sides of the cultural and political friction that keep it from being integrated in the Middle East. They are the contemporary equivalents of the ancient country's problems with its neighbors and its own non-Judaic population.

Like their ancient predecessors, modern Jews have trouble with themselves as well as with non-Jews. An Israeli with a sense of history may think of Jeremiah, Ezra, Nehemiah, and the Maccabees amidst the chronic efforts to legislate on the subjects of who is a Jew, secular marriage and divorce, regulations against abortions, the availability of nonkosher food, and the proper celebration of the Sabbath. The multiplicity of contentious perspectives apparent in the Hebrew Bible makes its appearance in the two dozen or so political parties that have competed in Israeli elections.

Extensive Diasporas are a feature of modern Jewry, as they were in ancient times. New York rather than Alexandria is the chief competitor of Jerusalem as the cultural center of world Jewry. Some words written about Diaspora and Judean communities of two thousand years ago have their parallels in what some Diaspora Jews say about Israelis today: "While the Jews of Judea . . . tended to be poor, backward, obscurantist, narrow-minded, fundamentalist, uncultured and xenophobic, the Diaspora Jews were expansive, rich, cosmopolitan, well-adjusted to Roman norms and to Hellenic culture, Greek-speaking, literate and open to ideas."[60]

One can find reason for either pessimism or optimism in the continuity of conflict among the Jews. One view is that that conflict is a precursor of civil war. Another view is that Jews have learned to deal nonviolently with their many points of view and that this trait makes Israel unique among new countries for the vitality of its democracy.

Unresolved issues are prominent among the costs that Israelis pay for a modern society that suffers from ancient problems. Old difficulties create periodic crises. Incomplete solutions leave Israel with religious-secular tensions, the cumbersome administration of occupied territories, physical insecurity, and a weak economy.

The conclusion of one commentary on the Hebrew Bible seems to be appropriate also for modern Israelis: "The future belongs not to those who must have certainties, but to those who can live with uncertainty, who can calmly and self-confidently explore the heritage of the past, the problems of the present, and the opportunities for the future, without the crutches of rigid and doctrinaire ideology."[61]

A messy pragmatism reflects the modern state's effort to cope with its traditions, dangers, and opportunities. Later chapters will describe a contemporary Jerusalem that is a frequent site of confrontations and adaptations. It is overtly secular on some dimensions but governed by religious law on others. Israel's posture with respect to East Jerusalem and other territories occupied during the war of 1967 is muddled by a partial application of Israeli law along with Jordanian law. While some Jews would occupy the territories outside of Jerusalem more fully as part of a policy strategy of domination, other Jews would relinquish control of areas as a way to accommodate demands by non-Jews that they view as justified.

CHAPTER 3

A Compelling History that Complicates the Present

Jerusalem's history elevates its importance far beyond that of a middle-sized capital of a tiny country. The same history that makes Jerusalem a world city complicates any efforts of the present generation to deal routinely with the kinds of problems that usually concern municipal officials. The city's history provides entry to local affairs of several interests that are foreign to the Israeli regime and some that are hostile to it, makes Jerusalem's problems a major element of Israel's problems, and contributes to the tenuous character of the entire country.

The most recent period in any city's history is likely to have the most direct influence on its problems and policies. A student of incremental decision making knows that the present year's budget and other policies are likely to be only marginally different from those of last year, while last year's will be only marginally different from those of the previous year. An incremental view of policy-making must also provide for occasional innovations, some of them dramatic.[1] Jerusalem's history is especially long, and the incrementalism that is evident has shown numerous interruptions. As a result of the most recent violent change in 1967, the city's area increased overnight by 2.8 times and its population by 17 percent. Perhaps even more problematic, Jerusalem acquired much of the West Bank as a Palestinian hinterland. More than twenty-five years later, the social and political problems associated with those changes are still high on the agenda of the city and country.[2]

The previous chapter dealt with the spiritual character of the city created by the Israelites, as well as geographical features that have shaped the city's opportunities. It discussed the themes of accommodation in the city's early regimes and described periods of domination that followed or preceded rebellion. This chapter begins with the Romans and moves quickly through several major historical periods. It slows considerably for a survey of developments having a more direct effect on the present, which began in the middle of the nineteenth century.

The Roman Emperor Hadrian pursued a policy of explicit domination after the failure of Bar Kokhba's revolt in 135 C.E. He renamed Jerusalem Aelia Capitolina and forbade the entry of circumcised persons under penalty of death. This excluded Jewish Christians as well as Jews, and the city sank below the Roman's provincial capital and port city of Caesarea. Perhaps as a studied insult to the Christians, Hadrian erected a market and a temple to Venus, the goddess of sexual love, on the alleged site of Jesus' tomb. Traces of the Romans are still apparent in the Old City. The primary east-west and north-south gates and streets are where the Romans placed them, and the market remains at the intersection of those streets.

Insofar as the early Christians viewed Jerusalem's destruction by the Romans as a divine act taken in punishment of the Jews for Christ's crucifixion, it was not a holy city in their eyes. This changed with Constantine's conversion to Christianity and the pilgrimage of his mother Helena in 326–27. She claimed to identify the sites of sacred events in Jerusalem and nearby Bethlehem, including the Sepulcher. Helena thus renewed the tourist industry that had lain dormant since the destruction of the Temple.[3]

Christian pilgrims have been unrestrained in the miracles perceived in Jerusalem. One visitor in the fourth century reported that water flows into the Pool of Siloam for six days and nights but ceases on the Sabbath. A guidebook produced during the Byzantine period described a cross in the Church of the Holy Sepulcher that was fashioned from the lance that Roman soldiers used to pierce the crucified Christ. The cross shone at night like the sun on the brightest day.[4]

Travel in the Holy Land was likely to be dangerous. Reports from ancient times through the nineteenth century speak of pirates at sea and bandits on the roads. Pilgrims who went up to Jerusalem from the east, or who went down from Jerusalem to the Jordan River, were preyed on by lions in the area of Jericho at least until the third century C.E. The inns used by pilgrims were described as dens of vice. It was partly to remove those temptations that European churches built hospices in Jerusalem and other sites of pilgrimage.[5]

The Romans and the Christians after them instituted a policy of denying to the Jews the opportunity to live within or even to enter their holy city. There is some dispute as to how well Roman and Byzantine rulers enforced these prohibitions. Nonetheless, the Romans (along with the earlier Babylonians and the later Crusaders) occupy a prominent role in Jewish nightmares. They are the model of a world power involved in the Land of Israel to the detriment of its Jewish residents.[6] Jews who distrust the promises of great powers also relate the story of the Persian invaders who reached Jerusalem in 614 C.E. They won the support of Jewish fighters by promising to restore Jerusalem as a Jewish city. By some reports, the Persians also promised that the Jews could rebuild the Temple. Neither promise was implemented. According to one historian, the Jewish population had dwindled to the point that the Persian promise was not tenable.[7] Another historian reports that Christians interceded with the court in Persia and sought to persuade the authorities not only to abandon the idea of making Jerusalem a Jewish city but even to bar Jews from living in the city.[8] The bones of Christians slaughtered when the Persians entered Jerusalem in 614 were unearthed by a construction project and became a political issue in 1993. Some rabbis insisted that there were Jewish bones in the collection and began a dispute with Christian clerics concerning the rites to be performed for their reinternment.

Jerusalem became Arab and Moslem as a result of Omar's invasion in 638. The Temple Mount was made a holy place for Moslems, with the Dome of the Rock and al-Aqsa its prominent shrines. The Moslems never made Jerusalem a political capital and initially had trouble settling it with their own people. By the end of the tenth century there may have been more Christians and Jews than Moslems in the city.

The Crusaders explained their conquest of Jerusalem in 1099 as a fitting response to Moslem attacks on Christian pilgrims and the violation of Christian holy places, especially the Church of the Holy Sepulcher. Modern historians quarrel about this. The harassment of pilgrims was a constant factor in the Near East, which began long before the Crusades, and did not cease once the Christians had established their kingdom in the Holy Land.[9] Scholars who doubt the Crusaders' own explanations point to a surplus of European gentry and a lack of land to provide for their support in Europe as leading the Crusaders to seek their fortunes elsewhere, in land they could take from others.[10]

According to one story, the holy nature of the Crusaders' mission led them to expect the city walls to fall upon their approach. When this failed to occur, their conquest was delayed until they could improvise equipment for a siege.[11] The Christians marked their entry to Jerusalem with a wholesale slaughter of Jews and Moslems. They may have killed seventy thousand Moslems in al-Aqsa alone, including many scholars who sought refuge there. A report from one Crusader reveals his pleasure in a bloody purge and his sense of righteousness with respect to Christian possession of the Holy City. "Some of our men—and this was the more merciful course—cut off the heads of their enemies; others shot them with arrows so that they fell from the towers; others tortured them longer by casting them into the flames . . . men rode in blood up to their knees and bridle reins. Indeed, it was a just and splendid judgment of God that this place should be filled with the blood of unbelievers, since it had suffered so long from their blasphemies."[12] Reports differ as to whether the Crusaders killed all the Jews or allowed some to be ransomed by other Jewish communities or sold as slaves.

At points of transition from Christian to Moslem rule, and then from Moslem to Crusader rule, the new regime changed the architecture on what Jews call the Temple Mount, and Moslems Haram al-Sharif. Each used soldiers to wreck the monumental buildings of the vanquished, sent in religious practitioners for a ritual cleansing, and then erected their own structures.

The Crusaders' regime was the least accommodating and most thoroughly dominating in the city's history. They transformed the Dome of the Rock into a Christian Church, and the Templar Knights used al-Aqsa as a residence, storehouse, and latrine. They are said to have banished all non-Christians from the city, but history is confused by travelers' reports of both Moslems and Jews living there during the Crusader period. The Jew Benjamin of Tudela visited the city in 1170 and found about 200 Jews with a monopoly of the dye craft.[13]

The Crusaders made Jerusalem the capital of their Latin Kingdom from 1099 to 1187.[14] They added considerably to the city's churches and hospices for pilgrims, and the population reached thirty-thousand. They treated Jerusalem narrowly as a holy city and did not concern themselves to populate and develop its hinterland. Their kingdom was heavily dependent on sea links with Europe. The ports of Acre, Tyre, and Antioch were larger and wealthier than Jerusalem.[15]

Saladin (or Salah al-Din) took Jerusalem from the Christians in 1187 and, except for a limited period of further Christian rule, began a Moslem period that lasted through several variations until British troops entered the city during World War I. The Ayyubid dynasty of Baghdad controlled the city until 1253. Then it passed to the control of Mamluks. The Mamluks lost it to the Ottoman Turks in the sixteenth century.

The Moslems cleaned the Haram al-Sharif of Christian symbols and human filth and took over other Christian churches for mosques or religious schools after their conquest of 1187. In order to avoid another crusade, they left the Church of the Holy Sepulcher in Christian hands. The Moslems sought to minimize the Christian population, without forbidding it entirely.[16] Moslem rulers tolerated a Jewish population. There are estimates of 70–250 families during the Mamluk period, some of them having come as refugees from Persia, Iraq, and Central Asian regions overrun by the Mongols in the thirteenth century.[17] An estimate from the middle of the sixteenth century places the Christian population at 1,800 and the Jewish population at 1,000–1,500.[18]

None of the Moslem rulers developed Jerusalem into a major city. It remained inferior to Cairo, Damascus, Constantinople, and even Aleppo, Gaza, Nablus, and Safed at various periods. Some Moslem rulers rebuilt the city walls that had been destroyed during their own entry. Other Moslem rulers destroyed the walls in order to make the city an unattractive focus of development and invasion.[19] The present walls resulted from a spurt of public building that occurred under the initial Ottoman ruler, Suleiman the Magnificent in 1537–41.

The Ottomans were accommodating in their strategy toward non-Moslems but fell far short of egalitarianism. They allowed the Jews to run their own affairs, with a Jewish sheik responsible for collecting taxes, guaranteeing debts, overseeing the baking of bread, ritual slaughter, and the reporting of deaths. The regime's lack of concern for social services is apparent from a list of officers in the Ottoman administration of Jerusalem: night guardian of gates, police inspector, chief architect, chief engineer, chief steward, chief cashier, treasurer, police officer, market inspector, mayor, and chief of the brocade bazaar.[20]

The Jewish community was desperately poor and could not afford to lose even meager personal possessions. The property of individuals who died without heirs reverted to the Moslem authorities. It was the task of the Jewish sheik to be alert to upcoming deaths of Jews who lacked heirs and to arrange gifts or fictitious debts within the community that would be repaid with the assets of the deceased.[21]

Jews served in many of the city's occupations as early as the sixteenth century but were subject to special restrictions. Jewish butchers were allowed to sell meat only on certain days in order to protect the market shares of Moslem butchers. Jews working for the government were likely to be in the loathsome positions of tax collectors or financial advisors. Leading Jews are recorded in the court files as having lent significant sums to Moslems. A modern historian concludes that these may have been bribes to pry favorable rulings from local authorities. Jews had to identify themselves with a yellow turban. Even in the bathhouse not all men were equal. A Jew had to wear a small bell around his neck and use a specially marked towel.[22] As late as the early nineteenth century, Jews avoided the area of the Holy Sepulcher for fear of being beaten by Christians.[23]

Amnon Cohen, Israeli historian of the early Ottoman period, concludes that the Jews were subject to discrimination but not overly so. They could get justice in Moslem courts, even against Moslem adversaries. Jews' testimony was accepted against Moslems, provided there was corroborating evidence. Bribery may have eased a Jewish plea before authorities but was not always necessary. There is evidence of local decisions against the Jews being overturned by appeals to officials in Constantinople.[24] One chapter in Cohen's book is titled "The Importance of Being Tolerated." It suggests the perspective of a Jewish intellectual after the Holocaust: Moslem rule could have been worse.

The Christians had more resources and international supporters than the Jews and thus presented the Turks with more problems and opportunities. The Latins and the Greeks were often at odds with one another over the control of the holy sites. A traveler of the late seventeenth century left the following report of violence in the midst of a religious ritual. "Greeks and Latins . . . in disputing which party should go in to celebrate their Mass . . . have sometimes proceeded to blows and wounds even at the very door of the sepulcher, mingling their own blood with their sacrifices."[25] At times the Turks would favor the Christians who were willing to pay the most to authorities in Constantinople or Jerusalem. The Crimean War, formally declared in 1854, owed something to Latin and Greek quarrels over the Church of the Holy Sepulcher and other holy places in Jerusalem and Bethlehem. France demanded that the Turks favor the position of the Roman Catholics with respect to the sites, and the Russians demanded the same for the Greek Orthodox. A number of historians conclude that the holy places were more an excuse than a genuine cause of a war that was fought to halt the expansion of Russian influence.[26] Whether cause or excuse, the holy places proved their capacity to ignite passions and to justify huge material outlays and organized slaughter. Arguments about which Christian church will have the right to make necessary repairs at holy sites have continued into the Israeli period. The severe winter of 1991–92 damaged a structure on the roof of the Holy Sepulcher shared by the Ethiopian and Coptic Churches. Senior officials of the Jerusalem Municipality and the Israeli Ministry of Religions, as well as the local heads of both churches were involved in negotiations to decide how the churches would divide the opportunity of repair.[27]

THE NINETEENTH CENTURY

The last century began like most of the previous nineteen in Jerusalem's history. It was a small town with eight to ten thousand residents and looked like many other cities in the Near East. There was still the outline of a rectilinear ground plan left over from the Romans, but a number of the streets had been blocked off to make cul-de-sacs. Family homes were built to enhance privacy and security. They were set around interior courtyards, often without any windows opening to the street. Quarters of the city were nearly homogeneous religiously, although there were some Jews and Moslems living in each others' quarter. There were also Moslems, but not Jews, living in the Christian Quarter. The Jewish Quarter was the smallest of the city's districts, with perhaps 12 percent of the city's area. It was also the poorest, most crowded, and least sanitary.[28]

The walls of the city functioned to keep out Bedouin raiders, and the gates closed each night. The domed stone roofs reflected the availability of stone and the lack of wood that could be used for beams. Many homes were dilapidated, with residents living in those rooms whose walls and ceilings had not fallen.

Sewers built in better days two millennia earlier had deteriorated; cisterns were neglected and water contaminated. Cholera and plague swept the city every few years. A visiting physician in 1834 found neither doctor nor dispensary. The general picture is one of decay in the Christian and Jewish Quarters, with the Moslem authorities refusing to permit new construction or even the repair of churches and synagogues. Piles of rubbish and dead animals were left to rot in the streets. Water was generally foul and usually in short supply. Mark Twain is widely quoted: "Rags, wretchedness, poverty, and dirt, those signs and symbols that indicate the presence of Moslem rule more surely than the crescent flag itself, abound.

Lepers, cripples, the blind, and the idiots, assail you on every hand, and they know but one word of but one language apparently—the eternal 'bucksheesh.' "[29] A British officer reported that the city was "one of the most unhealthy places in the world . . . [because of] the inferior quality of the water and the presence of an enormous mass of rubbish which had been accumulating for centuries."[30] An estimate as late as 1910 reported that 25 to 60 percent of the population suffered from endemic malaria.[31]

The city had no substantial industry. Its bazaar served as the trading center for a hinterland of marginal agriculture. The geographer and historian Edward Robinson estimated that only 3 percent of the Moslems were literate as of 1838.[32] There was not enough water to support the dyeing of cloth. The hygiene of the slaughterhouses was doubtful. A Moslem slaughterhouse adjacent to the Jewish Quarter and a leather factory next to the Church of the Holy Sepulcher were both sources of filth and stench and were thought by Jews and Christians to be placed so as to offend non-Moslems.[33] The major source of Jewish livelihood was donations collected by emissaries who traveled through Diaspora communities. Christian craftsmen supported themselves by making souvenirs and religious articles for pilgrims. Piracy at sea and bandits on the road from Jaffa served to limit tourism.

The quality of government was no better than the economy. Few Turks were attracted to live in Jerusalem during the whole Ottoman period.[34] Robinson wrote in 1838 that the city had "sunk into the neglected capital of a petty Turkish province . . . she sits sad and solitary in darkness and dust."[35]

Sources of Change

A series of changes began in the 1830s that continued to the end of Moslem rule in World War I. An Egyptian army under Mohammed Ali and Ibrahim Pasha took the city from the Turks at the end of 1831. The Egyptians increased the authority of the local officials and regularized their salaries to make them less dependent on what they could squeeze from the populace. The Egyptians added to the rights of non-Moslems and improved security outside the city. At least for a while, travelers to Jerusalem no longer had to pay a toll to the bandits of Abu Ghosh.

The Ottomans regained Jerusalem in 1839. By then the western powers had wakened to religious, commercial, and military interests in the Near East, and the Turks no longer had a free hand. Jerusalem consulates were opened from the 1830s through the 1850s by the Americans, Austrians, Belgians, British, Danes, Dutch, French, Greeks, Norwegians, Prussians, Russians, Spanish, and Swedes. France and Austria began separate postal services to Jerusalem in 1837. The beginning of steamship travel ended the threat of piracy at sea. A road from Jaffa to Jerusalem was begun in 1867, and carriages made travel more comfortable than riding mules, donkeys, camels, or horses over rough trails. Cook's began group tours to the city in the 1870s.[36]

Foreign governments and voluntary organizations established new churches, schools, hospitals, and orphanages in Jerusalem, as well as hospices for their country's pilgrims. Even the impoverished Ethiopians built a church owing to the personal commitment of Emperors Johannes IV (1872–89) and Menelik II (1889–1913). Ottoman authorities ended restrictions against non-Moslems that had required them to wear distinctive clothing and prevented them from riding horses. Among the prosaic signs of change were public toilets and street gas lamps, both of which appeared in the 1860s.[37]

Western consulates took the city's Jews under their wing. They provided foreign citizenship or protection and pressed the Ottoman authorities to allow them to acquire land. The successors of these consulates in the late twentieth century played a parallel role of representing Palestinians to Israeli authorities.

The activities of some nineteenth century consulates were designed to attract Jews to Christianity. Prominent in this movement was the London Society for Promoting Christianity Amongst the Jews. Although the incidence of actual converts remained small, Jewish leaders responded by forbidding Jews to take advantage of Christian hospitals or other social services under penalty of excommunication. Some Christian preachers were driven from the Jewish quarter under a hail of stones, dead cats, and other garbage.[38] The threat of missionaries also prompted the Jews to open their own schools, orphanages, and hospitals.[39]

The foreign concern for Jerusalem supported a growth of Christian and Jewish populations. Jews arrived in Jerusalem as refugees from a cholera epidemic that struck Safed in 1812 and as refugees from an earthquake that destroyed parts of Safed and Tiberias in 1837. Large-scale Jewish migration from overseas began with the onset of pogroms in Russian-controlled areas of eastern Europe in the 1880s. The number of Jews in the city grew from 2,000 in 1800 to 11,000 in the late 1860s, and then to 45,000 in 1910. The Jews reached 50 percent of Jerusalem's population in 1870 and 64 percent in 1910.

On the eve of World War I, the city's economy, based on pilgrimages, immigration, and financial contributions from abroad, was vulnerable to events overseas.[40] The economic hardships of World War I and the Turks' expulsion of nationals from the Allied Powers (especially Russia) produced Jewish emigration. Jews declined to 34,100 and 55 percent of the population in 1922. The Christian population had increased from 3,000 in 1800 to 16,750 in 1913, then declined to 14,615 in 1922 as a result of World War I. Meanwhile the Moslem population increased at modest rates: from 4,000 in 1810 to 7,500 in 1880, 12,000 at the outbreak of World War I, and 13,400 in 1922.[41]

It is difficult to decide how much of the foreign activity in behalf of Jerusalem was motivated by religious, economic, or political concerns. The nineteenth century was the era of imperial expansion. The British saw Palestine as an outpost on the way to India as well as the Holy Land. The increasing use of steamships and the opening of the Suez Canal in 1869 made Palestine more accessible and more important strategically. The British looked with suspicion at the German development of the Schneller orphanage, which serves today as an Israeli military base. Even more threatening were the elaborate preparations undertaken for Kaiser Wilhelm's visit in 1898 and the German construction of the Augustus Victoria hospice, with thick walls and a high tower upon a strategic ridge between Mount Scopus and the Mount of Olives, overlooking the Old City.

Problems among the Jews

The Jewish community was the most dynamic and fastest growing element in Jerusalem during the nineteenth century. It was also beset with internal problems. The tensions occurred along lines that could be described as old settlers versus newcomers, traditionalists versus moderns, with an overlay of what is now called ultra-Orthodox versus modern Orthodox, and religious versus secular. Details focused on the promotion of Hebrew as a daily language as opposed to using it as a holy tongue suitable only for religious ritual; the support of Hebrew-language newspapers; the development of a Hebrew library; the introduction of modern schooling as opposed to traditional religious instruction; and the continued reliance on charity as opposed to developing new crafts and occupations.

The Jewish communities of Jerusalem remained economically

dependent on outsiders. Although there was an increase in Jews engaged in handicrafts, trade, construction, and services, the distribution of charity collected overseas remained the economic mainstay. The distribution was not rationalized according to need among all the Jews but was organized according to *kolelim* (congregations) based upon Ashkenazi, Sephardi, and national origin. There were 27 *kolelim* among the Ashkenazi alone prior to World War I, each with their own emissaries who traveled abroad to collect funds for their schools and other institutions within Jerusalem and with their own criteria for distributing money among families.[42] The Moslem mayor of Jerusalem appealed to world Jewry in 1913 for donations that would pay for a sewage system for all the city's neighborhoods.[43] This reflected the still primitive nature of Jerusalem's sanitation and the impoverished condition of the Ottoman authorities. It also provided an example of a fund-raising technique that Teddy Kollek developed into the Jerusalem Foundation during the 1960s.

Most of the Jewish immigrants who came to Palestine from the late 1880s until World War I avoided Jerusalem altogether. Theirs was a new nationalism. Most immigrants were secular, and some were outspokenly antireligious. They were adamant in opposing the traditional Jerusalem religiosity and reliance on charity. They sought their Zionist future as farmers on their land or in the new cities along the coast.[44] One review of Zionist thinking about urban areas concludes that leading figures[45] "showed indifference and sometimes even outright hostility towards the city . . . strong emphasis was put on progress and modernity and enormous efforts spent on efficiency, innovations and the ability of the Jewish agriculture to compete in the market."

The development of cities was inevitable, but their growth was haphazard, without the planning that went into the agricultural settlements. "The high hopes of the Zionist leaders to establish a predominantly agricultural society in Eretz Israel thus gradually receded into wishful thinking . . . the exclusion of a major sector of society from planning and control [i.e., the cities] was bound to raise problems." The implications of the early Zionists' disinterest in the cities appeared after the first two decades of Israel's independence. There was unplanned sprawl in the urban areas and a collection of independent towns settled almost exclusively by new immigrants from the third world. These became small slums when the strongest of their residents left for the cities.

Secular immigrants of the late nineteenth and early twentieth centuries did not avoid Jerusalem altogether. They added their own diversities to the varieties of Sephardi and Ashkenazi communities whose roots extended back to the Middle Ages, and which had been made more diverse by nineteenth century arrivals from Yemen, Bukhara (in what is now Uzbekistan), eastern, and central Europe. By the end of the nineteenth century the Jewish communities of Jerusalem exhibited tensions as well as growth. Eliezer ben Yehuda, credited with the revival of Hebrew as a spoken language, expressed a view common among modern Zionists about the old religious communities that preferred to receive charity collected overseas rather than develop their own land. He proclaimed his intention "to destroy and lay waste the entire old edifice . . . life based on the abomination of haluka [distributions of charity], existence on hand-outs, the malignant leprosy that degrades the assembly of Israel developing in its land."[46]

The conflict between old and new Jews was not clear-cut. Some of new immigrants were religious and willing to fit themselves into the existing congregations, and the older communities were undergoing economic and cultural change. Arabic-speaking members of established Sephardi families served as intermediaries between Jews and Arabs and facilitated land purchases by newcomers. Some Sephardi offspring joined with the children of Ashkenazi families in the expanding commercial opportunities produced by the immigration. A number of rabbis stood against the aspirations of modern Zionists to create a new Israel in advance of a clear signal from the Almighty. Others, led by Rabbi Avraham Yitzhak Kook, saw even the antireligious Zionists as adding to the Jewish presence in the Promised Land and fostering God's plan of redemption.[47]

The New City

Events of the nineteenth century increased the population of Jerusalem, and especially its Jewish component, to the point where the Old City was no longer adequate. The steep valleys to the south and east of the city that had made the site defensible from the time of David retarded construction in those directions. As a result, new developments were to the north and west.

The move outward began tentatively in the 1850s. Security against bandits continued to be a problem, and it was not easy to persuade families to live outside the city walls. Nonetheless, the 1850s saw the beginnings of two European Christian institutions (the Schneller Orphanage and the Russian Compound) and one Jewish residential neighborhood (Mishkenot Sha'ananim). The construction of Jewish neighborhoods and Christian institutions, along with smaller developments of Moslem and Christian residential areas, continued from that point to remake the face of Jerusalem. Protestant congregations wanting a place in the Holy City created the American Colony to the north of the Old City and the German Colony to the south. Both remained small and came to be populated mostly by Moslems and Jews, respectively, after Israel's War of Independence.

Jewish neighborhoods came to dominate the new cityscape. The typical residential development was financed and promoted by foreign individuals or organizations with charitable rather than commercial motivations. The *kolelim* were heavily involved, with the result that most new neighborhoods were Ashkenazi or Sephardi, and homogeneous with respect to national origin.

The new quarters offered what modern Jerusalemites would view as tiny apartments. During the time when they were built, they differed from those in the Old City by being new and clean, with space between the buildings. The Jewish Quarter of the Old City was a crumbling ruin, with open sewers and garbage everywhere, and dependent on the foul water of cisterns. The associations in charge of the new neighborhoods sought to keep the residents from reverting to old ways. They required that residents keep their homes clean and deal with garbage in an orderly manner. Mea She'arim was established in the 1870s with the additional requirement that residents be pious in ways acceptable to the governing committee.[48]

The movement of Jews from the Old City began slowly, but gathered speed as the new neighborhoods proved to be safe. Estimates are that 2,100 among 17,000 Jews lived outside the walls by 1880, and 6,000 among 25,000 Jews by 1890. There were forty-six distinct Jewish neighborhoods outside the walls in 1897 and sixty-nine by 1914.

The terms "Old City" and "New City" remained geographical and cultural. The Old City was within the walls and became increasingly Moslem and Christian. The New City was outside the walls and mostly Jewish. Jews did not want to lose a connection with the Old City and resisted the division of the growing city into two local authorities. Arab riots of 1921 and 1929 added to the impetus for Jews to leave the Old City. When the fighting started in Israel's 1948 War of Independence, there were about 100,000 Jews in Jerusalem, with only 2,000–2,500 still living in the Old City.[49]

THE BRITISH

Great Britain was the first democracy to rule Jerusalem. The regime (1917–48) sought to accommodate the numerous groups with a stake in the city, but local rule was colonial rather than democratic. British officials with an eye on conditions far removed from the city decided whose interests would be accommodated and how much. The rulers' task was not enviable. British governmental and administrative ranks in Palestine were divided among those who favored the Zionist goal of creating a Jewish homeland, those who sided with Arab nationalists, and those who sought to placate both Jews and Arabs. One historian, Bernard Wasserstein, emphasizes the gradual cooling of the illusion that it was possible to meet the promises of the Balfour Declaration (both providing for a Jewish homeland and safeguarding the rights of non-Jews). He holds the British together with the Zionists responsible for strengthening Arab nationalism in Palestine. He concludes that British administrators in Palestine were more likely to be anti-Semitic than anti-Arab, but that many were one or the other. He quotes one ranking official who wrote about leading Jews as the "long-nosed friends"; another who described the Arab as "an admirable looter and jackal," "decadent, stupid, dishonest and producing little beyond eccentrics influenced by the romance and silence of the desert."[50] The British problem in Jerusalem was even more sharply focused than in Palestine as a whole. Sir Ronald Storrs, the governor of Jerusalem from 1917 to 1926, wrote that he relished the opportunity to bring peace to the Holy City but found himself criticized as being Zionist by the Arabs and pro-Arab by the Jews.[51]

The British provided some measure of local government to Jerusalem's residents, but not to the extent of recognizing majority rule. They were especially concerned not to offend Moslems and Christians by giving the Holy City over to the Jews. The Jews comprised some 55 percent of the population early in the Mandate Period,[52] but the government appointed a municipal council with two members each of Moslems, Christians, and Jews, with a Moslem mayor and Jewish deputy mayor. Early British rulers valued Jerusalem's spiritual quality and its beauty over its residents' concerns for their livelihood. They prohibited the construction of any industrial buildings but later amended this to permit them beyond the point where they could be seen from the Old City.[53] The local council was popularly elected by 1934. Then Jews comprised 75 percent of local taxpayers, but the council was structured to have six Moslems and six Jews.[54]

1948 AND BEYOND

Jerusalem's vulnerability was made dramatically clear during Israel's War of Independence. Arabs cut the water lines and the main road from Tel Aviv and created a situation in which numerous battles had to be fought in the city or on the roads to it. The city's importance to the Jews can be measured by the casualties that were suffered on its account. Approximately half of the six thousand Israelis killed in the 1948 war fell either in Jerusalem or in efforts to break the Arab blockade of the city.[55]

The borders defined by the armistice that ended the war put all of the Old City under Jordanian control, as well as neighborhoods to the north of the walls that were Christian and Moslem in their population. Only 3,500 Arabs remained in the Jewish part of the city, most of them in the village of Beit Safafa that was itself divided into Israeli and Jordanian sections.[56] Arab families abandoned neighborhoods of western Jerusalem, which were then populated by Jews who had fled the Old City or immigrated from Europe and Arab countries.

During the year after the war, Israeli policymakers found themselves in a quandary defined by some foreign proposals to internationalize the city and their own ambivalence. They wanted to control as much of Jerusalem as possible and to minimize Arab control of the city. To some Israeli views, internationalizing parts of Jerusalem (for instance, the Old City) or some functions (for instance, the control of holy places) might expand Israelis access to sites then in Jordanian hands. Yet other Israelis felt that agreeing to partial internationalization might lead to the city's full internationalization and their loss of control over its western section. There was some hope that a formal expression of internationalization might help, while the actual internationalization would not be achieved in practice. A ranking Israeli foreign ministry official expressed the problem:

> It is certainly true that we are trying to have our cake and eat it too, in other words, to maintain our hold on the New City while at the same time trying to keep the Old City from falling into Abdullah's hands. The reason for this is that we are caught in a trap which presents us with only two logical choices: either we agree to the internationalization of the entire

> city, which we do not want, or else we agree to Arab rule in those parts of the city which are not in our possession, which we also do not want. Under these circumstances we are forced to take a stand lacking all logic.[57]

In December 1949, Prime Minister David Ben-Gurion led his government to declare Jerusalem as the capital of Israel in response to a vote of the United Nations General Assembly to confirm the internationalization of the city. This set the stage for what has continued, with changes in detail, as the de facto Israeli control of Jerusalem (first western Jerusalem in its pre-1967 borders and later the expanded city in its post-1967 borders). Foreign powers did not press for the implementation of the United Nations' policy, but neither did most of them grant de jure recognition to Israeli actions.[58]

Both East and West Jerusalem suffered during the 1948–67 period. Each was isolated at the end of roads that led outward from the centers of Jordanian or Israeli economies. Each part of the city was cut off completely from the other, hindering its economic dynamism.

The period of Jordanian rule over a section of Jerusalem from 1948 to 1967 had elements of domination on the local scene but accommodation in a larger perspective. Jews were forbidden to enter the Jordanian section, including the Old City. Again as in late Roman, Byzantine, and Crusader periods, Jews assembled for prayer on religious occasions at high points outside the walls and strained to see areas sacred to them.

The Amman government also pursued a policy of domination with respect to Jerusalem's Palestinians. It proclaimed the city its second capital and promised to strengthen it economically but actually worked against its development. The government put its resources into the growth of Amman. Christian churches that offered to finance hospitals and other social services in Jerusalem were given permission to open them only in Amman. Only 30 percent of the homes in Jordanian Jerusalem had electricity prior to 1967, while all homes were electrified in Israeli Jerusalem. Income differentials between poor and wealthy income strata were a high 1:11 in the Jordanian city but a modest 1:3 in the Jewish city.[59] Tourism attracted to the Old City was the major industry of Jordanian Jerusalem. More than 50 percent of the city's workforce were guides, hotel or restaurant workers, or workers in small factories turning out souvenirs.

There was substantial out-migration from Jordanian Jerusalem. Its population growth was less than natural increase between 1948 and 1967. Migrants went mostly to Amman and the oil-producing countries of the Persian Gulf. The Christian population of Jerusalem declined by 49 percent during 1948–67. The intellectual and political center of Palestinian nationalism that developed in Jerusalem against the Zionists and the British turned against Jordan when it absorbed that part of the West Bank that was not taken by Israel and when it favored Amman and the East Bank in its development policies.[60]

Along with a Jordanian strategy of domination within Jerusalem and enmity between Jordan and Israel, there seems to have been a Jordanian policy of accommodation to divide with Israel what had been the British Mandate. Perhaps neither Israel nor Jordan wanted to control all of Jerusalem, in fear of provoking outside powers to implement the United Nations decision that the city be internationalized.[61]

Jewish Jerusalem grew at a substantially greater rate than Arab Jerusalem. The city received some of the mass migration that came to Israel in the late 1940s and early 1950s.[62] Many immigrants were housed in neighborhoods that had been abandoned by Arabs or in new buildings created alongside the cease-fire lines that divided the city. The border areas were dangerous on account of sniper fire and were avoided by Jerusalemites who could afford something better. The Israelis built long housing blocks facing the borders in order to protect other buildings from the gun fire. They put only small windows on the border side of those buildings in order to protect their residents.

Israel declared that Jerusalem was its capital and sought to attract additional population. However, the city's population grew at a lower rate than that of Israel as a whole during 1948–67. Some firms avoided Jerusalem because of transportation costs or because they feared a repeat of the physical isolation that the city suffered during the 1948 war. A Jewish out-migration was parallel to a similar movement on the Jordanian side. Upwardly mobile individuals left Israel's nominal capital for better opportunities on the coastal plain.

The committee in charge of naming the streets of Israeli Jerusalem sought to demonstrate the change in regime. St. Paul Street became Shivti Israel (Tribes of Israel), and St. Louis Street became King Solomon. Jaffa Road was renamed for Theodore Herzl but reverted to Jaffa Road in response to citizen protests. The founder of Zionism was compensated with a boulevard and a mountain in what was then the western outskirts of the city. King George V Street remained King George V Street, despite periodic demands that all traces of the British Mandate be removed from the city.[63]

Historians and ordinary Israelis quarrel as to whether the capture of East Jerusalem in 1967 was part of Israeli war plans or an improvised response to a Jordanian miscalculation. The Israelis sent a prewar message to King Hussein of Jordan to avoid attacking and committed themselves to refrain from hostile actions on the Jordanian border. Yet Hussein's forces opened fire on Jewish neighborhoods of Jerusalem, perhaps because he was misled by President Gamal Abdel Nasser into believing that Egypt was on the verge of destroying the Israeli military. In response to the Jordanian fire, the Israeli military mounted the attack that took the Old City and the remainder of the West Bank.

There are several indications that Israel's attack was not actively considered until it was forced by the Jordanians after the onset of hostilities. At various times during 1948–67 individual officers had prepared contingency plans and urged the Israeli government to attack East Jerusalem and other areas of the West Bank in retaliation for Jordanian violations of the cease-fire agreement. One of Jerusalem's city planners reports that during the 1948–67 period his colleagues tried several times to interest municipal and national government officials in the preparation of plans for a reunited city.[64] The government of David Ben-Gurion resisted any major departure from its agreement with Jordan, except for limited responses to Jordanian sniper fire and other provocation.[65] Another indication of the ad hoc nature of the Israeli conquest was the nature of troops who were used in the battle. Some of the units were composed of thirty- and forty-year old reservists, who were sent against Jerusalem only after the war had begun. Their age may have had something to do with the high rate of casualties they suffered. They were hardly the units that would be used in a major campaign, planned in advance, for a highly prized target.

Less than three weeks after the war ended, Israeli authorities began clearing the concrete blocks and barbed wire that had separated the city into Israeli and Jordanian sectors.[66] With the reunification of Jerusalem the city's population again showed the historic element of religious and ethnic tension, with latent or explicit conflict between rulers and a sizable Palestinian community that considered itself indigenous and conquered. Those who were out of power locally also had their foreign patrons. The successors of foreign consulates who protected Jews during the Ottoman period played a parallel role for the sake of Palestinians who acquired citizenship in Western Europe or North America. Even Israel's allies formally accept United Nations decisions that Jerusalem was to be internationalized.[67]

The Jerusalem municipality and the Israeli police absorbed a number of employees of the Jordanian authorities when the city was unified. Those persons risked being identified with the Israeli regime, but they facilitated the transition from one administration to another. They also continued to receive salaries from Amman as a symbol of Jordanian's continued claim of sovereignty. No members of the Jordanian municipal council would accept the posts offered for their service in the political ranks of the Israeli municipality.[68]

For the first time in history, Jerusalem local government during the Israeli period has been democratic. To be sure, critics of the Israeli regime claim that it is imposed on an unwilling Palestinian population and reserves its major positions and other benefits for Jews.[69] Few Palestinians from the area formerly controlled by Jordan have taken advantage of the political opportunities offered to them. Their participation in local elections since 1967 has never been higher than 22 percent of those eligible and has been as low as 4 percent. Virtually none have taken the Israeli citizenship required for voting in national elections.

Jerusalem policymaking has been open to scrutiny, documentation by scholars, and regime critics as never before. The period appears to fit within the accommodation strategy of governance. As in other periods of accommodation, the Israeli regime has not treated all communities equally. The primary beneficiaries have been the city's Jews. Some prominent Israelis would provide even greater proportion of benefits to the Jewish communities. The centrist character of the regime has been apparent in its efforts to find a path between those who would push its policy strategy to one of domination and those who condemn it for not being sufficiently accommodating to Moslem, Christian, or Jewish secular or religious communities, or to Palestinian nationalists.

Israel's first actions in taking control of the Old City and East Jerusalem in 1967 showed elements of the conquerors' taking sensitive sites for their own. Nonetheless, it was done within a policy to minimize the impact of conquest and to accommodate competing interests. Some of the first soldiers to reach the Temple Mount raised the Israeli flag above the Dome of the Rock. Defense Minister Moshe Dayan ordered the flag taken down and began what became Israel's policy of leaving the administration of the site in Moslem hands.[70]

The Jews focused their possessive feelings on the Western Wall and what had been the Jewish Quarter of the Old City prior to the 1948 war. Within three days of taking the Old City, they began to clear Palestinian homes from an area in front of the Wall and to create the plaza that has since been a site of daily prayer and mass gatherings for Jewish holy days and Israeli national holidays. The number of Jews living in the reconstructed Jewish Quarter increased from 720 in 1977 to almost 1,600 in 1981, and 2,200 by 1988.[71]

Also prominent in Israeli policy was the enlargement of Jerusalem's boundaries and the extension of Israeli law to areas formerly under Jordanian control.[72] The municipal area increased from 38,000 to 108,000 dunams (1 dunam = 1,000 square meters). Included within the new boundaries were the Old City, Arab neighborhoods to the north of the city walls, and a number of Arab settlements immediately to the east of the Old City, as well as extensive open areas to the north and south formerly under Jordanian control. The new boundaries went substantially beyond the pre-1967 Jewish and Jordanian cities of Jerusalem. They were crafted to include areas that would lend themselves to new housing for Jews and areas suitable for industrial development, as well as the airport north of the city. They stopped short of the Arab cities of Bethlehem and Beit Jallah to the south and Ramallah to the north, and they excluded a number of Arab settlements on the city's eastern boundary. In the north, the boundaries turned here and there to avoid Arab settlements. The point was to make Jerusalem more secure with a substantial Jewish majority.

As will be seen in subsequent chapters, Jerusalem's boundaries have served Israel's interests, but they have left some problems unresolved. The city map does not show the gross twists and turns of some gerrymandered congressional districts or municipalities in the United States. Jerusalem is a reasonably compact city whose sizable Jewish majority shares a commonalty of interests. What is left unresolved by Jerusalem's boundaries is the question of who will govern Jerusalem's hinterland, which is largely Palestinian, and what claims Palestinians may assert with respect to what they consider to be their holy city and sites now populated by Jews that they say were taken from them improperly by the Israeli regime.

The Israeli cabinet that served in the immediate postwar period divided over the status to be granted the Arabs of the newly created city. Ministers who would have given Israeli citizenship to the city's Arabs by fiat were opposed by those who opted for a minimum of Israeli intervention into the lives of East Jerusalemites. What emerged was something of a muddle. Israeli citizenship was offered but not imposed on the Arab residents who found themselves in the enlarged Israeli city. The city's residents were given the social services provided to Israelis, in contrast to residents of the West Bank outside of Jerusalem, who were not to receive those benefits. For religious purposes, East Jerusalem's Moslems remained under the same authorities that prevail in the West Bank and not those who govern religious matters for the Moslems who live in what had been Israel prior to 1967. Arab practitioners of professions and owners of businesses remained subject to the authority of existing Arab professional associations and the East Jerusalem Chamber of Commerce and have not been required to obtain Israeli licenses or to join Israeli associations that govern their members' practices. Israeli authorities initially sought to extend the Israeli educational network that serves Arabs to East Jerusalem but backed down and came to accept existing Jordanian curricula and private schools, with a minimum of Israeli supervision. Israel's tax authorities imposed their own rates and standards of administration gradually on East Jerusalem, which had been accustomed to much lower rates and the uneven quality of Jordanian enforcement.[73]

Soon after the 1967 war there began the task of rebuilding the Jewish Quarter in the Old City, creating new Jewish neighborhoods and suburbs at all points of the compass, and improving Jerusalem's highway connections with the coastal cities. The new construction was meant to realize the decision of the national government that Jerusalem be developed as a city with a large Jewish majority and to create physical facts that would discourage any further division of the city along the lines of 1948–67. The first new neighborhood was Ramat Eshkol, placed along the route to Mount Scopus and the former locations of the Hadassah Hospital and the Hebrew University. The neighborhood of French Hill was built alongside a strategic junction of roads that lead to the Old City to the south, Mount Scopus to the east, and Palestinian cities of the West Bank to the north.

The next stage put new neighborhoods for Jews in open areas that had been occupied by Jordan to the north, south, and east of the city. Neve Ya'acov was built on the site of a Jewish settlement that had to be abandoned in 1948 on the road to the Palestinian city of Ramallah. Ramot flanks the main road to Tel Aviv and serves to buffer Jerusalem and the highway from Palestinian villages to the north and west. Gilo and East Talpiot were built on the city's southwestern and southeastern flanks, positioned between it and the Palestinian locales of Beit Jallah and Bethlehem. To the east of the municipal boundaries is the new suburb of Ma'ale Adummim. It is alongside the main road between Jerusalem and the Jordan Valley and dominates the Judean desert. While some planners wanted to build other suburbs closer to the city on its eastern border, they were discouraged by the relatively dense Palestinian construction in the area and extensive landholding by Christian churches.[74] Figure 3.1 is a schematic map of post-1967 Jerusalem. It also identifies the 1948 cease-fire line that served as the boundary of Israeli and Jordanian Jerusalem that existed between 1948 and 1967 and locates new neighborhoods built since 1967.

A third stage of post-1967 building in the Jerusalem region includes new Jewish towns north and south of Jerusalem between the Palestinian cities of Hebron, Bethlehem, Ramallah, and Nablus. Pisgat Ze'ev fills in a spot within the boundaries of Jerusalem. Other Jewish settlements were located between Jerusalem and the coastal plain, in order to thicken the corridor that had been cut during 1948. The winding two-lane road through the mountains and rolling lowlands to Tel Aviv was replaced in stages with a four-lane divided highway that links up with the modern highway system between Beer Sheva, Tel Aviv, and Haifa. Traffic in the morning and afternoon reflects a post-1967 phenomenon of daily commuting between Jerusalem and Tel Aviv metropolitan areas. A network of additional roads is being built among the new settlements north, east, and south of Jerusalem, to connect them more quickly with Jerusalem, with bypasses around Palestinian villages to lessen impromptu blockades and stone throwing. Other roads have been planned or built directly to the coast from Jerusalem's northern and southern suburbs. All these developments lessen the isolation of Jewish Jerusalem in the Judean mountains and give Palestinians the impression that more of their land is being lost. By 1990, 132,000 Jews lived in new neighborhoods constructed on land that had been in the Jordanian sector prior to the 1967 war.[75]

Jerusalem's Mayor Teddy Kollek acquired a reputation for promoting Israel's policy of accommodation. He sought to maintain connections with leaders of the city's non-Jewish communities, local and overseas Jews, and key members in the national government. His task was not easy. On various sides were more overtly nationalist Jews who want to take more of Jerusalem, sometimes in an explicit and ostentatious manner; religious Jews who protested the municipality's policies on issues of religious law and custom; Palestinians and their supporters who felt that the mayor's expressions of accommodation were only a veneer that covered a policy of assuring

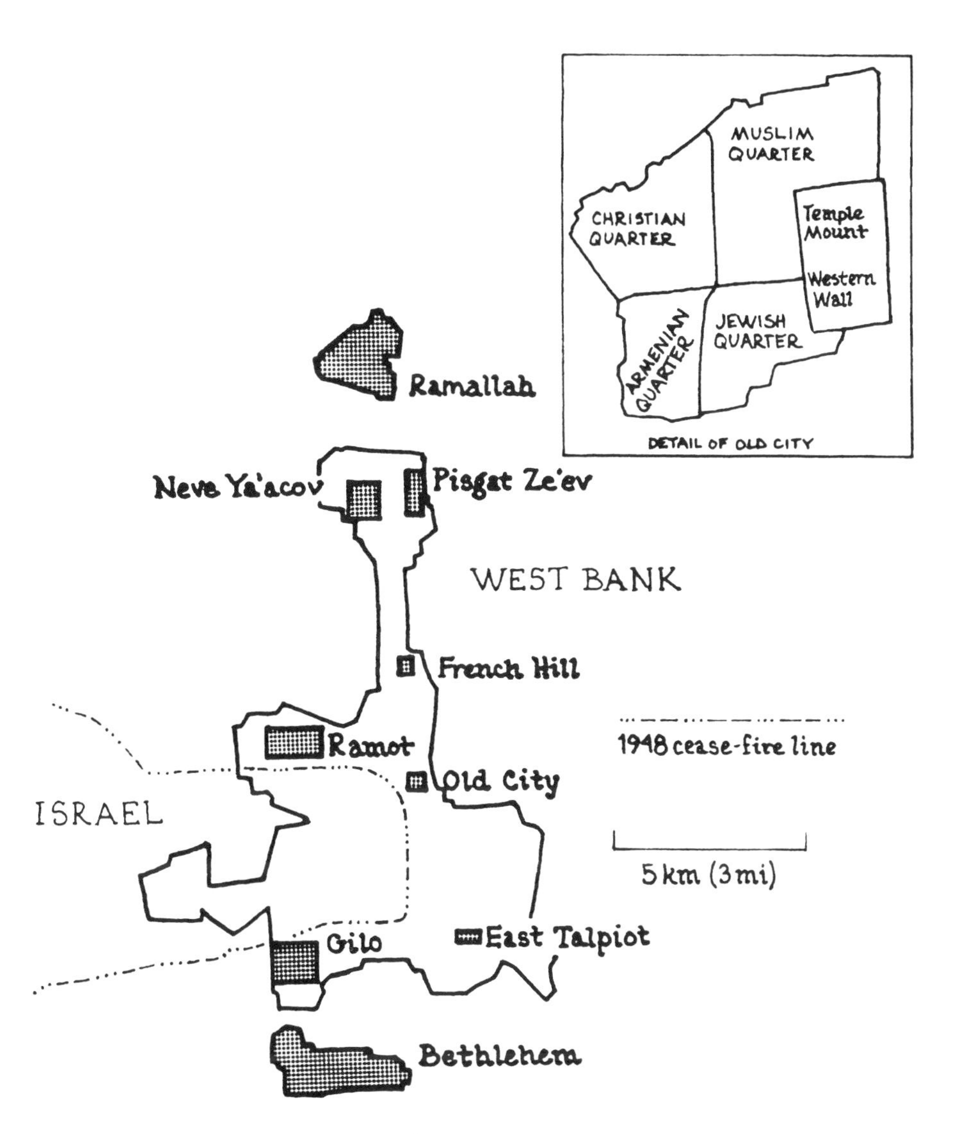

Figure 3.1
Jerusalem

Jewish control of the city and its environs; and Israeli national officials who wanted to make the important decisions for Judaism's showcase and Israel's most important city. Subsequent chapters will return to the activities and the problems of Kollek in more than a quarter-century as Jerusalem's mayor.

CHAPTER 4

Jerusalem as an Israeli Municipality

Jerusalem is not only the focus of the nation's aspirations and international interest. Its special features are fully apparent only when seen in the context of Israel's government structure, and relations between government ministries and other local authorities.

Israel is ruled from the center, with a large role for the professional staffs of national ministries and other government bodies. The International Monetary Fund ranks Israel among those democracies where the central government is most heavily involved in economic management. The combined budgets of governmental and quasi-governmental bodies sometime exceed gross national product.[1]

Centralization is made easy because of small size. Israel's five million people live in an area of 8,300 square miles (not counting the occupied territories). It is a bit larger than New Jersey and a bit smaller than Massachusetts. Most Jewish families arrived in the 1930s or later. Compared to countries of long- established settlement patterns, Israelis' national identity is stronger than feelings toward a region or locale. National politics operates with proportional representation in a single electoral district. No member of the Knesset is formally a representative of a city or region.[2]

The dominant Zionist ideology reinforces Israel's central government. The country's founders wanted to build a strong state in order to protect a people who had suffered from nearly two thousand years of statelessness. The fact that most founders came from eastern and central Europe, where centralized states are the norm, also contributed to Israel's development.

Economic conditions added to the power of national authorities. Most citizens were poor when Israel became independent in 1948. Only national institutions could amass resources from taxes and from loans and grants from overseas that were needed for developing agriculture, industry, housing, transportation, telecommunications, and social services. In these traits, Israel resembled many other new states that came on the scene after World War II. Like them, Israel provided a large role for the state in economic management.

Israel was pressed more than other new states by the animosity of its neighbors and massive immigration. These burdens added to the power of the central government. It had to organize and finance a large army and to integrate immigrants who more than doubled the national population in less than ten years after independence.

Israel has no written constitution. The majority of the Knesset is unrestrained by anything beyond political will in enacting new laws about the municipalities or in changing the laws which exist.[3]

In practice, the strong centralized regime does not operate quite as the rules suggest. The nature of Israeli politics assures that the formal rules of strict centralization are administered in a loose, somewhat chaotic fashion.[4] No political party has ever won a majority of the votes in a national election. Leading parties have had to put together coalition governments, with ministries passed out among the partners according to the number of Knesset seats they control. Prime ministers have been unable to impose their will on the partners, except with respect for a few key issues in the coalition agreement. Israel's concerns have been national security and economic stability. Problems of local governments have been lower on the list of priorities. Individual ministers have been free to operate as they wish on matters of local governments, without having to concern themselves for integrated national policies.

The "local state" of Jerusalem is largely one of official functionaries. Local and national bureaucrats and elected officials joust with one another, with local authorities doing better than suggested by the formal rules. Citizen groups are less prominent in Jerusalem policymaking than in the United States, and private entrepreneurs are less visible as investors than governmental or quasi-governmental organizations.

Israel governs itself with an extensive bureaucracy and rules that define competitive procedures of appointment and the rights of state employees. Yet there is a tradition of evading the rules to facilitate the appointment of persons who are politically allied with the minister. Reports of the Civil Service Commission show an incidence of appointments to national government offices not made according to competitive procedures in the range of 20–40 percent of appointments. Positions in local authorities and companies owned by national ministries or local authorities are not supervised closely by the Civil Service Commission and are thought to be even more open to political appointments.[5]

Jerusalemites concerned to know how their city operates have several sources of information. The Office of the State Comptroller is an independent auditor, responsible to the Knesset. It reviews the financial records and the programs of municipal authorities as well as other public bodies.[6] The State Comptroller has been an aggressive critic of governmental activities in sensitive fields of national security, economic management, political appointments to the civil service, and the financing of political parties. The State Comptroller's report about the financing of religious institutions via grants to the municipalities received considerable media attention in 1991.[7] It provided details on the ways that large sums were directed by Minister of Interior Ariyeh Deri to schools and other institutions associated with his ultra-Orthodox Sephardi party, Sephardi Observants of the Torah (SHAS). The report added to public interest in the long-running police investigation of the same issue.

The municipal comptroller has also been assertive in recent years. Its report published in November 1991 mentioned the planning authorities' practice of giving post hoc approvals to building violations, the distribution of funds by the religious council of the municipality without clear criteria, nepotism in the municipal education office, and faulty practices in the letting of contracts. Mayor Teddy Kollek responded defensively to the comptroller's report. He cited a growth of almost 30 percent in the city's population in the recent decade against a growth of only 3 percent in the municipality's workforce, saying that workaday problems in administration show only one face of his city.[8]

Jerusalem watchers concerned with the juicier side of local politics read the weekly local newspapers, *Kal Ha'ir* (All the City) and *Kol Yerushalayim* (Voice of Jerusalem). Israel's daily newspapers are national in their focus and provide limited coverage to local news. Like other local papers in Israel's major cities, those of Jerusalem aspire to the sensational exposé. They focus on the personal excesses of local personalities and controversial details of municipal and national government activities.[9]

THE STRUCTURE OF MUNICIPAL GOVERNMENT

The municipalities of Israel are formally subordinate to the state. The local council may take only those actions that are explicitly allowed in the Municipal Corporations Law. Numerous municipal actions require the approval of the Interior Ministry or other national bodies.[10]

Each municipality is headed by a mayor and local council. Local elections in all municipalities are held on the same day, every four years on the third Tuesday in the autumn month of Heshvan.[11] The mayor is chosen by a direct personal ballot. Council members are selected on a similar basis as the national Knesset: voters choose party slates in a single citywide district on the basis of proportional representation. Party committees rank the candidates on their list prior to the balloting, with each party's percentage of the popular vote determining the percentage of its list chosen for the council. Jerusalem's council, like that of other large cities, has thirty-one members.[12]

Eligible voters must be at least eighteen years of age and registered with the Interior Ministry as living in the municipality. Candidates for mayor must be citizens of Israel, but voters in local elections and candidates for the council need not be citizens.[13] The importance of this in Jerusalem's case is that Palestinian residents of East Jerusalem can exercise their weight in local politics without accepting Israeli citizenship. For the most part, they have declined to take advantage of the opportunity. The result is that all elected positions in the municipality are held by Jews, and political parties that are inclined to be forthcoming on Palestinian issues are weakened by the lack of Palestinian participation in local elections.

During Teddy Kollek's long tenure, Jerusalem's city council existed in the shadow of the dominant mayor on the one hand and powerful national government ministries on the other hand. The council provided a sounding board for elected politicians to criticize what was, or was not, happening in their city. It could back up its members' opposition to the actions of more powerful bodies by delaying approval of the city's budget or the projects that must be presented to the council when it sat as the local planning commission.[14]

The mayor serves as chair of the local council and is responsible for the execution of council decisions. Owing to direct personal election, the mayor's tenure is not dependent on the council's will, except for possible dismissal because of misconduct. The mayor's program depends on the harmony that the incumbent can achieve with the majority of the council. Teddy Kollek won 59 percent of the votes in the direct election for mayor in 1989, but his local party, One Jerusalem, won only eleven of the thirty-one council seats. After the 1989 election, the mayor's party entered into a "wall-to-wall" coalition with all of the seven other parties that held from one to four seats on the council. The election of 1993 produced a similar situation where Ehud Olmert defeated Teddy Kollek but where Olmert's Likud Party won only a minority of the city council.

The municipality is divided into departments of finance; engineering; water supply; town planning; family and community services; education; urban improvement; sanitation; public health; culture; fire brigade; youth, sport, and recreation; plus a department of general administration that includes the comptroller and ombudsman. Department heads are chosen from civil servants or other candidates with relevant professional experience.[15] Leading members of the political parties in the city council coalition are assigned department portfolios according to the coalition agreement. These positions are part- time, and the council members who hold the portfolios vary as to the time they put into their departmental activities and how much they seek to go beyond the ceremonial and seek to influence the decisions taken by their departments. The municipal workforce has ranged from 4,600 to 5,200 in recent years. The municipal budget was equivalent to US $315 million in 1990/91.[16] Jerusalem's municipal workforce is smaller than Tel Aviv's by about 1,500 and larger than Haifa's by 1,100.[17] None of these figures include the employees or the expenditures of national government bodies devoted to Jerusalem projects or quasi-governmental organizations to be described below.

Participants and observers quarrel about how the formal structure works in practice. Some episodes indicate the capacity of central government ministries to rule on the small details of local administration, while others indicate that local officials have more discretion in practice than the rules formally allow. Jerusalem's officeholders complain that the city's status attracts greater intervention than other municipalities by national politicians and ranking ministerial bureaucrats. This may be true for issues that become especially sensitive. In general, it seems that the city's status gives the mayor and municipal departments greater prominence and resources, and thereby more freedom than their counterparts in other Israeli cities.

MUNICIPAL FINANCE: HOW STRONG THE CENTRALIZATION?

Local government finance illustrates a situation of a formal centralization but actual administration that offers considerable flexibility to municipal authorities. The Interior Ministry must approve the local authority's taxes and expenditures and determine the general grant to be given each locality. The Finance Ministry must approve the budget of the Interior Ministry and may take an interest in the finances of individual localities.

The flexibility of local authorities begins with the inability of the Interior Ministry to learn the intricacies of local government finance and operations. According to one scholar who also served as a senior official in the Office of the State Comptroller: "The local authority invariably inflates its proposed budget prior to negotiations with the Ministry of Interior, so that even after cutbacks it is left with a budget which may be larger than strictly necessary . . . this may be closer to the truth during years of economic well-being, and less true during leaner periods when circumstances may diminish the 'negotiating margin.' "[18] When the Interior Ministry ordered that local authorities reduce their personnel as part of government-wide economy measures in 1984, a subsequent report of the State Comptroller found that most authorities did not implement the instructions.[19]

Also working in favor of clever municipal officials are the separate relations between local authorities and ministries that make expenditures on their own programs in the local communities and provide funds to local authorities for specific programs in ways that are not coordinated by the ministries of finance and interior. Ministry administrators operate under a large number of national government laws, ministry regulations, and precedents that reflect decisions taken over the years for different reasons. Some are held over from the period of the British Mandate, some reflect the considered judgment of prestigious commissions of inquiry or actions of the Supreme Court in response to a suit brought by a municipality or a private citizen. In all of these rules and regulations, there are numerous provisions for ministerial discretion.

Academic and governmental writers have commented on the problems in sorting through many years' worth of legislation, committee recommendations, court decisions, administrative rules, ministerial rulings, and financial records in order to identify the major lines of policy pursued by national authorities.[20] The ministries may not move together in response to the same policy themes. The mayor of Jerusalem and other cities have offered national politicians the opportunity to be the patrons of local projects. Ministers seek to advance their own reputations by favoring projects in local areas, whether or not they are not supported by the ministries of finance or interior.

The Interior Ministry provides a general grant for support of local activities. Procedures for figuring each city's grant include both objective criteria and ministerial discretion. This grant has been a target of frequent demands for reform by local officials who feel themselves unfairly treated. Commissions headed by prominent Israelis were appointed to study the problem in 1961, 1975, and 1978, and changes were made in the criteria for the general grant in 1955, 1965, 1974, and 1979.[21]

Interior Minister Ariyeh Deri was the subject of a prolonged police investigation on charges that he provided special allocations for municipalities to use in supporting programs sponsored by his political party, SHAS. The investigation began in 1990 and reached the stage of an indictment and the beginning of trial only at the end of 1993. SHAS has a higher percentage of supporters in Jerusalem than nationwide (8 percent of the votes cast in Jerusalem as opposed to 4 percent nationwide in the election of 1988, and 9 percent of the Jerusalem votes as opposed to 6 percent nationwide in the election of 1992), and a sizable number of Jerusalem's young people attend the schools supported by SHAS. Deri's relations with the Jerusalem Municipality figured prominently in press reports of the police investigation and in the State Comptroller's report on the allocations. On several occasions, Teddy Kollek seemed to go out of his way to praise the Interior Minister for proving one or another kind of help to Jerusalem.

The Ministry of Housing and Construction pays for the construction of housing and roads. The Ministry of Religious Affairs supports synagogues, ritual baths, churches, and mosques. The Ministry of Defense pays part of the costs of local civil defense. The Ministry of Health supports local clinics. The Ministries of Education and Culture provides funds for local schools and cultural events. Israeli education provides separate curricula and schools for secular Jews, religious Jews, and Arabs. The Palestinians of East Jerusalem can choose between an Israeli or Jordanian curriculum in secondary schools that are supported by Israel or Jordan, or take advantage of private schools operated by Christian or Moslem clerics without Israeli supervision. The choice of a Jordanian curriculum allows an Palestinian Jerusalemite to prepare for matriculation in a university within an Arab country.

The Ministry of Education chose Jerusalem for a pilot project of devolving greater responsibilities to local authorities. The municipal education department has more formal authority than in other cities with respect to supervising instruction, drawing school boundaries, and assigning pupils. The issues of school boundaries and pupil assignment are controversial insofar as they are made with an eye to the policy of integrating pupils from western and oriental families within the Jewish educational sector. The ministry has not relinquished its primary control over the content of school curriculum or its policy of integration. The policy means that the municipal education department receives numerous requests from Ashkenazi parents claiming special reasons for sending their children to a better school across town that is less integrated than their neighborhood school. There are no private schools in the Jewish sector that accept pupils on the basis of their parents' willingness to pay.

With the onset of massive immigration from the Soviet Union in 1989, the Ministry of Immigration Absorption became an important source of funds for social services. The minister from 1989 to 1992 was a rabbi with a record of strident orthodoxy, and the ministry was generous in supporting programs to inform the immigrants of Judaic traditions. There was a large void to be filled, insofar as the immigrants came from a regime that had suppressed religious training for seven decades. Jerusalem's Conservative and Reform Jewish congregations expressed their opposition to programs heavily loaded in favor of orthodoxy and their inability to obtain money from the ministry to support their own forms of Judaism.[22]

Municipal welfare departments used to receive funds from national ministries for distribution to needy residents. This provided opportunities for local patronage, along with a lot of noise and some violence. Clients learned that unrestrained emotions could earn more generous treatment from harried social workers. Now the distribution of welfare payments income has been routinized with little room for discretion in individual cases and centralized in National Insurance, an agency of the Israeli government. The Ministries of Labor and Welfare continue to support a number of locally administered social services. Municipal personnel provide counseling, referrals to other service agencies, and small amounts of emergency aid. Secular critics of the rabbi who served as the minister of welfare prior to the election of 1992 uncovered financial aid given to a library associated with a religious institution in Jerusalem and alleged that it was another example of religious politicians providing money to their supporters. When questioned about the appropriateness of the welfare ministry aiding a library, the minister replied that the library served aged and handicapped readers.[23]

Until a reform of 1992, each year's government budget had an item for special projects. The amount of this was generally no more than one-half of one percent of the national budget total. It was the honey pot of Israeli patronage and was likely to be debated actively by Knesset members who accepted with few questions the Finance Ministry's recommendations for the budgets of defense, debt-repayment, and other major activities. The budget item for special projects provided funding for programs operated by the political parties in each locality, including schools associated with the religious parties, athletic teams, centers for youth and the aged, housing, and other social services.

National and local officials can be aggressive players in an intergovernmental game that is something of a free-for-all among contending authorities concerned to guard their powers or stretch the resources at their disposal.[24] Ministers and senior civil servants withhold payments or approvals for local projects in order to force a municipality's compliance with a ministry ruling or to punish a municipality for overstepping its discretion. School principals may try to preserve smaller than average class sizes by telling newcomers to the neighborhood that there is no room for their children. Such tricks may work on timid parents, but many Israeli citizens have learned that they must inform themselves of their legal rights and insist on them against officials who would serve their own organizations rather than the public. There are occasional reports of citizens who pass through insistence to shouting and then upsetting the office furniture in pursuit of their interests, leading the police to intervene.

National ministries send inspectors to schools, welfare offices, and other activities that they support, but there are not enough inspectors to keep tabs on local authorities. Local politicians and administrators seek money where they can find it and do not always follow the rules about transferring funds between budget categories or the discretion they may exercise in program implementation.[25] Much occurs behind the scenes, with only the occasional story made available through the media or from insiders.

Annual financial reports are less helpful than they might be in revealing major lines of public policy at national or local levels. The categories used in budgets and financial reports may not be comparable from one year to the next, or from one local authority to another. They do not include the activities of quasi-governmental

Table 4.1
Percentage of Operating Budgets Derived from Locally Raised Revenues

City	1970–71	1989–90
Jerusalem	71	70
Tel Aviv	85	87
Haifa	77	83
Beer Sheva	71	65
All municipalities	78	74

Sources: Local Authorities in Israel: Financial Data (Jerusalem: Central Bureau of Statistics and Ministry of Interior, Annually).

organizations. Although the categories of "ordinary budget" and "extraordinary budget" suggest a division between operating and capital (investment) activities, items are assigned to one category or another on the basis of their financing by current income or loans. Thus, operating expenses may be included in the extraordinary budget if the local authority persuades the Interior Ministry that they be financed by a loan.

The categories of locally financed and government-supported activities do not reveal much about local initiatives or dependence on the national government. All incomes and expenses are formally provided or approved by national ministries. Jerusalem relies less than Tel Aviv and Haifa, but more than Beer Sheva, on revenues collected from its own residents or businesses. When it is viewed over time, Jerusalem is treated more or less like other cities on these issues of public finance. There have been periods of increased central government grants and periods of increased reliance on local revenues. The historical comparison fails to show any clear trend away from national government domination. Table 4.1 shows a similar ordering of reliance on locally raised revenues in Israel's largest cities in 1989–90 as in 1970–71. The table reports only the locally raised percentages of government revenue that flow through the municipalities. It does not include the revenues raised from donors and investors by voluntary and quasi-governmental bodies for use in Jerusalem.

Jerusalem benefits from special treatment in the rough and tumble of Israeli public finance. The municipality receives an allocation from the national government for being the capital. The mayor and ranking administrators argue in the national ministries that extra budget allocations for housing and public facilities are necessary to improve the city's standing as the nation's showcase, to attract Jewish residents, or to persuade Jews to remain in Jerusalem.

They seek matching allocations from national ministries in order to complete projects that are supported by overseas donors and investors who operate through quasi-governmental organizations. Such organizations offer Diaspora Jews the opportunity to put their family name on a piece of Jerusalem. The municipality's lack of a fiscal crisis owes something to the desires of national officials and overseas Jews to make Jerusalem as a world city, and thereby justify Israeli rule.

Municipal officials admit to being helped by the ministers, ranking national government bureaucrats, and members of Knesset who live in Jerusalem and feel the city's problems firsthand. The government's concerns for Jerusalem are expressed in the Cabinet Committee for Jerusalem that provides a forum to address issues dealing with the city that cross the boundaries of individual ministries. National government ministries have allocated funds directly to the construction of new neighborhoods, road-building in Jerusalem, and the construction of the Hebrew University campus on Mount Scopus without labeling them as aid to the Jerusalem Municipality.

The city's special opportunities free it from having to skirt around the edges of some regulations that govern Israel's cities. One study found that Israel's mayors had borrowed substantial funds in violation of the rules established by the finance and interior ministries. Jerusalem was distinctive among the large cities for the small size of its debt.[26]

Toward the end of 1991 municipal officials publicized a budget analysis presented to national ministries that showed the city receiving *less than it deserved* in comparison to Tel Aviv. On the item of education, Jerusalem claimed to receive less aid from the central government, despite having more children of school age. On the item of security, Jerusalem also claimed to receive less than Tel Aviv, despite having a greater incidence of terrorist incidents.[27] An outsider is hard pressed to know if this report shows the whole picture, including ministerial outlays in Jerusalem that do not pass through the municipality, or is just one more example of hyperbole in the pursuit of additional funding.

PHYSICAL DEVELOPMENT AND PRESERVATION: WHO PLANS?

The large role for the state in the management of Israel's economy, and the powers that central government ministries can exercise on local taxes and expenditures have their parallels in issues of physical development. Professional civil servants and elected officials dominate the determination of land use, the finance and construction of housing, and the development of roads, parks, and other urban infrastructure in Jerusalem and other Israeli cities. The role of private developers is not entirely absent but is less prominent than in more capitalist societies like the United States.[28] Companies involved in major development projects are likely to be public enterprises owned by national or municipal authorities or the Labor Federation.

Planning also reflects the dominant themes in Jerusalem politics that return time and again, in one field of policy or another. The most prominent physical developments since 1967 have expressed the national government's concern to strengthen the Jewish character of the city by building new neighborhoods for Jews at strategic points within and outside the municipal boundaries. Jerusalem's population has greater concentrations of Palestinians and ultra-Orthodox Jews than other Israeli cities, and the housing needs of those communities have figured in public disputes about who gets what in terms of land allocation. The religious parties of the Jews have exercised their weight in the municipal council and the national government to achieve their demands, while the abstention of Palestinians from local politics has contributed to their meager allocations. The care of the Old City figures prominently among the concerns of those who wish to preserve the spiritual and aesthetic character of Jerusalem. There are concerns for open spaces and scenic outlooks in the city of mountains and valleys. Against these may be arrayed demands of property developers concerned with housing and commercial construction, and government officials who want to strengthen the economic opportunities in a city that historically as trouble supporting itself.[29]

Jerusalem's physical development, like its finance, is governed by a combination of formal rules and pragmatic accommodations. The formal structure remains more or less as it was created by the British during the Mandate period. There are national, regional, and local bodies to do overall planning and review individual projects. There are legal provisions for the taking of land for public purposes, and permits required for each construction, demolition, and renovation.

The city engineer and the municipal council (sitting as the Local Planning Commission) have a role in planning and the detailed approval of building projects. The municipal bodies may be outmaneuvered by officials of national ministries, quasi- governmental bodies, property owners, contributors, and investors. Physical change may be especially complex and time-consuming if the project provokes religious sensitivities in the Jewish, Moslem, or Christian sectors, or aesthetic disputes focused on the Old City. Then the players may expand to include foreign governments, churches, and prominent individuals who demand to be heard.

Jerusalem's planning under the British emphasized conservation of historic sites and the restoration of what was exotic and charming, especially in the Old City. Economic development was not a high priority of the colonial officials. One early provision even forbade any building in Jerusalem for industrial purposes.[30]

Planning in Israeli Jerusalem is more oriented to economic development than it was under the British. There are overall city and regional plans that provide for industrial, commercial, recreational, and residential land uses. The mayor and other municipal officials recruit investors for individual projects. Official planners react to the initiatives of others, either from the private sector or government ministries and companies. Official planners prevent, control, preserve, and prohibit more often than direct.

The heavy hands of public officials in the planning process has not saved Jerusalem from a number of sins described for cities with overtly capitalist regimes.[31] Officials with grandiose conceptions of urban development have taken prized sites. Sometimes they have done this for the purpose of gentrifying run-down neighborhoods for the benefit of higher- income residents, at the expense of relocating established residents with limited political clout. Some projects promoted by overseas entrepreneurs may have been motivated less by sheer profit than the opportunity to do something for the holy city. The foreign base of the investors has spared them the consequences of what they have built and the noise of local critics. Some projects run much more quickly through the stages of land-taking and clearing than actual development. Delays may reflect the ancient finds that crop up in many Jerusalem excavations, and the laws that provide archaeologists opportunities to examine and preserve valuable items. Other delays are owing to limited funding or to opposition that takes hold only after a previous land-use has been destroyed but before a new land-use can be established.

City officials have taken the lead in some cases of restoring or preserving Jerusalem's notable buildings. They have been especially active in the case of Old City sites and have acted occasionally in preserving buildings outside the walls from the nineteenth or early twentieth century.[32] The process seems to depend on the political will and influence of those who want to stop a project of development that would destroy an old building, as opposed to the political will and influence of those who want it to go forward.

One such project involved St. John's Ophthalmic Hospital across Hinnom Valley from Mount Zion. A private developer who wanted to replace it with a 500-room hotel spent ten years preparing four separate plans for demolition and construction, all of which were rejected by municipal officials. Finally the developer perceived that the municipality would find one reason or another for rejecting a large project and reached an agreement whereby the old building would be preserved, with a modest addition, as a small prestige hotel with 130 rooms.

The municipality has allowed more dense development than it normally permits in exchange for an aesthetically acceptable restoration of an old building being made part of a new structure. It has traded approval of building rights on one site for a developer's willingness to preserve another site. A developer was about to demolish the turn-of-the-century Bnei B'rith Library and replace it with an eight-story commercial building. Mayor Kollek persuaded Bnei B'rith President Philip Klutznik (American businessman, political activist and philanthropist, and onetime U.S. Secretary of Housing and Urban Development) to forgo his organization's profit and restore the building as a municipal library.

The case of Sh'arei Tzedek Hospital illustrates the municipality's willingness to go beyond its formal authority in order to buy time or to pressure a developer. The hospital abandoned a restorable building when it moved to a new site across town. Some years later it applied for permission to demolish the old building and use its land together with an adjacent property for commercial development. As the city delayed the granting of a demolition permit, the hospital allowed the old building to stand open to thieves and vandals, in what seemed a strategy to allow the old structure to wither away. The city responded by mummifying the building by bricking up its doorways and windows. There was no permit for demolition and new development and limited further deterioration of a building that the city wanted preserved.

Like other cities of Israel, the municipality of Jerusalem does not have a monopoly of planning authority. It shares this function with regional and national committees appointed by the Interior Ministry. In issues of physical development, Jerusalem suffers the burden of being the country's most sensitive city, with numerous sites important to the programs of national ministries and other public bodies.

The Ministry of Housing and Construction is the largest single builder of housing and other infrastructure in Israel. Although its plans must now receive the approval of the Local Planning Commission, the resources and political connections of the ministry may overcome the opposition of commission members. Soon after the 1967 war, the Ministry of Housing and Construction moved forward with its intention to construct new neighborhoods on the city's outskirts. In plans then under discussion by the Local Planning Commission, areas in the new neighborhoods were identified as open land to be kept free from development.[33] The mayor expressed his opposition to huge developments outside the city core that threatened to swamp the capacity of the municipality to provide services and to reduce the resources that could be devoted to inner-city neighborhoods. National government planners and policymakers had identified the new neighborhoods as issues of prime importance, designed to frustrate anyone who would redivide Jerusalem as in 1948–67. Final decisions on the contrary plans of the municipality were delayed indefinitely, and the national priorities went forward.[34]

The hand of the Ministry of Transportation can reach past that of the city council and determine whether traffic on a city street will be one-way or two-way, and where the municipality can put a stop sign or prohibit parking. The ministry held up the implementation of an agreement between religious and secular parties on the city council to close a street through a religious neighborhood on the Sabbath because it opposed part of the agreement that would have opened another one-way street to two- way traffic only one day of the week.[35]

The Ministry of Education has several impacts on Jerusalem's physical development. It can make new neighborhoods more or less attractive by the resources it allocates to their schools. The head office of the ministry is also prominent on the landscape. It occupies the former Italian Hospital, built with a Florentine tower in the late Ottoman period. Municipal planners have listed the building as one of the sites that could be restored and made into a prestigious hotel.

The most prominent impact of the Ministry of Religions on the cityscape is the headquarters of the Chief Rabbinate and the adjacent Great Jerusalem Synagogue. Their facades recall the Holy Temple and are counted as examples of Jewish monumental building that was fashionable in the 1960s and 1970s.

The Ministry of Tourism looks on Jerusalem as its prime attraction. It promotes the city overseas and to Israelis living in other cities. The ministry also subsidizes the construction of hotels and the presentation of cultural programs that will attract tourists. Ministry of Tourism officials are likely to support plans for hotel construction with local planning officials and to support requests for financial aid from the Association of Hotels when there is a slump in overseas visits to Israel. The ministry also operates the program of inspecting hotels and may pressure hotel managers to reduce prices in order to attract more overseas visitors for the sake of Israel's foreign exchange balances.

The Israel Lands Authority has a role in local development by virtue of its management of public lands. This is a powerful body, insofar as most land in Israel is publicly owned and leased rather than sold to developers. The Authority's council is comprised of twelve representatives of the government and eleven representatives of the Jewish National Fund, an international organization concerned to purchase and develop land in Israel for public use. The Israel Land Authority can decide to lease its land only for purposes that are consistent with its own plans.

The Antiquities Authority can delay a project in order to save a sight that has archeological value. The developer who is kept from work is required to finance exploratory digging by archaeologists. Then there may be a tug of war between public and private bodies in behalf of preservation or continuing with construction. The result may be a delay of an entire project, or part of it, perhaps with a change in design in order to protect an ancient site of special importance.

The Ministry of Finance is always in the background of major construction projects, and sometimes the foreground, by virtue of its roles in budget allocations and lending.

The public was slow to become involved in planning. In this trait Jerusalem resembles other Israeli arenas in the deference provided to bureaucrats and other officials. The right to offer a formal comment on a proposed plan is available only to individuals who are materially affected by it and to public and professional bodies officially recognized by the Ministry of Interior. These provisions give a role to the recognized associations of architects and environmentalists but not citizen groups that create themselves on an ad hoc basis, unless they can demonstrate that harm will be caused to them by the project in question.

The international antennae of Teddy Kollek resulted in distinguished foreigners being invited to review and comment on plans that were not available to the Jerusalem public. The Jerusalem Committee was assembled in 1968 from what the mayor defined as "distinguished architects, urban planners, historians, philosophers, theologians, artists and writers, concerned with the restoration and preservation of ancient sites, and the aesthetic, cultural and human needs of Jerusalem."[36] The Jerusalem Committee roasted the first set of plans it was shown, that included monumental buildings and elaborate roadways. Its criticisms helped set the mayor and his underlings on a path of modesty.

The municipality's own city hall, including the mayor's office and council chamber, had long been in a small building not far from the Jaffa Gate of the Old City, with city offices spread throughout the city in nondescript quarters. Few who have visited city halls in North America or Europe would have accused Jerusalem's elected officials or employees of having a surplus of space, quiet surroundings, comfortable furniture, or other amenities.[37] A new municipal building opened in 1993. It is said to be excessive in bulk and grandeur, even while it is more modest than several earlier plans that were rejected on account of their size and expense.

The Ministry of Foreign Affairs makes its own point about the modesty of Israeli public buildings. It sprawls over the painted-up barracks of a former military compound. The ministry has no direct role in physical planning but is concerned with the overall status of the city as defined in other capitals. Most important, in this regard, are the formulations and the behaviors of the White House and the United States Department of State: whether East Jerusalem should be referred to as "occupied territory"; if the city should be treated as a unit or as separate entities that are currently unified pending a formal solution; and if officials are willing to treat Jerusalem as Israel's de facto capital, even if the de jure status of the city remains something else.[38]

Official policies in the field of physical planning have trouble being implemented as proclaimed, even after they have received all the formal approvals. In this trait, physical planning resembles other fields of policymaking in Israel and other countries.[39]

An example is the requirement adopted by British Governor Sir Ronald Storrs, and continued by the Israelis, that all Jerusalem construction be faced with stone. Even during the British regime, contractors ignored the provision when large numbers of German refugees arrived during the period of economic hardship in the 1930s. After the War of Independence, when even larger numbers of refugees came to Jerusalem from Asia and North Africa, local authorities did not impose the requirements in order to build large numbers of apartments as quickly and as cheaply as possible.

The stone requirement has also been overlooked for distinguished public buildings. The synagogue on the Hebrew University campus at Givat Ram and the Shrine of the Book repository of the Dead Sea Scrolls at the Israel Museum were built in white concrete. Other buildings have complied in a symbolic way with the requirement by including bits of stone amidst their glass, metal, or concrete.

Regulations appear strict in requiring authorization for the details of a building's design and any subsequent changes that are made. Occasionally a feisty resident will cite the law in objecting to the color that neighbors paint on the outside of their apartment door. Nevertheless, there hardly seems to be a building that does not have one or another style of aluminum windows used to turn balconies into spare rooms, virtually all of them in violation of planning regulations. Even the Knesset ignored the rules when it added a Star of David to the roof of its building without the approval of the planning commission.[40]

Jerusalem's planners operate in a political context. Developers often try and sometimes succeed in using their connections with national or local elected officials to overturn the planners' objections. Sometimes they win their case on the claim that a project will provide substantial tax revenues to the municipal treasury. Sometimes they assert that an international hotel chain will add its prestige to Israel and Jerusalem. The high-rise hotel built by the Hilton chain and now a Holiday Inn is said to offer the best view of Jerusalem because from it you cannot see that hotel. The Jerusalem Plaza Hotel was built by another well-connected group of foreign investors on a site that had been zoned to remain part of the only sizable public park close to the central business district. As in other cities, planning approvals are worth money and subject to illegal pressures. There have been police investigations and prosecutions concerned with building inspectors who overlooked contractors' violations of approved plans. Usually this has meant adding one or more additional floor or building closer to the street or a neighboring property. The local planning board has retroactively approved violations undertaken by builders who benefit from personal connections with members of the board.[41]

An area along what had been the boundary between Israeli and Jordanian Jerusalem prior to 1967 brings together numerous pressures that have worked to delay construction on land of high economic potential. The site includes plots owned by individual Palestinians as well as Moslem religious institutions and is bordered on the Jewish side by an ultra-Orthodox neighborhood. Its residents are likely to be provoked to mass action by anything that brings traffic on the Sabbath or immodestly clad tourists on any day of the week.

When a multilane, limited-access road was built through the area to connect the northern suburbs with the city center, the section of road alongside the ultra-Orthodox neighborhood was provided a high fence to screen the noise and the sight of Sabbath traffic. When the inevitable demonstrations accompanied the road's opening in 1991, the police announced that they would allow peaceful protest for a Sabbath or two, but then would be forceful in allowing traffic to flow without disturbance.

With the road's opening, the area's lack of completion became even more visible to city residents. City planners proposed park land, an area for street markets and exhibitions, elevated walkways to connect Palestinian and Jewish areas and to symbolize the city's unity, and even a plaza for political demonstrations. Meanwhile, Jerusalem's skeptics viewed the road and its undeveloped surroundings as providing a separation 100 meters wide, likely to last some time, between Palestinian and Jewish neighborhoods.[42]

The Mamilla project between the Jaffa Gate of the Old City and the central business district illustrates the clumsiness of Jerusalem's physical development. Municipal officials moved with dispatch to declare the region of low-income housing and small workshops an area for redevelopment and to remove the people who lived and worked there. Then the area of several square blocks on a highly prized site remained boarded up for more than fifteen years while the municipality dithered with a series of potential developers and their plans. When construction was well under way in the late 1980s, the *Intifada* cooled the enthusiasm of investors for what was planned as a commercial center oriented to tourists. After another spurt of construction began in 1991, the discovery of human bones produced other problems. Archaeologists demanded more time to investigate the significance of the findings, and religious Jews threatened to demonstrate against the desecration of ancient Jewish graves.[43]

As in other fields of public activity, the planning and control of Jerusalem's physical development is different within the Jewish and Arab sectors. There are many additions to private homes in the Jewish sector without the formal approvals that are necessary. With respect to original construction, however, the dominant picture in the Jewish sector is one of following the rules that require planning approval. The issue of illegal Palestinian building has emerged periodically in the Israeli media, with disputes about the extent of the phenomenon and which bureaucracy has failed in its tasks.

The style of Palestinian construction works against compliance with the formal rules. In contrast to the Jewish preference for high-density apartment blocks that make minimal use of land and are efficient to serve with roads and utilities, Palestinian buildings tend to be separate one-family structures that sprawl wherever there is vacant land, sometimes without concern for an orderly road network or utility connections. Many of Jerusalem's Palestinians work in the building trades, so families and friends can put up enough of a structure overnight to give the authorities a complicated legal task to destroy an unlicensed building.

Only 101 of 806 Palestinian houses built in East Jerusalem during 1968–74 had building permits.[44] Part of the problem was that no master plan had been created for those neighborhoods during the Jordanian period, which limited Israel's bureaucratic procedures for granting a building permit for a specific site. There were also a disinclination of the city's Palestinians to involve themselves with Israeli officialdom and a lack of public resources provided for the construction of Palestinian housing.

Between the city's reunification in 1967 and 1990, only five thousand apartments were built for Palestinians, against seventy thousand for Jews. During the same period, the Jewish population in the city increased by 80 percent while the Palestinian population increased by 96 percent. In the ten years up to 1991, only 10 percent of the housing construction was built for Palestinians, despite their comprising some 28 percent of the city's population.[45] Critics of the Israeli regime use these figures to explain the Palestinians' practice of building private houses, sometimes illegally, in a situation where there is little or no official encouragement for the building of Palestinian dwellings.[46] Supporters of the regime explain the same figures by the Palestinians' disinclination to invest in housing in proportion to their needs while the Israelis control Jerusalem or their unwillingness to live in the high-density patterns required by a planned urban setting.

A study conducted by the Jerusalem Institute for Israel Studies concluded that building permits were held up during the period 1967–83 by the failure of the planning commission to complete plans for Palestinian neighborhoods. The researchers concluded that this was not so much a case of simple delays as a response of bureaucrats to elected officeholders of the national government who could not decide how to deal with increasing Arab population in the city. Even when the commission completed plans and building permits became more freely available after 1983, there continued struggles over the quantity of permits to be issued. The municipality pressed for 18,000 Palestinian housing units for an area in the north of the city, while the Ministry of Housing and Construction succeeded in reducing the allocation to 7,500 units.[47]

Israeli planners have also sought to discourage the migration of Palestinians to Jerusalem from elsewhere in the West Bank by declaring "green areas" on land owned by Palestinians. There building would be prohibited, ostensibly for the sake of environmental protection. A report in 1993 revealed that some of those areas did not meet the official criteria as green areas, and they were opened to Palestinian construction.[48]

At the beginning of 1992, the Ministry of Interior estimated that there were 1,500 illegal dwellings in the Palestinian neighborhoods of Jerusalem, as well as some 100,000 Palestinian residents of the occupied territories living illegally in the city. Ministry officials criticized the municipality for lax supervision of building. A representative of the city rejected the estimates of the Interior Ministry and remarked that on one occasion ministry officials destroyed Palestinian dwellings for being built illegally in Jerusalem, only to discover that some of the dwellings had been outside the city's boundaries.[49] Some months later, Mayor Kollek announced that his conscience would not tolerate his signing demolition orders for Arab housing, despite their being built illegally. He cited one especially painful case, involving a family with fourteen children. In response, the District Commissioner of the Interior Ministry accused the mayor of encouraging illegal building and promised to use his authority to sign demolition orders if the mayor refused.[50]

NONGOVERNMENTAL AND QUASI-GOVERNMENTAL INSTITUTIONS

The organizational map of Jerusalem includes a number of public entities that are nongovernmental or quasi-governmental.[51] Some nongovernmental bodies reflect the appeal of Jerusalem for philanthropic organizations. Quasi-governmental organizations represent the tendency of Israeli government ministries and municipalities to conduct activities via units that are partly autonomous, which they establish by themselves or in conjunction with philanthropic organizations or private investors.

Overseas communities have long been attracted to support activities in Jerusalem. Jews of the Greek, Roman, and Babylonian Diasporas sent annual payments to the Temple that were used partly to support the poor of the city. During the long period of non-Jewish rule, emissaries from Jerusalem's Jewish communities traveled throughout the Diaspora seeking funds to support their poor families. Fund-raising became more extensive and formalized with the onset of modern Zionist immigration in the 1880s. This has continued with the activities of the United Jewish Appeal in the United States and the United Israel Appeal elsewhere to collect funds for allocation within Israel. Additional sums are collected by hospitals, universities, religious academies, and other social service agencies, many of which also receive Israeli government funding. Diaspora Jews who are suspicious of established organizations support separate bodies that advertise themselves as bringing change to Israel, by means of Jewish-Arab relations, or programs for women.

The non-Jewish communities of Jerusalem also have well- established patterns of international support. Overseas Christians built churches and monasteries, hospices for pilgrims, plus hospitals, orphanages, and schools for coreligionists resident in the Holy City, or to be used by missionaries to serve the unfortunate and attract converts. Officials of the British mandatory government created a Pro-Jerusalem Society that raised funds in Palestine, Europe, and the United States. It spent them on refurbishing historic buildings, town planning, cultural exhibitions, and publications.[52] Moslem authorities in Baghdad or Cairo, and more recently Saudi Arabia, have endowed schools and mosques in Jerusalem. The Moslem religious trust (Waqf) has extensive landholdings in modern Jerusalem that support religious institutions, social welfare activities, and political activities to advance community interests. The Jordanian government and the PLO have provided funding for organizations having economic, social, and political purposes, even though the Israeli government sought to prevent funding by the PLO.

Three quasi-governmental organizations were especially prominent during the Kollek era: the Jerusalem Foundation, the Jerusalem Development Authority, and the Moriah Company. The Jerusalem Foundation was created by Teddy Kollek soon after he entered the mayor's office in 1966. A distinguished group of Israeli and foreign personalities sit on the foundation's governing council. Its staff of some fifty fund-raisers, planners, architects, engineers, lawyers, accountants, and clerks identifies and develops projects in consultation with the staff of the municipality, other public institutions in Jerusalem, and donors. The staff also pays attention to financial regulations of Israel and governments in the donors' countries. Fund-raising branches of the Jerusalem Foundation work in the United States, Canada, Great Britain, Germany, Switzerland, Holland, and France.

A purist might insist that the Jerusalem Foundation is private and not "quasi-governmental." However, Teddy Kollek's positions as city mayor, foundation president, and prime fund- raiser blurred the meaning of "quasi-governmental," which is vague in any case.[53] More than other institutions, the Jerusalem Foundation confounded the issue of what is governmental and private and what is controlled by Israel, Jerusalem, or overseas friends of Jerusalem.[54] It remains to be seen how the foundation's relationship with the municipality will develop as a result of Ehud Olmert's election as mayor.

To the end of the Kollek regime, the Jerusalem Foundation had supported more than a thousand projects. Its playgrounds and flower gardens appear in every neighborhood. It helped build major facilities for museums, theaters, and cinema and subsidizes special attractions for schoolchildren. It funded community centers with gymnasiums, sports fields, and programs for dance, arts, and drama. It created social programs in poor neighborhoods, as well as those designed for the aged and new immigrants. It aids mother and baby clinics and built a clinic specially designed for Palestinian clientele. The foundation has tried to bring young Palestinians and Jews together in community centers located on the borders of their neighborhoods. A newspaper report described a library for Arabic readers in a Palestinian neighborhood, whose staff worried its way through the selection of volumes that would not be inflammatory politically.[55]

The foundation has built or refurbished churches, mosques, and synagogues. There are subsidized workshops for young artists, as well as apartments and studios for world-class artists, musicians, and intellectuals who visit the city. The foundation supports archaeological excavations and restorations. It is well along in developing a park around the walls of the Old City. It refurbished the walkway on top of the city walls and developed a museum depicting the city's history in the fortifications of the ancient Citadel alongside Jaffa Gate. It renovated buildings and streets in the Old City, repaired water, sewer, electric, and telephone lines and provided cable television to replace unsightly antennas. A promenade about one kilometer in length on a ridge overlooking the Old City is often crowded with strollers who enjoy its view, landscaping, benches, cafes, ice cream vendors, and ideal conditions for kite-flying. Like other projects of the Jerusalem Foundation, the promenade is divided into a number of distinct projects, each of which carries a plaque that identifies its donors.

The foundation's projects do not escape the barbs of Jerusalem's contentious groups. Palestinian sensitivities about Jewish incursions appear even when foundation programs are directed at the physical or social problems of the Palestinian community and staffed by Palestinians. Religious Jews have blocked or delayed foundation projects to construct swimming pools, a stadium, and cultural facilities that were said to threaten the Sabbath or the sensitivities of religious neighborhoods. Other critics question the capacity of the municipality to maintain the numerous facilities constructed by the foundation. Donors are more likely to pay for a new project that will carry their name than to support the undistinguished job of maintenance. The number of visitors to the rehabilitated Citadel of the Old City are not enough to pay for its operation. Foundation and municipal officials have turned to the Ministry of Culture for a budget allotment. The proposal is worthy, but the ministry's purse is already strained by cultural projects asking for public subsidy.

The foundation's financial contributions to Jerusalem amounted to about US $245 million from 1966 to 1991, and $20 million annually in recent years. Its outlays have been the equivalent of 10–15 percent of the municipality's operating budget, including those funds that go to projects not associated with the municipality. More than four thousand donors have contributed to the foundation, some 40 percent of them Americans, and two-thirds Jewish. Foundation personnel report that some donors show an intimate interest in details of their projects, while others are more concerned with the plaque that will include the donors' names and which of their relatives will be commemorated.

The Jerusalem Development Authority is a small organization with a handful of employees but a large mandate and first-class connections. By some claims, it became the tail that wagged the municipal dog. The authority was created by a 1988 act of the Knesset and headed by former city treasurer Uzi Wechsler. Its board of directors includes ten representatives of the municipality, nineteen representatives of government ministries, and nine other members. Its mandate extends to encouraging, planning, and initiating activities concerned with the economic development of Jerusalem and coordinating Jerusalem's economic development among government ministries, municipal officials, and other bodies.

Uzi Wechsler was described as Jerusalem's gray eminence or a member of its ruling triumvirate along with Mayor Teddy Kollek and Interior Minister Ariyeh Deri.[56] During the years he spent as Jerusalem's treasurer, Wechsler acquired Kollek's trust and exposure to the international contacts of the Jerusalem Foundation. Some donors to foundation activities became investors in authority projects. Because of Wechsler's willingness as city treasurer to support education and social services linked to the Sephardi religious party, SHAS, he earned the support of Interior Minister Deri.

The Jerusalem Development Authority works closely with the Moriah Company.[57] The Moriah Company is wholly owned by the municipality and was established by Wechsler while he was city treasurer. The Jerusalem Development Authority typically recruits overseas investors for major projects, arranges agreements about taxation and the repatriation of foreign currency with the Finance Ministry, and arranges the approval of plans by the municipality and Interior Ministry. The Moriah Company serves as prime contractor for the authority's projects.

The team of the Jerusalem Development Authority and Moriah Company took over the Mamilla project that had languished in a prized area, cleared of residents and boarded up while waiting the presentation of plans that could win acceptance. It also has responsibility for developments in the southwest quadrant of the city that include a stadium, a park for high-tech industry, a zoo, and a shopping mall; a building for international congresses adjacent to an existing concert hall and exhibition center; a project close to the central business district for the municipality and district offices of Israeli ministries; plus residential housing, commercial centers, and tourist sites. The Jerusalem Development Authority touted its present and future achievements, along with those of the Moriah Company, in an advertising supplement published by Jerusalem's weekly newspaper, *Kal Ha'ir,* in January 1992.[58]

One cluster of projects involving the Jerusalem Foundation and the Jerusalem Development Authority illustrates the organizational relationships that Teddy Kollek built around himself. The authority, together with the municipality, commissioned the Jerusalem Institute for Israel Studies to analyze a series of alternative proposals for extending the boundaries of Jerusalem.[59] Two decades earlier, the Jerusalem Institute for Israel Studies was established by a group that included Teddy Kollek and senior personnel of the Hebrew University, with overseas funding arranged by the Jerusalem Foundation. The institute has sponsored research into various public issues in Jerusalem. Its publications include the annual *Statistical Yearbook of Jerusalem*, produced in conjunction with the municipality, and a series of planning reports prepared for the Jerusalem Committee. As noted above, the Jerusalem Committee was another project of Teddy Kollek, appointed by him from distinguished international personalities to review proposals for Jerusalem's physical development.

The ostensibly private Hebrew University and Hadassah Hospital have earned the label of quasi-governmental. They collect sizable donations and research grants overseas, but Israeli government funds routinely exceed 50 percent of their revenues. In exchange for state money, government officials demand a role in setting salaries for their staffs, the fees charged to students or patients, and decisions about new programs. Both the Hebrew University and Hadassah Hospital have some clout in city affairs by virtue of their resources and status, the size of their staffs (they are the largest employers in the city except for the national government), and the status of their professional staffs. Like major institutions elsewhere, they have access to local and national policymakers on issues deemed vital to their needs.

Quasi-governmental organizations have several advantages. They can be structured to receive the money of foreign donors who wish to contribute to Jerusalem projects but whose laws in their home countries prohibit or discourage donations to foreign governments per se. American taxpayers can deduct from their taxable income the contributions made to the Jerusalem Foundation, whereas they could not take a deduction for money contributed to the Israeli government or the Jerusalem municipality. The Jerusalem Development Authority can offer foreign investors the prospect of profit, arrange economic surveys and loans, and contract with architects and builders more freely and more quickly than government ministries or ministerial departments that are tied to detailed procedures that require competitive bidding.

The Company for the Development of the Jewish Quarter illustrates the capacity of a quasi-governmental organization to remain alive beyond the completion of its original mandate. The company began work soon after Israeli forces liberated the Jewish Quarter in 1967 and a decade later had substantially completed its task of clearing the rubble and planning and constructing synagogues, other public buildings, and residential units that house some 2,200 individuals. The company was still extant in 1992. It was serving other aims of its parent Ministry of Housing and Construction, including the acquisition and development of parcels for Jewish residences in the Moslem Quarter of the Old City and nearby Palestinian villages.[60]

Quasi-governmental organizations have been praised for the structures and programs they have produced, without direct cost for Israeli taxpayers and more quickly than could be done by government bodies or local investors. They have also been accused of causing problems by their shortcuts through the official procedures for winning approval of their plans and by favoritism in selecting contractors or candidates for leasing the commercial structures that they own.[61]

The new municipal building illustrates how public sector entrepreneurs find a variety of resources from outside the normal government budgets. The Jerusalem Development Authority raised much of the money in a long-term loan provided by a prominent overseas Jewish building contractor who was given responsibility for the project. Lesser amounts came from donations, the sale of municipal assets, and the sale of commercial concessions in the project. When the project was already in the construction stage, a Knesset member with a record of conflict with the head of the Jerusalem Development Authority was quoted as demanding an investigation of the project by the State Comptroller. He claimed that the Jerusalem Development Authority was skirting the controls of the municipal council and was evading competitive bidding in letting its contracts. By the critic's reckoning, the cost of the project included in the planning was kept artificially low by not taking account of Value Added Tax (then 18 percent) and the cost of clearing the site. These items and other changes threatened to increase the cost from US $50 million to US $106 million.[62]

When the new municipal building was nearing completion, Teddy Kollek brought in a donation of $10 million and proposed that the city council rename the square in front of the new building in honor of the family that made the donation. Individual members of the council grumbled about selling pieces of the Holy City to wealthy foreigners, but the majority went along with the mayor.[63]

Kollek's dual role as mayor of the municipality and chairman of the Jerusalem Foundation provided him with the leverage of private resources over public resources and the leverage of public resources over private funds. Kollek extracted money from the municipality and the national government to match the nongovernmental funds raised by the foundation. He appealed to donors as a man who could use his status as mayor to push the foundation's projects through to completion and to supplement the private donations with public money. The intimate mixture of public and private roles also gave the mayor unusual advantages when he approached the voters for reelection as a man who added to Jerusalem's amenities. The attractions of these roles seemed to last until the election of 1993, when Kollek's age led even some enthusiastic supporters to withhold their support for yet another term.

The Jerusalem Development Authority presents an issue that is not present with the Jerusalem Foundation. The foundation deals with contributions and only offers its donors the opportunity to gain prestige for their family name in Jerusalem. The authority deals with investment and the potential of profit, as well as concessions with respect to the taxes to be levied on the profits and foreign currency controls affecting the remission of profits overseas.

The profitability of the authority's projects is not yet apparent. The largest investors have been prominent overseas Jews who have already contributed substantially to projects of the Jerusalem Foundation. They have coupled their investments in authority projects with sizable loans at modest rates of interest. Teddy Kollek's supporters asserted that the investors were more concerned to benefit Jerusalem than to assure themselves commercial gain.

One of the mayor's efforts to sidestep the formal procedures became the target of a police investigation. "Teddy's Fund" received moneys contributed directly to the mayor and was allocated by him personally without the institutionalized procedures of the Jerusalem Foundation or the Jerusalem Development Authority. Teddy's Fund seemed more private than public and too closely controlled by the mayor himself. Some money from Teddy's Fund paid for overseas trips of high-ranking city employees. These appeared to be the mayor's personal rewards for faithful support. The police closed the investigation without bringing formal charges when the mayor agreed to cease operations of Teddy's Fund.

There is no comprehensive measure of how much money foreign contributors and investors provide to Jerusalem. The sums made available to civilian activities in Jerusalem are part of the inclusive measure of financial transfers to Israeli institutions and individuals from foreign governments and nongovernmental sources for defense and civilian purposes. These sums approximated US $6.4 billion for 1991. They have amounted to 14–20 percent of annual Israeli government income or expenditures.[64] Jerusalem may have benefited from this aid more than other Israeli localities but less than the Israeli military.

The mix of governmental and nongovernmental bodies that operate in Jerusalem make it difficult to deal with classic questions of political science, such as "who governs?" "how?" and "who gets what?" Companies and other institutions beholden to different public authorities compete with one another, with private interests, ministries of the national government, and municipal departments for influence on major projects. Quasi-governmental organizations provide the mayor and ministers with speedy influence on land-use and construction that would be constrained by procedures that must be followed by the municipality or the national government per se. At the same time, the number of government bodies, private institutions, and quasi- governmental organizations with an interest in Jerusalem may delay or frustrate the mayor and other officials in the case of certain projects.[65]

The Egged Bus Cooperative is one quasi-governmental organizations that has used its political muscle to limit the actions taken by the municipality. Egged is owned by bus drivers and other personnel who purchase or inherit memberships in the cooperative. It is linked with the Labor Federation, receives substantial government subsidies, and has a virtual monopoly on intercity public transportation and local bus service in most Israeli cities. Its members have had enough electoral clout to select a representative in the Labor Party's Knesset delegation and to assure their access in local councils. This power was challenged by a free-enterprise-oriented member of the Jerusalem city council, who organized a mini-bus service between the Central Bus Station and the Hadassah Hospital. In the view of the promoter, it was to be the beginning of competitive public transportation. When Egged woke up to this threat against its monopoly, it mobilized public demonstrations against the mini-buses and then pushed through the council a cancellation of the authorization that had been granted to the mini-buses.[66]

Some Jewish religious academies (yeshivot) have joined the list of politically relevant nongovernmental organizations. They have been prominent recipients of special allocations pushed through the Knesset by their patrons in the religious parties. Members of the Belz congregations in Israel and overseas are creating a facility they say will include the world's largest synagogue. Believers hope that the Messiah will stop there on his way to the Temple Mount.[67] The academies together command the loyalties of thousands of students who can be turned out to demonstrate against an infringement of religious law.

One academy, Aterit Hacohanim (Crown of the Priests), has been aggressive in acquiring access to plots or buildings in Palestinian areas and turning them into Jewish residences or outposts of the academy. When the intense nationalist Ariel Sharon was Minister of Housing and Construction, there was a natural alliance between the ministry and academy.

EFFORTS AT DECENTRALIZATION

The municipality rules at the local level by means of bureaucracies in a way that is similar to the rule of the central government in the nation. Israel's style of government is foreign to Americans, who are reared in a culture that emphasizes citizen initiatives and the exposure of official actions by means of "freedom of information" laws. Jerusalem's municipal employees can make arbitrary decisions that are fateful for individual citizens, without explaining their reasons or providing access to the information that is used in making the decisions. Parents are incensed when stubborn clerks overlook explicit regulations in the assignment of students to schools and ignore written appeals to change their assignments. Disappointed applicants for municipal positions claim that the selection process was sewn up against them. Builders and architects accuse quasi-governmental organizations of favoritism in the awarding of contracts.

Several of Jerusalem's neighborhoods have associations of local residents that are part of a movement to counter the authority-centeredness that prevails in Israel. The associations received some of their early financing from American donors and were staffed by immigrants from the United States who were imbued with the American style of home rule. Neighborhood associations involve community residents in program planning and implementation and seek to improve communications between the municipality and its residents. Some of these associations are in Palestinian neighborhoods and have been a vehicle for the residents to express their concerns in a setting where they refuse to vote or otherwise take part in activities of the Israeli state or municipality. The Palestinian neighborhood associations have received quiet funding from Arab sources, perhaps Saudi Arabia, Jordan, or the PLO.[68] There were seven neighborhood associations in 1985, with seventy-seven employees and a budget of 510,000 New Shekels. By 1991 there were thirteen neighborhood associations with one hundred employees. In absolute terms, the budgets of the neighborhoods had increased by more than five times but declined from 1.06 percent of the municipality's total budget to 0.6 percent.[69]

Teddy Kollek tried on several occasions to divide all of Jerusalem into boroughs that would enjoy a measure of self- government. In his view, this would be a pragmatic way to deal with Jerusalem's diversity, while maintaining the city united under Israeli control. Each time the plan surfaced, it was opposed by Orthodox Jewish politicians who saw it as a way to evade Sabbath regulations in secular neighborhoods and by right-wing politicians in both national and local forums who saw it as the first step in the redivision of Jerusalem into Jewish and Palestinian cities.

The idea emerged again at the end of 1992. The borough idea was attached to the scheme of neighborhood associations. Twenty associations were identified for Palestinian neighborhoods and twenty-four for Jewish neighborhoods.[70] The initial responses were similar to those received by previous versions of Kollek's idea, and it did not move forward.

Another program meant to improve the quality of local decision making is Project Renewal. It was created by Prime Minister Menachem Begin in 1978 to serve as a focus of fund-raising among overseas Jewish communities, alleviate the social and economic problems of poor urban neighborhoods and small towns, and involve site residents and overseas donors in project planning and management.

It is not easy to summarize the record of the neighborhood associations or Project Renewal. The municipality labels the neighborhood associations "Self-Management Neighborhoods," but the term is exaggerated. Individuals involved with the neighborhood associations describe successful projects where local residents have influenced land-use decisions and educational programming in the neighborhood schools. Some residents feel more involved in public affairs as a result of the associations' activities. There have also been chronic disputes with professional bureaucrats of the municipality, who resist allocating to the associations anything more than symbolic discretion about minor issues. Participants in the neighborhood associations claimed that Teddy Kollek's attitude toward them ran hot and cold and that they were in danger of being swallowed or dominated by neighborhood cultural centers that have their own bureaucracy and professional employees.[71] Several Jerusalem neighborhoods have benefited from Project Renewal. There have been impressive physical improvements of run-down housing, as well as new social programs. There have also been frustrating confrontations between local residents, representatives of overseas donors, and Israeli bureaucrats.[72]

WHEN JERUSALEM IS DIFFERENT

The Jerusalem municipality is expected to administer policies established in national ministries, to soothe tensions, and to solve problems. Like municipal officials the world over, those of Jerusalem serve as buffers between citizens and the regime. Local authorities deal with problems caused by economic and social conditions, the actions or inaction of national officials. Local officials have more responsibility than authority. They receive the complaints of citizens when something goes wrong, even if the cause of the complaint has nothing to do with the municipality. Municipal officials suffer from a gap between what their city is expected to do and what it has the power to do.

In Jerusalem's case, the problem of responsibility is intensified by the importance of the city to so many international observers and the nation's tenuous hold on its capital. Municipal officials find themselves dealing with local problems exacerbated by the failure of national policymakers to resolve the international status of the city or to define clearly the rights and obligations of Palestinians and of religious and secular Jews.

The same holy and aesthetic aura of Jerusalem that attracts donors also attracts critics. The treatment of sensitive sites and their immediate surroundings can provoke a fanatic outburst or merely an intense controversy about taste. Once a Jerusalem issue reaches a certain degree of political importance, local officials may find that national officials step in and add their own complications to what the municipality is trying to solve. Outspoken foreigners may express their interest in making Jerusalem a city that is even more ideal. Some critics are bitterly opposed to the Israeli regime and find blemish wherever they look.

As the popular and aggressive mayor of Jerusalem, Teddy Kollek was harried by critics and a harrier of others. As the chief executive, the most prominent Jerusalemite, and an international celebrity, he commanded attention throughout the country. If there was a wave of stabbings of Jews by Palestinians or a charge of police brutality against Palestinians or Jewish demonstrators, it was technically matter for the national police. Yet the mayor has a concern for public order and his city's reputation. Kollek did not hesitate to prod the police. Insofar as keeping the peace is an especially sensitive issue in the ethnic and religious tinderbox of Jerusalem, he sometimes found that national politicians were prodding the police in another direction.

Jerusalem's special status was involved in the creation of a government Ministry for Jerusalem early in 1991. The idea of a ministry for the city had been around for a long time, often touted by politicians wanting to assert their concern for the leading city of Israel and Judaism. Critics asked what the ministry would do alongside the municipal authority on the one hand and other government ministries that have their own programs for Jerusalem on the other hand.

When the ministry was actually established, its purpose was more to solve a political problem in the composition of the national government coalition than to accomplish anything substantial in Jerusalem. It was created when the ultra-Orthodox political party, Agudat Israel, joined the government of Yitzhak Shamir. An Agudat Israel member of the Knesset was given responsibility for the ministry but only with the rank of deputy minister and a minuscule staff of six. It had funds to pay salaries but not for any projects. The legal advisor to the government ruled that the rank of deputy minister would allow the head of the ministry to attend cabinet meetings but to speak only on issues dealing with Jerusalem. The mayor was on record as opposing the creation of the ministry, but he complimented the deputy ministry for his help in arranging government approvals of projects requested by the municipality. A newspaper report about the ministry's first half-year of operations concluded that it had done no harm to the city, and not much that was good.[73]

The ministry found its project: a declaration of loyalty for Jerusalem that would be signed by Jews from the Diaspora and Israel on Jerusalem Day in 1992, the twenty-fifth anniversary of the city's liberation in the war of 1967.[74] When the declaration of loyalty was actually produced for signatures, Teddy Kollek and other secular politicians declared that they might not sign it! The declaration emphasized the religious character of Jerusalem's traditions and gave only a brief thanks to the Israeli Defense Forces for reuniting the city.[75] When Jerusalem Day arrived, Kollek agreed to sign but refused to make a speech at the signing ceremony. He appeared on that night's television news saying that he would have preferred that the money spent on the declaration be used instead to add an hour of instruction to Jerusalem's school day. No Minister for Jerusalem was named when Yitzhak Rabin formed his cabinet after the election of 1992.

CHAPTER 5

Social, Economic, and Political Traits

The expectations, explicit demands, and disputes of Jerusalem's half-million residents contribute to decisions made by the elected officials and professional bureaucrats of the municipal and national governments. In order to understand what happens in Jerusalem, it is helpful to describe the city according to conventional demographic, economic, and political indicators. They contribute to the analysis of Jerusalem, even if they are not the whole story. The data to be provided here describe the character of Jerusalem and its several communities. They show part of "who gets what?" in the city and will serve again in the final chapter's assessment of the city and its look toward the future.

POPULATION

Jerusalem is formally Israel's most populous city. The population of the municipality was 544,200 at the end of 1991, which was substantially larger than Tel Aviv's 353,200, and Haifa's 251,000. When the calculation is made according to urban area rather than municipalities, Jerusalem's area population of 600,900 is only about half the 1,131,700 in the Tel Aviv metropolitan area. The Jerusalem region is also less populous than Haifa plus nearby Acco.

The record of the city's population provides a summary measure of its changing importance over the ages. The data shown in table 5.1 prior to the 1920s are estimates, with those of the distant past being the least reliable. Despite their shortcomings, they provide the best record available of the city's changing fortunes.

Population peaks occurred prior to the destruction of the Second Temple, during the time when Jerusalem was the capital of the Crusaders' Latin Kingdom and again after the onset of major Jewish immigration in the latter part of the nineteenth century. During

Table 5.1
Jerusalem's Population

Date	Population
1000 B.C.E.	2,500
700	6,000–8,000
600*	24,000
537	10,000
0–70 C.E.	30,000
1099–1187	30,000
1200–1300	5,200
1500–1600	4,700–15,800
1800	8,000–10,000
1834	22,000
1840	15,000
1860	20,000
1876	25,000
1900	70,000
1913	75,200
1928	62,700
1931	93,100
1946	164,400
1961**	243,900
1967	267,800
1972	313,900
1988	493,500
1990	504,100
1991	544,200
1992	556,500

Sources: Howard F. Vos, *Ezra, Nehemiah, and Esther* (Grand Rapids, Michigan: Zondervan Publishing House, 1987); Joachim Jeremias, *Jerusalem in the Time of Jesus: An Investigation into Economic and Social Conditions during the New Testament Period* (London: SCM Press, 1969); Yehoshua Ben-Arieh, *Jerusalem in the Nineteenth Century: The Old City* (New York: St. Martin's Press, 1984); Amnon Cohen, *Jewish Life under Islam: Jerusalem in the Sixteenth Century* (Cambridge: Harvard University Press, 1984); Karl R. Schaefer, "Jerusalem in the Ayyubid and Mamluk Eras," Ph.D. dissertation, Department of Near Eastern Languages and Literatures, New York University, 1985; U. O. Schmelz, *Modern Jerusalem's Demographic Evolution* (Jerusalem: Institute for Contemporary Jewry, Hebrew University, 1987); F. E. Peters, *Jerusalem: The Holy City in the Eyes of Chroniclers, Visitors, Pilgrims, and Prophets from the Days of Abraham to the Beginnings of Modern Times* (Princeton: Princeton University Press, 1985). *Statistical Abstract of Israel, 1990* (Jerusalem: Central Bureau of Statistics, 1990); *Statistical Yearbook of Jerusalem, 1988* (Jerusalem: Municipality of Jerusalem and Jerusalem Institute of Israel Studies, 1991); *Statistical Yearbook of Jerusalem, 1991* (Jerusalem: Municipality of Jerusalem and Jerusalme Institute of Israel Studies, 1993); *Statistical Yearbook of Jerusalem, 1992* (Jerusalem: Municipality of Jerusalem and Jerusalem Institute of Israel Studies, 1994).

*After the arrival of refugees from the north following the Assyrian conquest

**Israeli and Jordanian sectors

most of the long periods of Moslem rule from the seventh to the middle of the nineteenth century, Jerusalem had importance as a site of Islamic holy sites and religious institutions but was politically and economically subordinate to the capitals of Cairo, Damascus, or Constantinople and never developed a large population.

The city's importance has reflected the changing status of that imprecise geographical area called the Land of Israel. The greatest periods of the city's development have occurred when it was a religious and political capital of a land heavily settled by Jews in the area between the Jordan River and the Mediterranean Sea and between Lebanon in the north to the Negev in the south. On those occasions Jerusalem has been close to the center of the country, on the junction of north-south and east-west routes. At other times Jerusalem was only a regional marketing center, with modest agriculture to the west but a desert to the east and 40 kilometers from major routes on the coastal plain that connect Cairo, Lebanon, and Damascus.

For the first time since Jerusalem's destruction by the Romans, post-1967 Jerusalem is again at the strategic heart of a country thickly settled by Jews. A book about the geopolitical importance of the city notes that it intrudes prominently into the center of Palestinian settlement on the West Bank. In what may be too final a conclusion, the author writes that no Palestinian state can be viable without the Jerusalem that Israel will never concede.[1]

Religion and ethnicity are the most obvious of Jerusalem's social categories. Table 5.2 shows estimates of varying quality for the city's major religious groups from 1525 to 1992. The Jews were the largest of the city's communities by the middle of the nineteenth century and have been a substantial majority throughout the twentieth century. Now they comprise 72 percent of the population. Israel's capital has the highest incidence of non-Jews among the country's major cities. Non-Jews are 9 percent of the population in Haifa and 4 percent in Tel Aviv. Jerusalem's population is also distinctive in having a larger proportion of ultra-Orthodox Jews than the country as a whole.

Christian fortunes in Jerusalem have waxed and waned with changes in regime. They reached the height of their post-Crusader development during the period of the British mandatory government and subsequently declined. Separate communities reflect the doctrinal and national divisions within Christianity and the concern of many congregations to maintain a position in the Holy City. There are Armenian Orthodox, Armenian Catholic, Greek Ortho-

Table 5.2
Jerusalem's Population by Religion

YEAR	MOSLEMS	CHRISTIANS	JEWS	% JEWS
1525	3,670	714	1,194	21
1553	11,912	1,956	1,958	12
1806	4,000	2,800	2,000	23
1844	5,000	3,390	7,120	46
1870	--------------11,000--------------		11,000	50
1876	7,560	5,470	12,000	48
1910	--------------25,000--------------		45,000	64
1913	10,050	16,750	48,400	64
1922	13,400	14,700	34,100	55
1931	19,900	19,300	53,800	58
1946	33,700	31,300	99,300	60
1948	40,000	25,000	100,000	61
1967	58,100	12,900	196,800	73
1985	115,700	14,200	327,700	72
1990	131,900	14,400	378,200	72
1992	------------155,500------------		401,100	72

Sources: Yehoshua Ben-Arieh, *Jerusalem in the Nineteenth Century: The Old City* (New York: St. Martin's Press, 1984); F. E. Peters, *Jerusalem: The Holy City in the Eyes of Chroniclers, Visitors, Pilgrims, and Prophets from the Days of Abraham to the Beginnings of Modern Times* (Princeton: Princeton University Press, 1985); U. O. Schmelz, "Modern Jerusalem's Demographic Evolution" (Jerusalem: Hebrew Institute of Contemporary Jewry, 1987); Schmelz, "Jerusalem's Arab Population since the Mandatory Period (1918–1990)," in Aharon Layish, ed., *The Arabs in Jerusalem: From the Late Ottoman Period to the Beginning of the 1990s—Religious, Social and Cultural Distinctiveness* (Jerusalem: Magnes Press, 1992), 6–42, Hebrew; Sarah Markovitz, "The Development of Modern Jerusalem: An Evaluation of Planning Decisions and the Effectiveness of the Planning Process," Senior thesis, Princeton University School of Architecture and the Woodrow Wilson School for Public and International Affairs, 1982; and *Statistical Yearbook for Jerusalem, 1988* (Jerusalem: Municipality of Jerusalem and Jerusalem Institute for Israel Studies, 1990); *Statistical Yearbook of Jerusalem, 1992* (Jerusalem: Municipality of Jerusalem and Jerusalem Institute of Israel Studies, 1994).

dox, Greek Catholic, Roman Catholic, Ethiopian, Copt Orthodox, Copt Catholic, Syrian Orthodox, Syrian Catholic, Maronite, Anglican, Lutheran, Baptist, other Protestant, and Mormon congregations in the city.[2] A survey of Christian clerics revealed an increase in antipathy toward the Israeli regime since the onset of *Intifada*, especially among sects whose local spiritual leaders are ethnic Palestinians.[3]

The city's most prominent minority is variously described as Moslem, Arab, or Palestinian.[4] The terms overlap to some extent, although the Arab and Palestinian designations include a sizable number of non-Moslems (mostly Greek Orthodox and Greek Catholics). The non-Jewish population grew in percentage terms more than the Jewish population between 1967 and 1992. Moslems and Christians together increased by 119 percent, compared with a 104 percent increase for Jews. The Jewish percentage dipped from 73.5 to 72.1 percent during that period.

It should be kept in mind that the demographic data for the Jerusalem municipality and the Jerusalem metropolitan region does not include Palestinian settlements that are in the occupied territories outside the borders of Jerusalem and Israel. As noted in chapter 3, the municipal boundaries were crafted in 1967 to exclude a number of Palestinian settlements and to maximize the Jewish percentage of the Jerusalem population.

It will be noted below that Jerusalem's economy is weakened by a lack of natural resources or proximity to a large market for industrial output. Yet the economy is strong enough to serve as a magnet for the Palestinian population of the Judean mountains. The city is a center for shopping, education, religion, and politics, as well as a source of jobs. Although there was an economic decline in East Jerusalem during 1948–67, a Palestinian intelligentsia remained and continues to provide a focus of nationalist activity. Jerusalem's Palestinian newspapers and opinion leaders are more prominent than others in the occupied territories. Al Aqsa mosque is both a national symbol and a place of worship that attracts thousands of Moslems from the surrounding area each Friday and Islamic holy days.

Population records for the occupied territories have not been updated since a census of 1967. Officials of the Central Bureau of Statistics concede that even making estimates has been difficult since the onset of the *Intifada* in 1987. Israeli regulations permit Palestinians from the occupied territories to enter Jerusalem and other Israeli cities to work, shop, or visit on a daily basis but bar them from establishing residence within Israel. Enforcement is haphazard. Estimates or guesses by officials of the municipality and the Interior Ministry range between 10,000 and 100,000 residents of the occupied territories living illegally in Jerusalem.[5] Being without proper documentation, those residents would not qualify for the social services available to the Palestinians of East Jerusalem. They would encounter no problem finding work, renting a dwelling in an Palestinian neighborhood, and sending their children to a private school. Israel's Central Bureau of Statistics estimated that 20,000 Palestinians entered Jerusalem on a daily basis from the territories in order to work during 1989.[6] An estimate for "metropolitan Jerusalem" that includes an area in the West Bank from which there is sizable daily migration to Jerusalem estimated 510,000 Palestinian residents as of 1982.[7] This means that the population in and around Jerusalem is at least one-half Palestinian, compared to the 72 percent

Jewish population recorded for the municipality per se. A report published in 1992 estimated that 180,000 Palestinians and 90,000 Jews lived in metropolitan Jerusalem outside the city boundaries.[8] If these figures are added to the Central Bureau of Statistics estimates of city population in 1990, they produce a metropolitan profile that is 58 percent Jewish and 42 percent non-Jewish.

East Jerusalem has remained outwardly more peaceful than the West Bank. According to one observer, much of Jerusalem's Palestinian-Jewish violence has been "imported" from elsewhere in the occupied territories.[9] The Palestinians of East Jerusalem have several reasons to accept the status quo, or at least to avoid violence. They benefit from Israeli social services that are not available to residents of the West Bank. They are closer to the economic opportunities offered by the city than West Bank residents and less likely to be kept from work by a military curfew. Jerusalem's Palestinians have not been roused to violence by the extensive building of Jewish suburbs. This may be because Palestinians have benefited economically by doing almost all of the manual labor involved in the construction and because Israelis have built mostly on vacant land.

The Jordanian government exercises a conservative influence in the Jerusalem Palestinian community by its connections with the religious establishment (Waqf) and the Arab Chamber of Commerce. East Jerusalem's neighborhoods are diverse in their socioeconomic and religious profiles, and so far have not moved in large numbers to Islamic fundamentalism.

The Jewish municipality has dealt with Palestinians partly through the institutions of the traditional mukhtar (village headman) and modern neighborhood associations. By one view, the intention is to deal with problems at the lowest possible level, in order to forestall the development of a citywide, all-Palestinian confrontational organization. Jerusalem's Palestinians have not formed their own political party for municipal elections, and individual Palestinians have not stood for election to the municipal council. Palestinians have either boycotted the electoral process or given their support to Teddy Kollek's One Jerusalem party. In the 1985 municipal election, One Jerusalem received 95 percent of the votes of those Palestinians who participated but only 18 percent of those eligible to vote. As will be shown below, Palestinian voting dropped to its lowest post-1967 level in the local elections of 1989 and increased only slightly in the election of 1993.

A discussion of its relative calm should not lead to the optimistic conclusion that East Jerusalem is totally different from other

Palestinian communities in Israel or the occupied territories. Palestinian neighborhoods of Jerusalem have had incidents of stone throwing, tire burning, killings within the Palestinian community, and casualties in encounters with Israeli security forces. There have been waves of stabbings of Jews by Palestinians. The most explosive recent event occurred during Succoth, in October 1990, when twenty-one Palestinians were killed by police on the Temple Mount, after the Palestinians began stoning Jews who were praying below at the Western Wall. Public opinion surveys, to be described below, find widespread hostility to the Israeli establishment among Jerusalem Palestinians.

Social contacts between Jews and Palestinians are rare. With few exceptions, Palestinians and Jews live in their own neighborhoods, read their own newspapers, send their children to their own schools, use their own bus lines and taxi companies. Palestinians in East Jerusalem academic high schools generally prepare for higher education in Arab countries, and few have the command of Hebrew that is typical of Arab students elsewhere in Israel. As a result, most of the Arabs who study at the Hebrew University are from outside of Jerusalem. Intermarriages are discouraged in both Jewish and Palestinian communities and are rare.[10]

There are numerous Palestinian political movements. The community is not organized as a formal authority and does not conduct regular elections. It shows the fluidity of irregular organizations that are partly clandestine. Numerous Palestinians shun contact with Israeli authorities. Some groups employ violence against nonconforming Palestinians and/or Israelis. It appears that the vast majority of politically active Palestinians in Jerusalem identify with the PLO. It is less clear how much support is enjoyed by groups affiliated with various factions of the Palestinian organization and how much support is enjoyed by Yassir Arafat or other individual leaders.[11]

Israeli critics of the policies pursued by the national and municipal governments have asserted that the Palestinians of East Jerusalem are more integrated with the Palestinians of the West Bank than with the Jews of Jerusalem. They conclude that Jerusalem is divided de facto and that its Palestinian sectors might as well acquire formal status as the capital of Palestine.[12] Supporters of the status quo, including Teddy Kollek, have expressed pride in the united municipality and see its operation as linked to a continuation of voluntary segregation in Palestinian and Jewish enclaves, as well as the voluntary segregation of ultra-Orthodox and other Jewish neighborhoods.[13]

The separation between Jerusalem's communities is an emotional and political topic. One study of Jewish-Palestinian relations in Jerusalem departed from its professional posture to speculate that the city is more divided than Montreal and Brussels, or even Nicosia and Beirut.[14] The quality of that speculation has been exaggerated and cited as authoritative by critics of Israel's administration.[15] In contrast is another study that is explicitly comparative in its coverage of ethnic tensions in Jerusalem, Washington, D.C., Singapore, Belfast, and Montreal. It concludes that Jerusalem is its own special case, and that there are no simple lessons to be learned from the comparisons.[16]

Jewish-Palestinian issues are not always at the top of Jerusalem's agenda. Occasionally a Roman Catholic-Greek Orthodox dispute reaches the headlines, usually about an incident involving the Church of the Holy Sepulcher. More common are disputes between religious and secular Jews or Jews of different ethnic backgrounds and political perspective. In late 1994, after Israel had signed an accord with the PLO and a peace treaty with Jordan, there surfaced a dispute between the PLO and Jordan over Jerusalem's Moslem religious functionaries. Both parties appointed a mufti, each of whom claimed that he was the supreme religious authority for the city's Moslems.

The Jews of Jerusalem are divided in about the same proportion as those of Israel with respect to their ethnicity. Some 53 percent trace their origins to Asia or North Africa and 47 percent to Europe, America, and Oceania.[17] The concept of "blocked amalgam" has been used to describe the situation of Israel's oriental Jews (Sephardim) from Asia and Africa. Most oriental Jews arrived in the late 1940s and 1950s when the foundations of Israeli society were already well established. Cultural patterns emphasized European values and skills, along with democracy, secularism, and the absorption of newcomers into the western Jewish society.[18]

Religion and ethnicity are associated with variations in occupation, family traits, and living standards. Secular Jews from European and American backgrounds are most likely to have small families, be housed in relatively spacious dwellings, and work in professional, managerial, or clerical occupations. They are followed in these traits by Jews born in Israel, Jews born in Asia or North Africa, and then by Palestinians. Jerusalem's Christians tend to have higher standards of living than Moslems, and on some measures

Table 5.3
Jerusalemites Employed in Professional, Managerial, and Clerical Occupations, 1983

	Men (%)	Women (%)
Jews, total	52.7	73.8
Origin Israel	53.3	78.3
Origin Asia		
Born in Israel	38.8	70.9
Born abroad	35.1	57.6
Origin Africa		
Born in Israel	42.7	72.0
Born abroad	44.3	56.8
Origin Europe-America		
Born in Israel	69.5	87.2
Born abroad	67.6	78.0
Non-Jews, total	21.1	72.5
Moslems	17.3	74.0
Christians	45.2	70.8

Source: U. O. Schmelz, *Modern Jerusalem's Demographic Evolution* (Jerusalem: Jerusalem Institute for Israel Studies, 1987), 105.

higher standards of living than Jews from Asian or North African backgrounds. (See table 5.3.) Some of these Christians are clerics of European or American origin. Religious Jews, especially the ultra-Orthodox, tend to marry early, have large families and low incomes. They are off the conventional scales that link income with education. The males, in particular, spend much of their lives in intense study of religious materials.

There is no simple way of estimating that proportion of Jerusalem's Jewish population that is secular or religious, ultra-Orthodox, simply Orthodox, or traditional. The labels mean different things in different contexts. A demographer has estimated that 20 percent of Jerusalem's Jews are ultra-Orthodox on the basis of voting results.[19] In recent elections Jerusalem's voters have supported ultra-Orthodox religious parties (Degel Hatorah, SHAS, and Agudat Israel) with about twice the percentage of votes that those parties have received nationally.

The demographic trend of the city is apparent in the 60 percent of Jewish primary school pupils who study in religious schools (state religious and independent ultra-Orthodox schools). Table 5.4 shows a dramatic increase in the proportion of primary school pupils in religious schools from 1972–73 to 1992–93, especially the independent sector operated by ultra-Orthodox congregations.[20] The

Table 5.4
Changing Incidence of Religious Education

Jewish primary school pupils by sector	1972/73 (%)	1992/93 (%)
State secular	53	32
State religious	28	19
"Independent" religious (including Talmud Torah)	17	42

Sources: Jerusalem Statistical Data (Jerusalem: Jerusalem Municipality and Jerusalem Institute for Israel Studies, 1983), 176; and *Statistical Yearbook of Jerusalem, 1992* (Jerusalem: Municipality of Jerusalem and Jerusalem Institute of Israel Studies, 1994), 257.

ultra-Orthodox schools appeal to many parents because of free bus transportation, meals, a longer school day, and shorter vacations, as well as the religious content of their curriculum.[21] Secular Jerusalemites look with some concern on the growth of ultra-Orthodox education and its implications for coming disputes about the imposition of religious laws in the city.

The large families of ultra-Orthodox Jews result in chronic pressure to expand their neighborhoods. Secular Jews accuse the ultra-Orthodox of "block busting" by opening a yeshiva in a secular neighborhood on the fringe of an established religious area and paying high prices for the first flats to be sold to religious families. Once an area seems destined to be religious, secular families leave en masse and apartment prices decline. For a secular family who remains in a largely religious neighborhood, life can be made difficult by harassment against driving, doing laundry, or listening to the radio on the Sabbath. It may be difficult to find a kiosk that dares sell secular newspapers.

Ultra-Orthodox Jews charge secular Jews with using their own unfair tactics to counter the expansion of religious neighborhoods. Religious groups opposed the plan to build a sports complex, including an outdoor swimming pool, in the new neighborhood of Ramot. Some ultra-Orthodox said that the sports center was planned in a manner to discourage the further development of religious housing in the area. They claimed that the sight of mixed bathing would offend religious families and keep them from moving into a project planned for a nearby hillside.[22]

During the decade of the 1980s Jerusalem's Jews and non-Jews moved closer to one another on some social indicators. Non-Jewish birth rates dropped from 42.8 births per 1,000 population in 1979 to 32.4 in 1991. The rate for Jews increased slightly during the same period from 26.7 to 27.0. Infant mortality dropped substantially for both Jews and non-Jews, with that of Jews remaining lower than that of non-Jews. The two groups' rates were 16.2 and 28.9 infant deaths per 1,000 live births in 1978, then 7.4 and 11.4 in 1990. Divorce rates continue to favor the Palestinian population: .07 cases per 1,000 population in 1990, as opposed to 1.5 cases among the Jews. This reflects a more closed, traditional society, and a strong family structure among Jerusalem's Palestinians.[23] For purposes of international comparison, United States rates for 1988 were 15.5 births per 1,000 population, 10.4 infant deaths per 1,000 live births, and 4.8 divorces per 1,000 population.[24]

JERUSALEM'S ECONOMY

The increase of Jerusalem's population by a factor of seven times since the beginning of the century and its tripling since World War II indicate a spurt of prosperity unequaled in its history. The city's Jews, in particular, are a long way from the wretched population that was barely kept alive by donations collected overseas and lived in the most crowded and run-down quarter of a filthy city neglected by its Ottoman rulers. They are the now the dominant element in the capital city of a Jewish state.

Despite the growth of Jerusalem to a size unprecedented in its long history, the city's fortunes remain tenuous. Its economic base is propped up with government outlays and donations from overseas. The hinterland has been constrained by the political context that closed most of Israel's neighbors to normal commerce. There is taxi and truck service between Jerusalem and the Jordanian capital of Amman, some 70 kilometers (40 miles) across the Jordan Valley. Until the peace treaty signed with Jordan in 1994, neither Israel's Jews nor their products could formally make the trip. All of Israel has limited appeal to multinational corporations because of the Arab boycott, the small national market, and the lack of natural resources. The coastal plain remains the economic heartland of Israel and contains the seaports and airports that provide connections with overseas markets and sources of supply.

As ever, Jerusalem lacks a firm base of nearby natural resources. Its immediate hinterland is small, without sufficient population to provide the markets for extensive industry. Jerusalem is dependent on resources provided by a state that is hard-pressed economically. Manufacturers would rather locate their plants close to suppliers, markets, and international ports on the coastal plain. Forty-four percent of Jerusalem's workforce is employed in public and community services and only 10 percent in industry. Comparable figures for Tel Aviv and Haifa are 21 and 28 percent in public and community services and 19 and 22 percent in industry.[25]

The Israeli regime has sought to broaden Jerusalem's economic base. It continues to emphasize the service sector and has sought to preserve the special character of Jerusalem. The Hebrew University, Hadassah Hospital, Jewish religious academies (yeshivot), and institutions affiliated with non-Jewish religious bodies are more prominent in the local economy than any industrial plants. Jerusalem is lovely, with the cleanest air of any Israeli city and modest family incomes that reflect the residents' dependence on salaries from government and other service organizations.

As in times past, tourism is a major component of Jerusalem's economy. Its hotels provided 1,818,000 person nights to foreign visitors in 1988, compared to 1,384,000 for the hotels in Tel Aviv and 145,000 for Haifa.[26] There are no figures for receipts, by Israeli locality, of foreign contributions. Jerusalem's university and hospitals, as well as numerous religious schools, orphanages, synagogues, churches, and mosques continue their historic practices of sending emissaries to responsive communities overseas.

The state treasury that provides the basis of Jerusalem's economy is by no means enviable in its strength. Israel is notable for an international balance of payments that is chronically negative, military expenditures that have been in the range of 20 percent of gross national product (five or more times greater than those of other western democracies as a percentage of gross national product), an international debt that may be the world's largest on a per capita basis, inflation that has ranged between 10 and 20 percent annually in recent years (down from 400 percent in 1984), and substantial financial aid from foreign governments and overseas Jews.

Jerusalemites have a modest standard of living by North American or Western European standards and are clustered toward the middle of the income scale. Net income per household was 3,710 New Shekels per month in Jerusalem during 1991 (equivalent to US $1,627), while it was 3,620 New Shekels in Tel Aviv and 3,990 in Haifa. A lower percentage of salaried families in Jerusalem have incomes in the upper three deciles than in Tel Aviv or Haifa (see table 5.5). Only 12 percent of Jerusalem's families live in a dwelling of at least 100 square meters (1,100 square feet), while 43 percent live in 60 square meters or less (see table 5.6). There were only 163 registered motor vehicles in Jerusalem per 1,000 residents in 1988, compared to 431 in Tel Aviv and 286 in Haifa.[27] Jerusalem had 466

Table 5.5
Israeli Household Incomes

City	Upper 3 deciles (%)	Middle 4 deciles (%)	Lower 3 deciles (%)
Jerusalem	26.6	41.2	34.4
Tel Aviv	43.6	32.0	23.5
Haifa	43.6	37.9	18.5

Source: *Statistical Yearbook of Israel, 1988* (Jerusalem: Municipality of Jerusalem and Jerusalem Institute for Israel Studies, 1990), 73.

Table 5.6
Dwellings in Jerusalem, 1992

Size in square meters	%
More than 100	12
81–100	16
61–80	28
41–60	29
less than 40	14

Note: 100 square meters = 1100 square feet
Source: *Statistical Yearbook of Israel, 1991* (Jerusalem: Municipality of Jerusalem and Jerusalem Institute for Israel Studies, 1993), 206.

telephones per 1,000 residents. Americans, in comparison, have 680 telephones and 575 automobiles per 1,000 residents.[28] By way of compensation, most Jerusalemites live close to a bus line, with service ranging from every four minutes to every half-hour between 5:30 A.M. and midnight.

A lack of economic opportunities is prominent among the explanations for the continued out-migration of the city's Jews. During eight of the ten years between 1979 and 1988, more Jews migrated from Jerusalem to other locales in Israel than migrated to Jerusalem from elsewhere in Israel. During four of the ten years, there was a negative migration to the Tel Aviv metropolitan area, reflecting its employment opportunities. During each of the ten years until 1988, there was a population movement of Jews from Jerusalem to the West Bank and Gaza,[29] reflecting the availability of lower-cost housing. Israel's governmental and quasi-governmental bodies provided land in the Jewish settlements of the territories at substantially lower prices than the cost of land in Jerusalem, as well as more generous mortgage terms. Moreover, construction in the territories avoids the costly provision that all buildings in Jerusalem be faced with stone. Despite these indications of a negative internal migration, Jerusalem's Jewish population grew as a result of natural increase and migration from overseas.

A combination of ethnic separation and Palestinian dependence on Jews is the rule in Jerusalem's economy. Numerous Palestinians work for the municipality or other public bodies or in the Jewish private sector, typically in lower-level positions. A study done in the 1980s showed no Jews working in Arab enterprises. Most shopping occurs in one's own sector. For some of their contacts with Israeli officialdom, Palestinians can visit a branch office in their own part of the city and deal with clerks in their own language. Jewish and Palestinian business firms purchase one another's products and services. There seem to be few Jewish-Palestinian partnerships, except for what are said to be joint ventures among car thieves, drug dealers, and other criminal entrepreneurs.[30]

JERUSALEM'S NEIGHBORHOODS

Jerusalem's neighborhoods translate the city's statistical traits into contending interests, political postures, and voting behavior. They also contribute to the city's charms. The Old City's Moslem, Christian, Armenian, and Jewish Quarters are defined by religion. Beit Safafa and Silwan are Palestinian villages in the midst of the metropolis. The Greek, German, and American Colonies preserve some of the houses constructed by nineteenth-century Christians who sought to make a home in their Holy City. Now the Greek and German Colonies are populated by middle-class Jewish families, and the American Colony is in the heart of Palestinian East Jerusalem.

The Katamonim are working class areas with concentrations of Jews who immigrated from Morocco and Kurdistan. Old Katamon had been an upper-class Palestinian neighborhood in western Jerusalem whose residents fled or were pushed out by Israel's War of Independence. Now their former homes show the remnants of grandeur amidst four decades refurbishing and new building. Abu Tor occupies a spectacular site on a hill overlooking Mount Zion and the Hinnom Valley and is unusual in having both Jewish and Palestinian families. However, those who are looking for an integrated neighborhood will find an invisible line between Abu Tor's Palestinian and Jewish sections.[31] Rehavia was known for its population of well-educated German Jews who came to Israel in the 1930s. Now families with young children are moving into homes vacated by senior citizens. Portions of Rehavia have been recycled into student apartments and the offices of physicians, attorneys, and accountants.

Mea She'arim is the archetype of Jerusalem's ultra-Orthodox religious neighborhoods. The flats are small and crowded with large families. The residents are poor materially, with many of the men studying full-time in religious institutions. Vendors of used clothing do a lively business in Mea She'arim, and there is a community soup kitchen. Newer religious neighborhoods have more space within and between their buildings. They resemble Mea She'arim in the dress of the residents, the large number of children, and being closed to vehicular traffic on the Sabbath and religious holidays.

Baaka was an Palestinian neighborhood before the War of Independence that was abandoned and then taken over by Jewish immigrants from North African and Asian countries. In recent years a number of its crumbling homes have been gentrified or replaced by new apartment buildings filled by younger Jews of European and North American origins. There are disputes between the old and new Jewish populations. Baaka's neighborhood association has sought to smooth the cultural tensions, as well as to improve the area's physical amenities and social programs.

Shmuel Hanavi is a feisty lower-class neighborhood that began as a group of blocks built along the dangerous border of 1948–67. At various times it has been a site of illegal drug trafficking and a source of support for the ultra-nationalist Kach movement founded by the late Rabbi Meir Kahane. It is one of the places where police congregate in order to protect passing Palestinians from reprisals after a case of anti-Jewish violence. An Israeli social scientist found that residents of Shmuel Hanavi were more likely than residents of a similar neighborhood in the town of Ramle to feel themselves deprived and to express dissatisfaction with government institutions. He reasoned that the closeness to better-off neighborhoods explained the harsh feelings in the Jerusalem neighborhood. In contrast, the lower-class neighborhood of Ramle fits into the homogeneous character of that small city.[32] Shmuel Hanavi received a major face-lift as part of Project Renewal after 1977, but it still suffers by comparison to Ramat Eshkol, an adjacent middle-class area.

Also distinctive are the newer Jewish neighborhoods that are further away from central Jerusalem. Many French Hill residents are European or North American in origin and include a number of faculty members from the nearby Hebrew University. Neve Ya'acov has a sizable community of Jews who immigrated from the former Soviet Republic of Georgia. The neighborhoods of Ramot, Gilo, and

East Talpiot provide homes for young Israeli families and new immigrants of varying national origins and socioeconomic traits.

POLITICS IN JERUSALEM

There is little in Jerusalem that is not touched by politics. In this it resembles other national capitals. Politicians assemble there to make decisions that affect the nation. Many of the city's residents work in government offices. Jerusalem is at the focus of news stories that attract attention throughout Israel and the world. Intimacy is made closer by the small size of the country and its capital. A resident is occasionally led to say hello to a familiar face, which is recognized only later as belonging to a prominent politician or television personality.

The Israeli and Jerusalem polities feature struggles between professional position holders and elected officeholders. The playing field on which their politics occurs is the city's mosaic of communities. Depending on the issue, subdivisions may be more important than the major blocs. Jews are divided into secular, ultra-Orthodox, and Zionist Orthodox or nationalist-Orthodox communities, and further divided by Sephardi-Ashkenazi, national origin, socioeconomic class, and political party. Disputes between secular Likud, Labor, or One Jerusalem parties on the city council have erupted when they have not stood together against the religious bloc. Within the ultra-Orthodox (or Haredim) and Zionist Orthodox communities are quarrels among individual rabbis and their congregations. They argue about points of religious law and claims of being more pious or law-abiding than one another.[33] Some religious Jews will not eat in a restaurant without determining which rabbi issued its certificate of being kosher. There is a story of one ultra-Orthodox rabbi who was asked what religion is closest to Judaism. He answered "Chabadism," the name of a rival ultra-Orthodox community. On occasion the yeshiva students of one group will paste their accusations of one another on the poster-boards of religious neighborhoods or even attack one another with fists and sticks.

Palestinians are divided among a Moslem majority and a Christian minority. The Armenians are the most prominent non-Palestinian Christian community. Like other Christian religious communities, the access of their leaders to the offices of the mayor and national officials is assured more by international clout than numbers of voters in local or national elections.

As in other democracies, the citizens' record of participation

Table 5.7
Voters Per 1,000 Residents, Knesset Election of 1988

Jerusalem	355
Predominantly Jewish areas	410
Non-Jewish area in city since 1948	
Beit Safafa	481
Non-Jewish neighborhoods absorbed in 1967	
Christian Quarter of Old City	13
Armenian Quarter of Old City	164
Moslem Quarter of Old City	3
Beit Hanina-Shu'afat	7
Sheikh Jerrah	2

Sources: Statistical Yearbook of Jerusalem, 1988 (Jerusalem: Jerusalem Municipality and Jerusalem Institute for Israel Studies, 1990), tables 3.4, 19.2; and Maya Choshen, "The Elections to the Knesset in Jerusalem: Statistical Outlook" (Jerusalem: Jerusalem Institute for Israel Studies, 1990), Hebrew.

in elections and their choice of parties provide one indicator of political importance. Israelis in Jerusalem vote at about the same rate as the country's citizens. Turnout in the four Knesset elections of 1977, 1981, 1984, and 1988 was 77–78 percent of eligible citizens voting in Jerusalem and 79–80 percent in the country.

Most of the Palestinians who were included within the city when Israel annexed a large area after the 1967 war have refused the offer of Israeli citizenship. That step is a prerequisite for voting in Knesset elections but not for voting in municipal elections. The willingness of Palestinians to identify with Israel can be judged by the incidence of residents in non-Jewish areas absorbed in 1967 who vote in the Knesset elections, in comparison to the incidence of voting throughout Jerusalem. This is not a conventional measure of voting turnout insofar as it does not take into account age differentials within the various sectors of the population. Nonetheless, the differences shown in table 5.7 are so stark as to make the point.

The residents of the Armenian Quarter in the Old City demonstrated their greater rapport with Israel than other non-Jewish residents of post-1967 neighborhoods by their participation in the 1988 Knesset election. Even their rate of participation was less than one-half that of the norm in predominantly Jewish areas of Jerusalem. The voting data for the Christian Quarter of the Old City (whose population is 85 percent Christian and 15 percent Moslem) shows the slight degree to which Christian Palestinians exceed Moslem Palestinians in their rapport with Israeli institutions. The rate of participation in the Christian Quarter was greater than that of post-1967 districts noted in table 5.7 that are almost entirely Moslem in their population. However, the election participation of residents in the Christian Quarter was only 3 percent of the norm in predominantly Jewish areas.[34] The election participation of post-1967 neighborhoods that are predominantly Moslem varied from 0.4 to 1.7 percent of the norm in predominantly Jewish areas.

The northern sector of the Palestinian village of Beit Safafa found itself within Israel at the end of the 1948 war. Its residents are Israeli citizens by fiat and can vote in Knesset elections without taking a step that can be deemed an active acceptance of nationality. These Jerusalemites are more integrated than other Palestinians into the political fabric of the city.[35] They suffer from being viewed as Palestinians by Jews and as Israelis by Palestinians. Table 5.7 shows that the incidence of voters in Beit Safafa was even higher than the norm in predominantly Jewish areas. In the election of 1988, 51 percent of those voting in Beit Safafa supported left-of-center parties that are predominantly Jewish and 40 percent left-wing parties that are predominantly Palestinian.[36]

Noncitizen Palestinians can be candidates for the municipal council and vote in municipal elections by virtue of being city residents. Palestinians refused to stand as candidates throughout the Kollek era. No Palestinian political party has emerged in local elections, and most Palestinians refuse to vote in local elections. An estimated 7,500–8,000 Palestinians out of the 35,000 (21–22 percent) who were eligible voted in the municipal election of 1969, and the boycott of the election proclaimed by some Palestinians was called a failure by Jewish commentators. Later elections indicated an end to that doubtful honeymoon. In the election of 1973, held soon after the Yom Kippur War, only 3,150 out of 43,000 eligible Palestinians are estimated to have participated (7 percent). In the election of 1978, 7,000–8,000 out of the 55,000 eligible Palestinians cast ballots (14–15 percent). The municipal election of 1985 saw 10,000–11,600 Palestinians participating out of perhaps 66,000 Palestinians who were eligible (18 percent). The election of 1989 occurred almost two years after the onset of the *Intifada*. The boycott held as never before, and the Palestinian vote dropped to 3,000.[37]

There is no shortage of politics in the Palestinian sector of Jerusalem, but it is outside the municipal framework. Much of it is concerned with the struggle against Israel. This chapter will not go beyond mentioning the existence of these politics. Their description is made difficult by the number of groups involved, their existence in a gray area or outside the framework of Israeli law, as well as by the fluidity and violence associated with clandestine activities.

Table 5.8
Selected Knesset Election Returns, Percentages of Total Vote

Party	1992		1988		1984		1981		1977	
	Isr	Jer	Isr	Jer	Isr	Jer	Isr	Jer	Isr	Jer
Likud	25	26	31	24	32	26	37	32	33	31
Labor	35	21	30	15	35	18	37	20	25	12
Right-wing secular parties (Tehiya, Tzomet, Moledet)	10	17	7	8	4	5	2	3	2	4
Left-wing secular parties (Citizens Rights, Change, Mapam, Merets)	10	10	9	9	5	7	3	3	14	15
Ultra-Orthodox (Agudat Israel, SHAS, Degel Hatorah)	8	22	11	18	5	11	4	9	3	8
National Religious Party	5	7	4	4	4	2	5	4	9	8

Source: Statistical Yearbook of Jerusalem, 1988 (Jerusalem: Jerusalem Municipality, 1990), table 19.1; *Statistical Abstract of Israel, 1990* (Jerusalem: Central Bureau of Statistics, 1990), table 20.2; daily newspapers after 1992 election.

In the long run Palestinian leaders may prove themselves able to maintain their distance from the Israeli regime and preserve their community in readiness for the day when they create their own polity. In the short run they have lost the opportunity to translate 25–30 percent of the city's population into a significant voting bloc. With the power they could achieve in the city council and Knesset, they might enhance the economic and social conditions of their sizable community. With skillful politicking, Palestinian leaders might multiply their weight in the electorate by joining Jewish political parties in permanent coalitions or floating alliances. By choosing to wage the fight of "whose city is Jerusalem?" the city's Palestinians have conceded their loss of political competition about "who gets what?"

Jerusalem's voters have tilted to the right in recent Knesset elections. The right-of-center Likud list has generally outpolled the left-of-center Labor list in Jerusalem by significant margins, while the two blocs have been more closely matched nationally (see table 5.8). Ultra-Orthodox religious parties and right-wing secular parties have also done better in Jerusalem than throughout Israel. The National Religious Party (described as Zionist-Orthodox, nationalist-

Orthodox, modern- or neo-Orthodox)[38] has done less well in Jerusalem than in the country as a whole during three of the five recent Knesset elections.[39]

A mapping of Jerusalem's Knesset voting behavior by neighborhoods shows the sources of various parties' support. Likud's strength is greatest in working-class neighborhoods south and west of the city center. These neighborhoods (Katamonim) gave Likud more than 50 percent of their votes in the Knesset election of 1988. Even more uniform is the voting behavior of several neighborhoods north of the city center heavily populated by ultra-Orthodox Jews. Sanhedria, Mea She'arim, Geula, and a religious section of Ramot gave the ultra-Orthodox parties more than 70 percent of their votes. Labor received its most concentrated support (at least 40 percent of the vote) in three upper-income neighborhoods heavily populated by professional people, as close to a "Yuppie" population as can be found in Jerusalem: Beit Hakerem, Ramat Dania, and Neve Sha'anan.[40] The upper-class appeal of Israel's Labor Party was not limited to Jerusalem during the period 1977–88 and helps to explain its failure to win any national election during that time.[41] Likud continued to outpoll Labor in Jerusalem in the national election of 1992. Labor's success in increasing its percentage of the Jerusalem vote from 15 to 21 between 1988 and 1992 reflected a national swing that brought the party to power. During his tenure as mayor, Teddy Kollek sought to blur his own Labor Party roots by creating a local party and calling it "One Jerusalem."

Political parties deserve modest treatment in this discussion of Jerusalem politics. During the Kollek administration they existed in the shadow of the mayor's personal influence and the weight of national ministries, municipal departments, and quasi-governmental organizations. Local branches of national parties did not do well in competition with Kollek's own local political party prior to the election of 1993. One Jerusalem enjoyed a working majority of the city council after the elections of 1978 and 1983 and a dominant plurality of eleven out of thirty-one seats after the 1989 election. With Teddy Kollek as its star, One Jerusalem was the dominant actor in coalitions that include all major secular and religious parties. In the Knesset, the national branches of these same parties were often at odds with one another.

Interest groups in Jerusalem and elsewhere in Israel operate in the context of a dominant public sector. Citizen groups emerge to protest and promote a variety of issues, but they aspire to join the public sector rather than remain independent sources of pressure.

The Society for Nature Preservation has acquired quasi-governmental status as a provider of school trips, summer camps, and other nature-related programs, as well as being a voice of Israeli conservation and environmental protection. The Manufacturers Association has a formal role as the representative of Israeli employers in economic negotiations with the Labor Federation and the Finance Ministry. The Labor Federation not only represents workers but is a prominent member of the Israeli establishment by virtue of its association with the nation's largest health service and bank, plus pension funds, bus cooperatives, and the kibbutzim and moshavim that comprise most of the country's agriculture. Gush Emunim (Bloc of the Faithful) pursued its program of assuring continued Israeli control of the West Bank by winning substantial government aid for its settlement projects.[42]

Symbolic politics rank high in the public activities of Jerusalem. As the term is used by political scientists, this means conflict that focuses not so much on the distribution of material resources as on issues that have intangible importance, sometimes of high intensity.[43] The spiritual feelings triggered by religion and nationalism are the prime objects of symbolic politics in the Holy City. Jerusalem's case also shows that politics about symbolic and material goals can be intertwined. There are both substantial and spiritual stakes involved in the issues of who controls the Holy City or holy sites within it and whether religious or secular law will govern commerce on the Sabbath.

Sometimes it seems that the meager value of the tangible results stand in inverse proportion to the emotions exhibited by those who participate in symbolic politics. Jerusalem's established place at the center of international interest assures wide audiences for those who can ignite a local issue into a world crusade. Moslems and Palestinian nationalists play to their international followings in religious communities, the United Nations, plus campus and third world groups committed to the liberation of the oppressed. Christians plus Orthodox, Reform, and secular Jews also have their own overseas communities of sympathizers who provide financial and political support.

Bombast, hyperbole, unbounded threat and promise are the stuff of symbolic politics. Chapter 1 includes some examples of the language used by Moslems, Palestinian nationalists, and Zionists against one another. The style is no less extreme in conflicts within the Jewish sector. Reform and secular Jews accuse the Orthodox establishment of religious persecution. Orthodox politicians accuse

Reform and secular Jews of blasphemy and apostasy. Each side accuses the other of anti-Semitism and says that their adversaries within Judaism are fomenting a civil war that will bring about Israel's destruction. Religious and secular activists seek the attention of the mass media by citing the scandalous behavior in the rival camp, demand the intervention of the police or the State Comptroller, and predict dire consequences if their demands are not met. According to the rhetoric of intense conflict, sports clubs and swimming pools proposed by secular organizations should be turned into religious academies and ritual baths. Structures built by a religious academy against zoning regulations should be torn down and the organization subject to police investigation. Neighborhoods must be made totally religious or completely secular.[44] An observer may wonder how much of this activity is meant to realize an actual change in public policy and how much is meant to vitalize organizational or individual reputations by arousing supporters.

TEDDY KOLLEK

Jerusalem politics revolved around Teddy Kollek between his initial election in 1966 and his defeat in 1993. Historians are likely to debate what he contributed personally to the city, as opposed to influences coming from national or international figures, the errors of Arab leaders, or the relative power of Israel and the Arab states.

Kollek received at least three times the vote of his nearest competitors in the elections conducted in 1978, 1983, and 1989 after the city began direct, personal elections for mayor. He received 63 percent of the vote in 1978, compared with 15 percent for the second-placed finisher; 64 percent (compared with 20 percent) in 1983, and 59 percent (compared with 17 percent) in 1989. Kollek's local party, One Jerusalem, did less well in voting for the municipal council, with 47, 49, and 36 percent in the elections of 1978, 1983, and 1989.[45] It did well enough in comparison with three to eight other parties in order to dominate council coalitions.

Kollek's dominating personality figured prominently in the 1989 municipal elections. A coalition of secular parties campaigned to help him hold back the ultra-Orthodox. Religious parties ran countercampaigns against what they described as antireligious incitement. A small party campaigned on the promise to join Kollek's coalition with the slogan, "Only Teddy can."

As in the case of other sophisticated politicians, an observer cannot document what Kollek believes or thinks. Even he may have had trouble doing this in the midst of numerous cross-pressures. Keeping one's options open and ambiguous expressions are a chief executive's stock in trade. Especially where the job is to pacify and lead a contentious community, a politician may be ill-advised to think in the heroic terms of solving difficult problems once and for all times. Success goes to the leader who can cope with conflict, blur the issue of who wins and loses, and prevent any group from being so disappointed that it embarks on violence.

The record of what Kollek has said and done is open to inspection. There is no challenging his credentials as a Zionist concerned with the survival and development of a Jewish state. Like many of the individuals to reach prominence in Israel's first generation, he was born into a European bourgeois family, left the comforts of his parents' home and migrated to Palestine as a young adult, and was a founding member of a kibbutz. He acquired experience from the late 1930s in Europe and America as an organizer of youth groups, mover of Jews and arms to Palestine (legally and illegally), fund-raiser, and intelligence operative. He rose during the era of Israel's founding prime minister, Labor Party leader David Ben-Gurion, and sharpened his administrative and political skills as director general of the prime minister's office.[46] He formally left the Labor Party along with Ben-Gurion in 1965. This move demonstrated Kollek's flexibility with respect to his party roots that appeared again in his creation of a local party, One Jerusalem. This is a stand-in for the Labor Party and has helped him appeal to a broad spectrum of the electorate in a city where the Labor Party is weak.

Kollek's most striking success was as the mayor of Jerusalem for twenty-six years after its reunification in 1967. He had the good fortune to find himself in a small holy city that changed its strategic configuration a year after he came to office. As a result of the Six-Day War of 1967 Jerusalem was no longer isolated at the end of a narrow corridor from Jewish settlements along the coast. It became the center of a Jewish country after a hiatus of nineteen hundred years. Kollek seized the opportunity for all it was worth. What he did not accomplish with the Jerusalem Foundation in the field of cultural and social programming his administration pursued in land development and major construction with the Jerusalem Development Authority and the Moriah Company.

During Kollek's career as mayor he had to work with national figures of other political parties. The Interior Ministry was controlled by religious parties concerned with the Jewish character of the capital. For all but two of the years between 1977 and 1992 either

Menachem Begin or Yitzhak Shamir served as prime minister. Both rose to power in Jewish underground militia prior to Israel's War of Independence and were labeled terrorists for their anti-Palestinian and anti-British activities. Then they served as leaders of the right-wing nationalist Herut (Freedom) Party, the leading element in the Likud Bloc and the opponent in national politics of the Labor Party that was Kollek's original home.

Kollek's international reputation rested on his sensitivity and deft dealing amidst Jerusalem's religious and ethnic tensions and his patronage of the arts. Residents with limited tolerance for European tastes criticized the theaters supported by the Jerusalem Foundation for their "foreign" productions and questioned the need for so many parks in a city with unmet social needs. Kollek's appearances at youth concerts and traditional Palestinian and Jewish celebrations conveyed the impression that he enjoyed loud and crowded discotheques and oriental bands no less than classical music.

The mayor was involved in numerous skirmishes with other authorities and developers over the face of Jerusalem and who should own what or live where. He played a role in persuading Israel's prime minister, minister of justice, and the president of Hebrew University to cancel the sale of the imposing but war- damaged structure of Notre Dame de France to the university after the Vatican objected to the decision of a religious order to sell its property. He helped persuade the Ministry of Education to allow both Jordanian and Israeli Arab curricula in the schools of East Jerusalem, after an earlier policy of replacing the Jordanian with the Israeli curricula led many parents to withdraw their children. He succeeded in preserving some empty space and a striking landmark when he kept developers from building villas on the hillside below the tomb of the prophet Samuel. He turned the walls of the Old City into a floodlighted centerpiece of the city's attractions, although David Ben-Gurion suggested tearing them down as a symbol of the city's reunification.[47] Yet it was in Kollek's regime that Israeli and overseas developers built high-rise apartments, office blocks, and hotels that receive few words of praise.

Kollek protested against the efforts of nationalist and religious Jews to take too much, too quickly, and with too much bravado. In his view, they inflame passions in a city that is destined by history for intergroup suspicion. Tension disturbed Kollek's city and the foreign donors and investors whose money he sought to attract.

Kollek's centrist posture within the Zionist community appeared not only in his condemnation of Jewish politicians who would take too much land, in too flagrant a fashion. He stood for the right of Israel to develop Jewish areas in the new neighborhoods of Jerusalem that other governments recognize as "occupied land." In early 1992 he was speaking out both against right-wing Israelis who would settle more Jews in areas traditionally Arab and senior officials of the United States government who demanded that Israel cease all development for Jewish settlement in areas annexed to the city after 1967.[48] Kollek's municipality integrated the urban area physically so that it will be difficult to take apart. "New electrical grids, water lines, and sewage systems . . . will make Jerusalem the hub of a modern system of pipes and lines. Whatever happens politically, services will emanate to the entire area from a united Jerusalem with a clear Jewish majority—but again with opportunities and benefits for Arabs who wish to cooperate, with or without Palestinian ethos."[49]

Kollek stood against Jewish politicians who would go too far, by his standards, in meeting Palestinian aspirations. Moshe Amirav was a member of the city council who moved ever leftward in a political career that began in the right-wing nationalist Likud Bloc. After his Likud colleagues expelled him for his challenges of their dogma, he joined the city council as a member of the left-of-center party, Meretz, and spoke out against the municipality's failure to provide services to the city's Palestinians. He exceeded Kollek's threshold when he published a proposal, along with a Palestinian activist, to divide Jerusalem into Jewish and Palestinian municipalities. At about the same time, Amirav added to the mayor's annoyance when he spoke out against an ultra-Orthodox campaign to prevent the construction of a new roadway when the work uncovered ancient Jewish gravesites. Kollek claimed that Amirav's comments added to the heat of the discussion and prevented a quiet resolution. Amirav had administrative responsibilities both for citywide transportation and the examination of conditions in East Jerusalem (Palestinian neighborhoods) and claimed to be acting within his mandate in both fields.[50]

Amirav also offended his colleagues in Meretz with the extent of his posture for the Palestinization of city areas. He lost out in the party primary for a place on its ticket for the 1993 election to the city council. Then he announced his intention to form a political party along with Palestinians, committed to the principle of reaching an accommodation that would allow Jerusalem to be the capital of a Palestinian state as well as Israel. When local Palestinians expressed their reluctance to join with Amirav, he said that he would visit PLO leaders in Tunis in order to acquire an endorsement of his campaign and a green light for Jerusalem Palestinians to join his ticket or at least vote for it in the municipal elections.[51] This occurred several months before it was clear that the Israeli government and the PLO were on the verge of an accord, when it was still customary to denounce the PLO as an organization of terrorists. At this point, the mayor announced that Amirav had broken with the city council coalition and removed his administrative responsibilities for citywide transportation and conditions in East Jerusalem.

Kollek stood by the principle of respecting each community's right to voluntary segregation even while he admitted that every resident has a right to live anywhere in the city. He noted that just as secular Jews avoid living in ultra-Orthodox neighborhoods, he would like Jews to avoid choosing a residence in the Moslem or Christian Quarters of the Old City.[52] He described segregated schooling, with separate Arab and Hebrew curricula and languages of instruction, as a vital component of communal peace. This stand caused him problems with potential overseas donors to the Jerusalem Foundation who were convinced that integration in the American way is the secret to Jerusalem's future.

By one report, the mayor sought to persuade Prime Minister Yitzhak Shamir to order other ministers to moderate their purchases of Palestinian land in the Jerusalem area during 1991. What he is said to have received for his efforts were the prime minister's congratulations on his eightieth birthday and a copy of a book of poems written by Abraham Stern, a prominent Jewish fighter of the 1940s who had led Shamir and others in attacks on British and Palestinian targets.[53]

Kollek harbored no illusions that his efforts would produce a solution for Jerusalem's problems in the short term. "Here it is clear beyond all doubt that Arabs will continue to speak Arabic and be educated with the Koran. The same for the Armenians or other Christian Churches that have guarded their languages and their doctrines over the generations. We have no aspiration to integrate. That would not be good for us, and it is not possible."[54] "We entertain no illusions that this will defuse the existing political contradictions; these, with patience and tolerance, may be solved in another generation or two. . . . We pursue our goals expecting neither sympathy nor gratitude from a population which cannot alienate itself from its national emotions."[55]

A scholar concerned with Arab affairs has written that Kollek followed the strategy of checking major moves with the Jordanian capital of Amman and keeping open lines of contact with different factions among local Palestinians, including young people. He "adheres to the Ottoman principle of keeping the wolves satisfied and the sheep happy. . . . a certain amount of autonomy, socioeconomic self-indulgence, and indeed 'progress' is granted to Arab society."[56]

Kollek employed a network of contacts with Moslem and Christian religious leaders and heads of prominent families, appointed representatives of neighborhoods (mukhtars), neighborhood councils, and aides and advisors in order to keep him informed about Palestinian concerns and to provide individual Palestinians with personal points of contact that could help them with the local or national bureaucracies.[57] Palestinians appeared at the mayor's receptions on Israeli national holidays and expressed their admiration for him. Kollek failed in his efforts to persuade Palestinians to stand as candidates for the city council. His One Jerusalem party did well among those Jerusalem Palestinians who voted in local elections, but it did not compete well against Palestinian efforts to boycott Jerusalem elections. The decline in Kollek's margin during 1989 and his loss in 1993 reflected the success of Palestinian boycotts.

One of Kollek's skills was being able to deal pragmatically with contentious interests, even while life in the cross-pressures produced outbursts of temper. When one constituent threatened not to vote for him, the mayor responded, "Kiss my ass."[58] Kollek stood against a sizable national majority when the Knesset enacted the Jerusalem Law in 1980 that added symbolic verbiage to the extension of the municipality that had been implemented by the Interior Ministry in 1967. Kollek said that the 1980 law was unnecessary and would produce only international condemnation for Israel. He would have preferred a Jerusalem Law that provided the municipality with greater rights and autonomy from Israeli national authorities.[59] He said that Israel's sovereignty with respect to Jerusalem can coexist with a pragmatic concession that leaves the Temple Mount in Moslem hands. He suggested taking the additional step of enacting a law to that effect and having the decision anchored in a United Nations resolution.[60]

During his first decade or so as mayor, Kollek acquired a reputation for personal involvement in the details of program administration. He rose early in the morning to check on garbage collection and street cleaning, served as tour guide for potential contributors, and walked the streets to see how his city worked. Later he focused on major appointments and policy issues. The coincidence in 1991 of his eightieth birthday and the twenty-fifth anniversaries of his being the mayor and president of the Jerusalem Foundation was the occasion for numerous celebrations, awards, cultural events, and fund-raising opportunities in Israel and overseas that raised $12 million for the Jerusalem Foundation.[61] By the informal reckoning of one senior municipal official, the mayor was spending about half his time in Jerusalem.

An observer who is skeptical about the prospects for peace in Jerusalem described Kollek as the city's last optimist.[62] Critics charged that he exploited his status as the incumbent by including campaign material along with the salary slips of city employees and by touting the city's growth and development as his personal accomplishment. Those who admire Kollek's skill as a fund-raiser say that he squeezed contributions to the Jerusalem Foundation from the overseas Jews who invest in projects of the Jerusalem Development Authority. Until 1993, his supporters pointed to the election results as the ultimate justification for whatever he did.

The issue of Kollek's retirement became prominent in 1992, the year before the municipal election. City hall gossips, as well as local and national newspapers reported that the mayor was tired of his position and fatigued physically. His well-known practice of dozing on public platforms was said to be increasing in frequency. A commentary published by the prestigious daily, *Ha'aretz* was headlined, "Kollek's Twilight Period," and urged the mayor to help his city and his own reputation by announcing a firm date for his retirement.[63]

Likud members of Knesset positioned themselves as mayoral candidates as the election neared, hoping to take advantage of their party's advantage in the Jerusalem electorate. Ehud Olmert, a Likud member of Knesset and minister of health in the national government that served until 1992, won his party primary as mayoralty candidate. Olmert campaigned on themes similar to those identified with Kollek: a concern for openness in Jerusalem and sensitivity for the interests of all the city's communities. He took care to praise Kollek's achievements and sought to establish himself as similar but younger.[64]

The prospect of losing Israel's major city to the opposition led the Labor Party prime minister to urge Kollek to run once again. In June 1993 Kollek announced that he would run. Those close to him indicated that he would resign shortly after winning election and turn over the office to the second on the electoral list of One Jerusalem. Kollek announced that his number two would be the former spokesman of the Israel Defense Forces. This candidate had no political experience but had won substantial public recognition during the Gulf War of 1991. Press reports recalled that Kollek had indicated that he would resign after the election of 1989 and turn over his position to Deputy Mayor Amos Mar-Chaim. Mar-Chaim adopted a posture of chagrin at the news that he would not be second on the Kollek list for 1993. The morning after the mayor announced that he would run again, the country's most prestigious newspaper featured a critical editorial titled, "Kollek as Surrogate Mother."[65] A short while later Kollek's designated successor took himself off the election list.

The election campaign dealt with Kollek's age as well as his accomplishments since 1966. After the signing of an accord between the Israeli government and the PLO, the last two months of the mayoralty campaign also became something of a referendum on the policy of making concessions to Palestinians. Kollek defended the actions of his Labor Party colleagues in the national government, while Olmert expressed the Likud bloc's reservations and promised to extend the Jewish neighborhoods of the city. A few days prior to the election, an ultra-Orthodox mayoral candidate withdrew his candidacy and supported Olmert, in exchange for Olmert's commitment to appoint nominees of the religious party to municipal positions and to support the party on policy issues. Religious party activists worked hard to bring out the vote for Olmert. Turnout was 85 percent in religious neighborhoods, compared with 34 percent citywide.

The mixture of personal and policy issues made it difficult to interpret the election results, beyond indicating that Ehud Olmert won with about 55 percent of the vote. The city's Palestinians seemed torn between wanting to oppose the Likud candidate in the context of the Israel-PLO accord and wanting to continue their practice of not endorsing the Israeli regime in Jerusalem with their votes. Some 7 percent of the eligible Palestinians voted, more than in the early *Intifada* election of 1989 but at a lesser rate than in elections of 1969, 1978, and 1985. Nationwide, Likud won thirty-six of the mayoralty contests in Jewish local authorities, while Labor won only twenty. Candidates running as independents or as heads of local parties won in another thirty localities. While such figures might indicate some opposition to the peace accord associated with the national Labor party, a low overall turnout in Jewish municipalities of 36 percent suggests that apathy also played its part in election results.[66]

The new mayor assembled a city administration of department heads from the right wing and the religious sectors of the political spectrum. This profile was not markedly different from the profile of Jerusalem's voters in national elections. Teddy Kollek left the mayor's office but not the Jerusalem Foundation. He continued to host major contributors and other distinguished visitors to the city.

Despite these alterations in detail, several factors seemed likely to moderate any change in local affairs. The dependence of the municipality on national ministries calls into question the value of the new mayor's postures on controversial issues as long as the Labor Party controls those ministries. The heavy weight of professional bureaucracies at both the municipal and national levels counsel that "business as usual" rather than major change would accompany the changes at the top of the local polity. Mayor Olmert has expressed himself in favor of negotiating the issue of Jerusalem sooner rather than later. This puts him at odds with the established Israeli policy of postponing bargaining about Jerusalem until the settlement of all the other disputes between Israel and the Arabs. To date, national officials who deal with the peace process have asserted the priority of the established policy, without engaging the mayor in a public debate.

The institutionalization of the Jerusalem Foundation as well as the mutual dependence of the foundation and the municipality seem likely to lessen any change in the foundation's activities. To the extent that Kollek continues to be involved in the foundation, he may be disinclined or unable to use the foundation to affect major developments in opposition to municipal departments or national ministries.

A newspaper survey of Olmert's first year in the mayor's office gave expression to a feeling of transition but a lack of certainty as to direction. One article expressed a concern about the weight of the ultra-Orthodox in the mayor's coalition. Another described the disappointment of ultra-Orthodox groups that they had not achieved more. Another article indicated that Olmert made promises to the city's Palestinians before the election but then overlooked their needs after they failed to support him. An interview with Teddy Kollek was conducted in the presence of a public relations officer from the Jerusalem Foundation. It indicated that all sides are concerned to handle the relations between the foundation and city hall with a delicacy appropriate to their mutual dependence. A separate article in the same issue of the local newspaper reported that the new mayor had not replaced the head of the Jerusalem Development

Authority, a longtime confidant of Teddy Kollek. As noted in chapter 4, the authority is one of the most prominent institutions involved in physical planning and construction in Jerusalem. The newspaper section that carried the survey of Olmert's first year was headed, "Already a Year, We Hardly Felt It."[67]

ATTITUDES ABOUT JERUSALEM AND THE TERRITORIES

Israeli Jews have been so united on the issue of Jerusalem that few pollsters bother to include a specific question on the issue. In one poll taken in 1980, 86 percent of Israeli Jewish respondents were against giving up East Jerusalem if that was necessary in order to reach a peace settlement. A slightly different question from 1980 provided an opportunity to compare Israeli Jewish and Palestinian opinions. Forty-two percent of Palestinians but less than 2 percent of Jews said that they were willing to return to pre-1967 borders, including East Jerusalem, in order to reach a settlement. Sizable numbers of Palestinians preferred other arrangements even more favorable to their side, while only a handful of Jews supported them. The option of the 1947 United Nations partition plan, which included the internationalization of Jerusalem, drew the support of 26 percent of Palestinians and only 0.3 percent of Jews. The option of turning all Israel into Palestine received the support of 12 percent of Palestinians and 0.1 percent of Jews.[68]

On other issues involved in the Israeli-Palestinian dispute, Israeli Jews divide into doves and hawks, with the proportions changing over time and in response to the particular question that is asked. A 1986 poll showed 30–40 percent of Israeli Jewish respondents willing to talk with the PLO if it recognized Israel and renounced terrorism or willing to talk with the Jordanians about giving back parts of the West Bank. Larger pluralities opposed such options. Seventy percent agreed with the position that Jews have rights to the Land of Israel that are more just and compelling than those of Palestinians, and 58 percent rejected the option of a Palestinian state in the West Bank and Gaza that would not threaten Israel.[69] Another 1986 poll found that 47 percent of an Israeli Jewish sample would leave the territories as they were (under Israeli military occupation), while 32 percent would give up the territories if Israel's security was assured. Only 16 percent would agree to return all the territories, with minor border modifications and a special arrangement for Jerusalem. Forty-nine percent of the same sample expressed the opinion that Israel has a right to the territories.[70]

More dovish were the results of a poll made in 1991, as the United States government began its effort to begin a dialogue for peace after the Gulf War. Then 50 to 60 percent of the Israeli public responded positively to questions about their willingness to make territorial compromises in the interest of peace. No question in this poll asked if Israelis were willing to make concessions about Jerusalem.[71]

American Jews are a potential reference group for Israelis and appear to be more dovish. During 1986 only 51 percent of American Jews, as opposed to 70 percent of Israeli Jews, agreed with the position that Jews have rights to the Land of Israel that are more just and compelling than those of Palestinians.[72]

Palestinians also have compatriots and other supporters in the United States, although they are fewer and less well organized than those of Israel. The results of what researchers called a nonprobability, "semi-snowball" survey were reported in 1989. A semi-snowball survey seems to be one in which known Palestinians are contacted and asked for the names of additional Palestinians. The survey was based on the 240 replies received from 350 questionnaires distributed. It showed 61 percent expressing support for the position that Jerusalem be "completely restored to Palestinian control" (begging the question if complete or even partial Palestinian control ever existed), while 24 percent opted for internationalization of the city as envisioned in the 1947 United Nations Partition resolution, and 15 percent would have Jerusalem the capital of both Israel and a Palestinian state.[73]

The Palestinian posture was less successful in four referenda conducted in American localities during 1988. Items did not deal specifically with Jerusalem but with Palestinian statehood, the creation of a sister-city relationship with a refugee camp, or condemning Israeli violation of Palestinian human rights. Pro-Palestinian referenda lost by 2:1 margins in San Francisco; Berkeley, California; and Newton, Massachusetts, and won by a margin of 53–47 percent in Cambridge, Massachusetts.[74]

JERUSALEM IN THE SHADOW OF *INTIFADA*

From the 1967 war through the early 1980s, it was common for friendly foreign writers to express cautious optimism about Jerusalem's future. They praised the mayor for his sensitivities toward

Palestinian feelings and the projects financed by his Jerusalem Foundation in Palestinian neighborhoods and noted his support by the Palestinian electorate.[75] A study of Palestinian public opinion in Jerusalem as late as the summer of 1987 (six months prior to the *Intifada*) concluded that Palestinian fragmentation based on religion, extended families, and socioeconomic status had prevented the citywide development of Palestinian political expression.[76]

The center of gravity of the *Intifada* was outside of Jerusalem. It was in the Gaza Strip and the West Bank that the uprising began in December 1987 and where most stones were thrown, tires burned, and Palestinians killed by the Israeli security forces or by other Palestinians. East Jerusalem merchants observed numerous calls for strikes or limited working hours issued by the leaders of the *Intifada*, despite the efforts of Israeli authorities to force them to open their shops. There was some violence in Jerusalem's Palestinian neighborhoods and suburban villages. Israelis ceased the pre-*Intifada* practice of shopping in Palestinian neighborhoods, where stores are open on the Jewish Sabbath and offer lower prices than shops in the Jewish sector. Israeli and overseas tourism in the Old City experienced its ups and downs, along with the tempo of violence.[77]

Survey results offer sobering findings about the feelings of Palestinian Jerusalemites.[78] Eighty-six percent answered "No" or "Not at all" when asked if they were satisfied with the services rendered by the Jerusalem municipality. Almost 90 percent chose "Palestinian state" when asked, "If confronted with a choice, which would you choose: Palestinian state, economic well-being, family and community, or religion?" Less than 40 percent reported that they have some relationship with an Israeli institution.

Israeli readers might find cause for optimism in the finding that 26 percent of the Palestinian respondents indicated their support for an open city of Jerusalem where residents could move freely between Jewish and Palestinian sectors. Yet 55 percent responded to the same question by saying that the city should be divided east (Palestinian) and west (Jewish).

A review of Jewish public opinion throughout Israel after two and one-half years of *Intifada* found that many people clung more firmly to their earlier postures with respect to the Palestinian-Israeli conflict. There was also an increased rejection of the "status quo" option and an increase in dovishness, which anticipated the left-wing shift in the 1992 election. Although the survey was designed to test the outer limits of Israeli dovishness, it did not include a question about withdrawal from East Jerusalem.[79]

Surveys taken in Jewish and Palestinian sectors after the announcement of the Israel-PLO accord in September 1993 showed initial support in both communities from about 60 percent of the respondents. As some Palestinian violence continued and snags occurred in continuing discussions, however, support in both sectors declined below 50 percent. The accord was formulated to exclude any immediate changes in Jerusalem, so the early poll results cannot be read to indicate any firm changes in the two communities' postures toward the city.

CHAPTER 6

Policymaking: How Jerusalemites Cope with Themselves and Their History

Residents and officials of Jerusalem deal with problems typical of a middle-sized city plus those associated with being the national capital. Visitors expect that the city's roads, parks, museums, and other public services will accommodate them, although they pay their local taxes somewhere else. Political demonstrations for the benefit of national politicians and the mass media add to the problems of congestion and public order. As a reader may already expect, these are not the problems that are high on Jerusalem's agenda. Jerusalem is not a typical city or the capital of a typical country.

The previous chapters dealt with Jerusalem's history, the structure of its government, traits of the local economy, people, and their politics. They provide the background for this chapter's discussion of policymaking. How the authorities of Jerusalem and Israel deal with the city's problems and what they decide reflect the city's history, the hierarchy of authorities and formal procedures, and the immediate pressures presented by the population and outsiders. Perhaps no clear linkages can be described between the materials presented in chapters 2–5 and details of Jerusalem policymaking or the substance of public policy. It is not possible to assert with certainty that a certain factor produces a style of policymaking or brings about a specific policy. Nonetheless, we can see the influence of the material examined earlier.

It is also impossible to identify policies that are the product of municipal authorities acting alone. National politicians and civil servants determine the school curriculum (except in the schools run by ultra-Orthodox congregations and schools in East Jerusalem answerable to Jordanian, Moslem, or Christian authorities), the character of police protection, health and welfare benefits, and local taxes. National ministries must approve the allocations that appear in the municipal budget, as well as local decisions about the city's physical development. Even where the rules do not require ministerial involvement, the priority of Jerusalem in Israeli affairs may lead to consultation between local and national officials or a determined intervention by a national official. Quasi-governmental organizations are prominent. As explained in chapter 4, they are better situated than municipal agencies or ministries to recruit funds from overseas individuals who are willing to donate or invest in Jerusalem. The quasi-governmental organizations also add to the problems in determining who influences policymaking.

The categories of *macro* and *micro* are useful in thinking about the influences that shape policymaking for Jerusalem. Individuals and institutions that are classified as micro actually produce the decisions that become public policies. They are national and local politicians; employees of national ministries, municipal departments, and quasi-governmental organizations; activists in political parties and interest groups. In Jerusalem's case, a number of macro conditions may weigh more heavily than equivalent factors in other cities. The long history of the city and its spiritual legacies produce intensities of feelings that constrain the actions of policymakers. The social geography and economics of the city and its surroundings produce chronic concern for the city's security and the government's need to support a city without nearby natural resources or a market for industry. Tensions between Palestinians and Israelis, as well as between religious and secular Jews, reify the history of Jerusalem at the end of the twentieth century. Each misstep of policymakers or administrators that rubs the exposed nerves of religion or ethnicity raises the image of yet another crusade, perhaps this time encouraged by a resolution of the United Nations, declared by a crowd in an Arab city, and supported by western university students.

The raw materials of this chapter are numerous policy-relevant episodes that have occurred in recent years. They illustrate themes already apparent in previous chapters: the intensity and multiplicity of problems that policymakers face in dealing with Jerusalem; competition between Israeli advocates of accommodation versus domination with respect to the city's Palestinians; the prominence of officeholders in city affairs; the struggles of local officials against formal procedures that empower national officials; and the appeal in such a context of coping, as opposed to comprehensive problem-solving. This chapter also feeds into the assessment of policymaking in Jerusalem and scenarios toward the near future that are the subjects of chapter 7. The details here are interesting in their own right and for their message that Jerusalem responds to the micro as well as the macro. It is a locality as well as a world city. Squabbles between personalities and the pressures coming from neighborhoods mix with international institutions and foreign governments, plus events in the region and the wider world to affect what happens in the city.

POLICY PROBLEMS AND THE STYLE OF POLICYMAKING: THE MUNDANE AND THE DRAMATIC

A discussion of Jerusalem policymaking and policy must deal with the mundane and the dramatic. Both are necessary in order to provide a complete picture. The emotional charge that pervades Jerusalem can transform a pedestrian issue that would be of municipal or neighborhood interest elsewhere to something that attracts international attention. An administrative blunder that seems innocent and insignificant can be exploited by those wishing for another confrontation on basic issues. It is never clear what starts an international crisis or what is simply used as an excuse by those who want a crisis. In Jerusalem's case, what one person describes as a small issue will be seen by others as a cause of war.

The explosive nature of what might be described as small or large issues is not something that is new to the current Israeli regime. The ancient Judeans revolted against the Greeks and the Romans after the imperial rulers had placed pagan statuary in the Temple. Arab desecration of the Church of the Holy Sepulcher contributed to the Crusades. Some eight hundred years later Greek Orthodox and Roman Catholic disputes over repairs to the same church were among the problems that led to the Crimean War. During the British Mandate, Jewish efforts to pave the alley in front of the Western Wall and to erect temporary barriers to separate men and women who would pray there on the Holy Days contributed to the growing ill will between Palestinians and Jews, as well as to animosities between Jews and the British. Once the Israelis gained control of all Jerusalem in 1967, local Christians and Moslems sought to arouse international concern in response to the demolition or construction of individual buildings at sensitive sites or the efforts of Jewish families to live in areas that others said were "not for Jews."

Several styles of policymaking appear in Jerusalem. Professional bureaucrats of the national or local authorities decide routine issues according to formal rules. Planning is widely in evidence, with committees concerned with everything from deciding about sizable parcels of land to persuading apartment dwellers to erect shields in order to hide from public view the areas where they hang their laundry. When a problem escalates from the routine, the formal rules and established plans may bend to the weight of elected officeholders at national or local levels or the influence of distinguished persons from overseas. At times it is difficult to determine if one or another figure is genuinely moved to improve conditions in Jerusalem or takes an action in order to score points in another forum. Policymaking on prominent issues appears to be reactive and sometimes panicked, with the persons actually making decisions responding to threats or fears of yet another crisis that might weaken Israel's hold on its capital.

Within the Jewish Sector

Some issues of purely local, Jewish import gain special status because they occur in Jerusalem. The wave of immigration from the Soviet Union that began in the spring of 1990 added to the pressures on housing. Rents increased along with the demand for housing. The immigrants had an advantage over local families on account of the allocation for housing in the funds provided to them. A number of local families declared themselves to be homeless and erected tents at a prominent site opposite the Knesset. The municipality provided the settlers with water and electric lines and toilet and shower facilities. The municipality, the Ministry of Housing and Construction, and housing companies owned by the municipality and the ministry said that they were trying to help. It did not advance the cause of the homeless when the mother of one family said on Israeli radio that she could not accept the apartment offered to her because it had only two rooms and lacked a balcony. The "tent city" of perhaps ten units became a tourist attraction for Jerusalemites and others. It returned to the headlines at the beginning of September when the municipality assigned the children to schools, again when the onset of autumn cold and rain led the authorities to renew their offer of quarters for the homeless, and again when Iraq missile attacks led the authorities to provide temporary quarters in hotel rooms that could be sealed against the possibility of poison gas.

A separate group of religious tent dwellers set themselves up in a religious neighborhood. They refused offers of temporary housing in hotel rooms on the argument that they would prohibit the maintenance of a kosher lifestyle.[1]

The problem of homeless families evoked an ethnic and class issue that has simmered since the 1940s. Most of the homeless were lower-income families of Asian and North African origin who compared the benefits provided to new Russian immigrants with the lack of benefits provided to their own parents when they arrived in Israel. The homeless claimed to be the residue of a social problem derived from poor and crowded housing that Israel must solve before turning its attention to European immigrants with professional qualifications.[2]

Another problem connected with immigrant housing emerged in the early months of 1991. An area of Pisgat Ze'ev, a new neighborhood of upwardly mobile families, was chosen as the site for trailers as temporary immigrant housing. This produced a demonstration of residents who noted their support for the national cause of Soviet immigration but said they were sure the municipality could find a more suitable place for the immigrants. The protest fit the pattern of "not in my backyard" (NIMBY), familiar to policymakers in many settings when residents demand that an undesirable facility be located elsewhere.[3] The municipality reduced the number of trailers to be put in Pisgat Ze'ev and began to investigate a number of alternative sites. Once burned by publicity, the city engineer refused to disclose the locales being considered.[4] When the alternative sites were made known a few weeks later, the neighbors of each indicated their reasons for opposition. "Why not put them in Rehavia or Beit Hakerem?" was the question asked by one angry resident, indicating older upper-crust areas with little open space for any of the several hundred trailers at issue.[5]

Hadassah Hospital worked out a deal whereby it would provide land to the municipality for temporary housing, on condition that it could use some of the units for the immigrants it recruited to its own staff. The hospital and its international funding arm, Hadassah Women, also won some plaudits for serving the cause of immigration.[6]

When ground preparation was underway at another sight for the placement of trailers, archaeologists of the Antiquities Authority announced that part of the area had been inhabited from the time of the First Temple until the Byzantine period. The contractor continued to excavate until the Antiquities Authority produced a stop order from the police. Archaeologists surmised that they would have to halt all site development for at least three months and hoped to preserve part of the area for continued research. Meanwhile, immigrant and homeless families would continue in the temporary quarters of hotels or tents until they could be moved to the somewhat less temporary trailers.[7]

The press of more than three hundred thousand immigrants who arrived in Israel during 1990 and 1991 proved too much for the existing housing stock or that which could be assembled quickly from new construction or temporary dwellings. The government took over entire hotels, whose owners saw this as a welcome relief from a slump in tourism. Tensions seemed bound to emerge when whole families were put for months on end in hotel rooms, having to prepare their food on tiny electric units or in shared kitchens. There was the additional problem of cultural clash when several hundred Russian and Ethiopian families were placed in the same Jerusalem hotel. The hotel's name, the Diplomat, added to the stories carried in newspapers throughout the world when the friction escalated through name-calling and fights among the children and then to fights among the adults.[8] A few weeks later, there was a similar problem at the Hotel Shalom, this time pitting Ethiopians against homeless Israelis in the hotel.[9]

Charges of favoritism in the allocation of financial resources appear in many political arenas, as a signal of competition over who gets what. Among the prominent noises in Jerusalem politics are the charges of getting too much directed against ultra-Orthodox Jewish institutions and political parties. An explicit or implicit feature of these charges is that ultra-Orthodox institutions receive special funding, and ultra-Orthodox males and females enjoy exemptions from the military service that is a difficult part of other Israelis' lives.

The media paid close attention to allegations about Interior Minister Ariyeh Deri and his colleagues in the Sephardi Religious Party, SHAS. They detailed each stage of a long-running police investigation that began in 1990 and touched on Deri's personal finances, his ministry's grants to local authorities that were made on condition that the municipalities pass some of the money to SHAS-related institutions, and allegations of forgeries by ranking SHAS personalities. Some of the activity seemed to be traditional patronage, but on a scale and with an brazenness that exceeded recent Israeli norms. Deri defended his actions as corrective discrimination, or an Israeli version of affirmative action that made up for years of deprivations suffered by the community of Sephardi ultra-Orthodox.

The story of SHAS became more spectacular when it was

linked to a family squabble in a prominent rabbinical family. One Sephardi rabbi and the son of SHAS's patron, the former Sephardi Chief Rabbi of Israel, accused SHAS leaders of forging checks made out for large sums of money. Party defenders said that the accuser was jealous because he had been left out of SHAS's patronage. He was also the subject of accusations that have special significance in the religious community. He was called a rebellious son, who had not invited his distinguished father to the circumcision of the older rabbi's grandson.

A bar mitzvah celebrated by a prominent ultra-Orthodox family received media attention because it occurred on the memorial day for members of Israel's security forces.[10] Prominent figures at the bar mitzvah were a Knesset member and his son, who was a member of the municipal council. The point was that ultra-Orthodox parties have a long history of not honoring the institutions of the Israeli state. Once again the leaders of Agudat Israel had been found celebrating on a day of mourning for secular Israelis whose sons had been killed during service in the armed forces. The celebrants responded that a bar mitzvah is a sacred duty that takes precedence over mourning, even in the case of a death in the immediate family. Other Jerusalemites responded that the celebration could have been more modest out of respect for dead soldiers.

During the early 1980s the question of Jerusalem's sports stadium set the largely working-class, oriental Jewish football (soccer) fans against various groups of upper-income western Jews and against religious Jews. The problem began when it was decided to demolish Jerusalem's small and outmoded stadium located in an upper-income neighborhood of western, secular Jews. A proposal to build a new stadium on the same site provoked the opposition of local residents who demanded that they be free, once and for all, of the noise and traffic associated with Saturday football games. A proposal to rent the seldom-used stadium of Hebrew University brought the opposition of university officials, who feared that unruly fans would trample the botanical garden they were developing in the vicinity of the stadium.

Mayor Teddy Kollek was opposed by leaders of the city's ultra-Orthodox Jewish communities when he sought to build the new stadium on the city's northern outskirts with funding from the Jerusalem Foundation. Religious Jews stood against the project on account of its violation of the Sabbath, which is the occasion for most of the country's football games. The city's ultra-Orthodox neighborhoods were expanding in the northern direction. Sooner or later the noise and traffic of the stadium would disturb their Sabbath rest and worship. Some religious leaders opposed the construction of a football stadium anywhere in the Holy City, in a move that recalled the opposition of Jewish zealots to Greek athletic contests during the Hasmonean period (167–37 B.C.E.). Opponents of the stadium recruited allies from Jewish communities overseas. In a period when the religious parties held the balance of power in national politics, Prime Minister Menachem Begin and the Minister of Interior Yosef Burg, a member of the National Religious Party, decided that Jerusalem could not build its football stadium.

There is now a modern structure, named "Teddy's Stadium," in a working class area of the city far removed from religious neighborhoods, whose construction survived a court challenge. In contrast to the situation during the Begin administration, the religious parties held no balance of power in the government that ruled after the election of 1988.

The issue of Jerusalem's stadium should be viewed in the perspective of the modest interest in sport throughout Israel. It is not only the religious parties who think that athletics is something for the *goyim* (non-Jews). Neither universities nor high schools maintain teams in competitive leagues. The major spectator sports of football and basketball do not come up to European or North American quality. Israeli football teams have trouble keeping their occasional world-class star from defecting to Europe. Basketball teams are limited in the number of players they can recruit from overseas but nonetheless put on the floor a number of African-Americans. Jerusalem has had trouble producing a team to compete successfully even in Israeli basketball, and it did without a football stadium for ten years without crisis. The city's football teams played on the rough grass of the YMCA field, with several hundred fans looking on from the scruffy bleachers.

The involvement of the prime minister and the interior minister in stopping the construction of a stadium in northern Jerusalem showed that national authorities would intervene in a local issue against the wishes of the popular mayor. Another example occurred when the government wanted to build a ring of new Jewish neighborhoods surrounding Jerusalem following the 1967 war. Kollek viewed the proposal as taking resources away from the established sections of the city and threatening the deterioration of the central core. For national ministries these considerations were less important than expanding the national capital in a way that would add to

Jewish housing at all points of the compass and make it impossible to redivide the city.

In order to minimize disputes about the application of religious as opposed to secular law, policymakers use the principle of preserving the "status quo." Conditions are said to have been frozen according to the status quo that prevailed when Israel achieved its independence. Practices then allowed in individual localities were to continue, while practices forbidden were to remain unlawful. The problem comes in interpreting the status quo. What about new neighborhoods whose religious residents want to close the streets to Sabbath traffic, including bordering streets that are major thoroughfares? When such issues arise, religious politicians accuse their secular colleagues of wanting to violate the status quo, which they may define as no Sabbath traffic in *all* neighborhoods with a religious population.

The religious community is especially concerned to minimize violations of religious ordinances in Jerusalem. It is the Holy City that should live according to the highest standards. Religious leaders have demanded that swimming pools outside of their own neighborhoods forbid the mixed swimming of men and women. They have settled for having certain hours set aside for segregated swimming and having the pools fenced and roofed so that religious people would not be offended by the sight of immodesty. There have been demonstrations and occasional violence against shops that sell pornography or pork. In order to assure that a religious person who died suddenly would not be subject to an autopsy according to a police order, yeshiva students have organized body snatchings and quick burials.

One season of religious outbursts was directed against advertisements posted in sheltered bus stops. Religious Jews burned some bus stops on account of the immodest attire of women in the posters. Liberal Jews from Israel and overseas decried the lack of free expression in Israel, while Orthodox Jews from Israel and abroad decried the lack of decency in the Holy City. The police arrested some perpetrators, and the advertising company negotiated with religious leaders in an effort to define the kinds of pictures that would be inoffensive. Such negotiations seemed futile when a bus stop was burned that carried a picture of a mayonnaise jar without any human forms.

Residents of the religious neighborhood of Sanhedria caused problems when they insisted that the main road to the new neighborhood of Ramot, which skirted their own neighborhood, be closed on the Sabbath. This was not a demand that the municipality could accept. It threatened to blockade the twenty-five thousand secular residents of Ramot in their homes during their one-day weekend. Sanhedria claimed priority on the basis of religious law and the disturbance of their own Sabbath by the noise of the traffic. Yeshiva students escalated the conflict by standing on a cliff above the road and pelting cars with stones. The municipality built a detour that would allow drivers to skirt the point of contact with Sanhedria. Then some secular residents of Ramot refused to take the detour in order to avoid giving pleasure to their religious antagonists. In response to them, the municipality erected signs asking drivers to take the detour in a spirit of accommodation, and police officers directed cars onto the detour. By some views, religious Jerusalemites stopped their disturbance of Sabbath traffic only when secular residents of Ramot conducted their own nighttime pogrom against parked automobiles and other property in Sanhedria.[11]

City planners employed by the municipality contend that the Ministry of Housing and Construction erred in locating Ramot's access road alongside the older religious neighborhood of Sanhedria. They asserted that the Ramot lesson is to isolate religious neighborhoods more completely, so their residents' insistence on their own lifestyle does not impinge on their secular neighbors.[12] It is typical of the infighting that occurs in Israel that officials of one agency accuse another of error. The Housing and Construction Ministry did not admit any mistakes in planning Ramot.

An issue with a long history moved toward the top of the secular-religious agenda in the middle of 1987. Secular Jews in Jerusalem sought to change the status quo with respect to the opening of cinemas, cafes, and discotheques on Friday evenings, after the onset of the Sabbath. Mayor Kollek lent his support to those seeking entertainment on the Sabbath. He said that secular young people should not have to leave Jerusalem in order to enjoy their weekends. Overseas Jews expressed themselves for and against. The Jerusalem branch of the Hebrew Union College, an American-based seminary for the training of Reform Judaism's rabbis and teachers, added to the animosity of Orthodox Jews when it began showing cultural films on Friday evenings.[13]

The movement to open sites of public entertainment on the Sabbath was given a boost by a court decision that municipal bylaws that forbid their opening were flawed and could not be enforced. By this point, masses of religious Jews were blocking traffic on Friday evenings and Saturdays. The issue faded when the Israeli Cabinet committed itself to legislation that would enable the municipalities to outlaw public entertainment on the Sabbath and when Palestinians began the *Intifada*. Palestinian-Jewish violence took precedence and helped to submerge communal violence among the Jews.[14]

More than seven years later there was still no comprehensive law to govern the issue of Sabbath entertainment, and Jerusalem's young swingers had grown accustomed to enjoying themselves on Friday evenings. It seemed too late to turn back the clock and impose restrictions.

In a flare-up of the issue during 1991, the Agudat Israel deputy minister of labor announced that he would bring a criminal action against places of entertainment that employed Jews on the Sabbath without having a formal exemption from the labor laws. A cinema manager that was about to be charged said that she had been unable to find non-Jews to work the Sabbath shift. She asked if the ultra-Orthodox deputy minister would like her employees to convert to Christianity or Islam in order to comply with the labor law.[15]

Teddy Kollek supported a proposal to divide Jerusalem into secular and religious districts and allow or forbid activities in each district according to the residents' lifestyles. Then some religious members of the city council threatened to leave the coalition with Kollek's party and cause a political crisis. According to one council member affiliated with a religious party, the proposal ran counter to the status quo and threatened to legitimate intolerable violations of Jewish law in the Holy City. Leaders of right-wing secular parties had their own reason for opposing the mayor. They saw his proposal as a precedent that could lead to the redivision of the city into Jewish and non-Jewish districts and end Israeli control over the city.[16]

Another proposal would update the status quo by allowing those places of entertainment that had opened on the Sabbath since the 1987 court decision to remain open. A variant on this would close those in the central city near religious neighborhoods but allow Sabbath openings in an outlying commercial district on the extreme opposite side of the city from most religious neighborhoods. Insofar as it is difficult for religious politicians to admit that they have accepted any violation of Sabbath, anywhere, the council members concerned with this issue had to find a way to agree without formally agreeing.[17] In what was termed a "cease-fire," the religious parties on the city council were said to have agreed tacitly to allow a new status quo of entertainment on the Sabbath, while secular parties agreed not to attempt the formalization of the status quo in an ordinance.[18]

The activities of Reform Judaism present their own red flags to Orthodox Jews concerned to guard the purity of Judaism as the Orthodox believe it should be observed, especially in the Holy City. One encounter focused on a community center that provided space for a new Reform congregation that was too small to obtain its own building. An Orthodox rabbi and his followers vandalized the site when they failed to persuade the community center manager to oust the Reform congregation. Another encounter began when the Municipal Department of Education offered an empty school building to a primary school affiliated with Reform Judaism that was looking for quarters. The building at issue was empty because the neighborhood had become increasingly Orthodox, and there was no longer need for a secular primary school. As a primary school with a Reform emphasis in its curriculum, the school could draw pupils from outside its immediate area. Orthodox residents in the area promised violence if the plan went forward.[19]

Ethiopian immigrants have also been at the center of a Jewish religious problem. Some Orthodox rabbis questioned the authenticity of the Ethiopians' Judaism. Ethiopians charged that their children were not accepted in some Orthodox schools and were segregated in other Orthodox schools from non-Ethiopian students.[20]

Jews are not reluctant to criticize city and national government planners in the sharpest of terms about the most sensitive of issues. The redevelopment of the Jewish Quarter is touted as the jewel of Israel's reunification of Jerusalem. It returned more than two thousand Jews to a part of the Old City that was taken by the Arab Legion in 1948, then despoiled during twenty years of Jordanian rule. The project has earned praise for its architecture, its use of costly stone, wood, and iron to the exclusion of asphalt and plastic, the lack of individual television antennae, and the care with which the builders dealt with sites of religious and historical relevance. Local critics, in contrast, call the Jewish Quarter Hollywood kitsch.[21]

The plaza created in front of the Western Wall immediately after the Israelis regained the site was meant to be the beginning of a more extensive development. More than twenty-five years later the project is frozen at an early stage of completion, and antagonists seem to have tired of trying to convince one another about the merits of contending plans. One controversy sprouted when former Chief Ashkenazi Rabbi Shlomo Goren erected a modernistic monument to Holocaust victims by sculptor Ya'acov Agam on the roof of a building overlooking the plaza. The monument was less flashy than Agam's computer-programmed, multicolored water fountain in the center of Tel Aviv. Nonetheless, what to the rabbi was an artistic achievement was to others an abominable desecration of a site that should be left unadorned. Four years after the squabble began, the sculpture was still in place while municipal officials were unable to obtain the rabbi's agreement to erect a stone parapet that would partially obscure the monument, in exchange for retroactive authorization from the planning commission. The rabbi was quoted as saying that the monument would remain until the Messiah arrived to move it to his newly erected Temple.[22] Meanwhile, the monument would commemorate Jerusalem's problems in implementing decisions of its planning authorities.[23]

An episode involving a major road construction and ancient graves erupted toward the end of 1992 and included a number of issues typical of Jerusalem policymaking. There was secular versus religious, economic development versus the city's sacred heritage, and actions of the national government to take a hot problem out of the municipality's jurisdiction. The problem also reflected the difficult topography of a mountain city whose opportunities for road building are limited by ridges and valleys. The city found itself with one intersection having to handle multiple streams of heavy traffic: the major north-south road from Ramallah, Nablus, and other Arab and Jewish settlements to the north of Jerusalem, as well as the new suburb of Pisgat Ze'ev; and the major east-west route connecting Jerusalem with Jericho and the Jordan Valley, including the new suburb of Ma'ale Adumim. Travelers often waited an hour or more to negotiate the junction during the morning peak. The condition threatened to worsen significantly because Pisgat Ze'ev was the major site for building in the face of continuing immigration from the former republics of the Soviet Union, with apartments for an additional forty thousand residents nearing completion.

When excavation for a two-level interchange was well advanced, contractors uncovered gravesites from the period of the Second Temple (535 B.C.E.–70 C.E.). Then began a controversy not unusual in Judaism. Some rabbinical sources favored moving remains to other gravesites in order to facilitate the city's development, while other rabbinical sources were cited as opposing any disturbance of the dead. Secular observers asked why these graves should prove a barrier to the city's development on a matter concerned with a major roadway, when contractors managed to find solutions for gravesites found while building housing in ultra-Orthodox neighborhoods.

Israel's archaeologists inserted themselves as a third factor between those wanting to leave the graves as they were and those wanting a new intersection as soon as possible. The country's laws provide for a halt to construction when ancient sites are discovered and a period for archaeologists to ascertain the importance of the findings and to make some provision for preservation or removal. When archaeologists demanded their rights for the site in question, they triggered memories of numerous previous conflicts with religious Jews over the excavations of other gravesites. Some religious leaders seemed willing to move the remains to other graves but not to have them pass through the hands of the archaeologists, while archaeologists insisted on their legal rights to examine the graves and to preserve the stone coffins for further research or exhibition.

Just then another gravesite at a different construction site provoked two days of trash burning and demonstrations by tens of thousands of ultra-Orthodox men that tied up traffic and sent demonstrators and police officers to the hospital. The mayor's opponents charged that the issues of graves and construction were beyond an old man's ability to find a solution. The prime minister sided with those who claimed the problem exceeded Kollek's capacity and appointed a committee of ministers to produce a solution for the troublesome intersection.

What emerged from this committee was a decision to move the planned intersection eight meters westward in order to avoid the gravesites in question. This could add more than ten million shekels (US $3.5 million) to the cost of the project and a delay of perhaps six months in its completion. It did not satisfy the archaeologists, who began a suit to realize their rights to excavate the gravesites. The proposal satisfied religious leaders only until another gravesite was discovered along the revised roadway chosen by the committee. Then, in a process that ends numerous controversies in Jerusalem, a delay helped to cool tempers and work continued.

Jews and Others

Troubles among Jews in the Holy City are difficult enough for the municipality. When Jewish and Christian or Moslem sensitivities rub up against one another, the waves may go even further afield.

The Temple Mount, or Haram al-Sharif, has long been Jerusalem's most sensitive locale. It was there that Israelite kings provoked the writers of the Books of Kings and Chronicles by the abominable behaviors of placing foreign idols in the Temple. Greeks and Romans stimulated Jewish revolts by placing their own statuary there, and Christians and Moslems provoked one another from the Byzantine period onward. Problems continue even now when the Israeli government controls all of Jerusalem but has conceded de facto Moslem control of the Temple Mount. Moslems have sought international condemnations of Israeli archaeologists who are said to be undermining the site or weakening its structures by nearby diggings. Religious Jews have protested against archeological digs in the same area on the basis that they are desecrating ancient Jewish graves. An Australian tourist demonstrated the vulnerability of Jerusalem to outbursts of communal rage that are not of its making when he set fire to al-Aqsa Mosque in August 1969. His identity as a Christian with a record of mental instability and the responsibility of Moslem guards for the mosque's security were not sufficient to calm Moslem convictions that the fire was a Jewish plot to prepare the way for a new Temple.

Jewish organizations that proclaim their rights for the Temple Mount have organized prayer sessions and marches on the site, often timed for religious occasions of heightened feelings. Some Orthodox Jews oppose these demonstrations out of concern that the celebrants would unknowingly violate the biblical prohibition against entering the place of the Holy of Holies, whose exact location on the Temple Mount has not been determined. Israel's television news showed a hapless Palestinian truck driver, who was in the employ of Jews wanting to lay the foundation for the Temple, seeming apathetic when the police would not let his rig with a huge stone approach the Old City. The Institute for Research and Construction of the Temple received the small sum of 6,600 New Shekels (US $2,750) in the 1991 municipal budget. A spokesman of the institute explained that it was concerned with historical research and preparing ritual artifacts against the day when it may be possible to construct the Third Temple.[24]

Succoth is one of the Holy Festivals that brings thousands of Jews to pray at the Western Wall just below the Temple Mount. During the holiday in 1990, it was also an occasion for several hundred Palestinians to gather on the Temple Mount and to lob stones on the Jews below. In the panic that resulted several Jews were injured, while twenty-one Palestinians were killed by police gunfire. This brought an outcry of international protest about the behavior of the

police, which in turn provoked Israeli protest about the unbalanced nature of international statements that did not also condemn Palestinians who attacked Jews praying at their own sacred site. It also provided a boost to the *Intifada,* whose intensity had lessened in the preceding months.

The Moslem religious authorities who administer the Haram al-Sharif responded to the violence by limiting the hours that non-Moslems were allowed to visit the area. Israeli police prevented Moslems from using an entrance to Haram al-Sharif next to the Western Wall. The police also limited access to Friday prayers in al-Aqsa mosque (located on Haram al-Sharif) by Moslems from the occupied territories, especially young men who fit their profile of potential troublemakers. Seven months after the Succoth incident, Moslem authorities and police commanders met, along with a representative of the municipality, in order to relax the limitations that each had taken against the other.[25]

Moslems have their own problems with respect to their sacred places. The early months of 1992 witnessed a row between the kings of Jordan and Saudi Arabia over who would have the honor of financing repairs on the Haram al-Sharif. Jordan's King Hussein claimed priority on account of the Hashemite family's traditional responsibility for the Moslem holy places of Jerusalem. The Saudi royal family, which ousted the Hashemites from the Arabian holy cities early in the century, seemed intent on scoring more points in intra-Moslem rivalries. While King Hussein insisted on his own right to finance the repairs, Yasir Arafat gambled on improving the PLO's status, or his own, when he publicly thanked the Saudi King Fahd, but not Hussein, for offering to finance the repairs.

The Jerusalem Center of Brigham Young University became the center of controversy while it was being constructed on a prized site on the Mount of Olives overlooking the Temple Mount. Religious Jews became alert to the Mormons' commitment to proselytizing some dozen years after the Mormons first opened a Jerusalem Center in temporary quarters and after construction of the new facility was well under way. Mass demonstrations stopped construction. Member of Knesset Rabbi Meir Kahane proclaimed that the partly finished building should be completed as a rabbinical academy. Senators from the Mormons' home state of Utah spoke about their support for Israel and expressed their concern about the rule of law in Jerusalem. Teddy Kollek supported the project's continuation. An Israeli court ruled in favor of the university, and construction continued. A committee chaired by an official of the Justice Ministry was given responsibility for supervising the university's commitment not to proselytize in Israel. Some years later, Teddy Kollek visited Utah and returned home with contributions from the Mormons to his Jerusalem Foundation.

The efforts of Jews to establish homes or schools in the Moslem or Christian Quarters of the Old City guarantee protest. Nationalist Jews, including former Minister of Housing and Construction Ariel Sharon, have moved into apartments in those quarters. They assert that such locations will discourage Palestinians from attacking Jews on their way to and from the Western Wall.

When some Jews moved into an empty building near the Church of the Holy Sepulcher in 1990, they provoked a condemnation from Greek Orthodox clergy that recalled the historic Christian practice of permitting no Jews to live in Jerusalem when they controlled the city and stoning Jews who wandered near the Church of the Holy Sepulcher when the Moslems controlled the city. The Greek clergy made it clear that they did not want Jews living near their Church and brought suit to expel the Jewish residents from the building they had occupied. The church claimed that as owner of the building it had a right to bar Jews, while the Jews asserted that they had a legal sublease, granted by an Armenian who had a lease on the property from the church. The issue put Mayor Kollek in the delicate position of chastising Jews who chose Easter as the season to become neighbors of the Holy Sepulcher while defending the right of Jews to live anywhere they could legally secure residence in Jerusalem. An Israeli court imposed a temporary order for most of the Jews to vacate the building, while it allowed some of them to continue living there in order to safeguard their claims.

The ghoulish problems of 1992 involving graves and new construction also set the rabbinate against the patriarch of the Greek Orthodox Church. The long-delayed Mamilla project was threatened once again by the discovery of the several thousand sets of bones in a mass grave. Israeli archaeologists concluded that they mostly likely were the remains of Christians slaughtered during an invasion by Persians in the seventh century C.E. Some rabbis asserted that there were also Second Temple Jewish graves in the area and demanded that all the remains be reinterred in a Jewish cemetery according to Jewish burial rites.

One troublesome settlement of Jewish families in an Palestinian neighborhood (Silwan) occurred during October 1991. The Bush administration was trying to cobble together an international peace conference and spoke against provocative Jewish settlements in Palestinian areas. During the same week, United States officials had criticized Israel for sending its air force over Iraq to gather intelligence. Israeli critics of the settlers expressed the view that the settlers were primarily concerned to scuttle a peace process that might end with Israel withdrawing from some of the occupied territories. The neighborhood chosen for the settlement was less than two kilometers (a mile and one quarter) from the main shopping street in the predominantly Jewish section of Jerusalem but had been a particularly violent spot in the *Intifada*. Even some members of the right wing Likud government criticized the settlers for poor timing. Teddy Kollek called the action a bad dream that was certain to increase local tensions. The police initially moved against the settlers but then committed themselves to protecting the settlers from their new neighbors when a court ruled that the settlers had a legal right to the dwellings.[26]

In March 1992, the Ministry of Housing and Construction provoked another outburst from the mayor when it indicated that it would ask the approval of planning authorities for a new Jewish neighborhood of two hundred apartments on one of the few remaining vacant plots within the Old City.[27] At about the same time, Israeli newspapers reported that the Ministry of Housing and Construction was considering a plan to locate a number of trailers in the Old City for the temporary housing of new immigrants.[28] A reader could only hope that it was the ministry's effort to provoke the mayor. Kollek's humor seemed to have reached its limits. He was reported as saying at a local council meeting that "the Cabinet was shit."[29]

Another move in the effort to Judaize sensitive areas came when the Ministry of Housing and Construction offered a plan to build 205 housing units in the City of David. This was the site of the Jebusite city taken by David some three thousand years ago, located on a ridge that extends south and west just outside the present walls of the Old City. In this case the plan was opposed by a formidable group of city council members who identified with the mayor's campaign against the ministry, as well as architects and archaeologists who object to any construction of private homes on land with historic and scientific value.[30]

The number of occupations, building starts, and plans that surfaced in 1991–92 suggested that key officials in the Ministry of Housing and Construction feared that they would not be serving after the 1992 election. They sought to locate Jewish families or institutions in Christian and Moslem Quarters of the Old City, as well as sensitive locations just outside the walls. They tried to use provisions allowing speedy approval of planning changes that had been implemented in response to the wave of immigration that began in 1989. Their opponents sought to use the complications of the planning process against them, as well as appeals to moderate opinion through Israel's mass media. The projects seemed likely to be in the headlines for some time, until they were removed from the agenda when the Labor Party and the left-of-center Meretz Party became major components in the national cabinet after the 1992 election.

KEEPING THE CITY BEAUTIFUL

Preserving the beauty of Jerusalem has been a major goal of public policy since the British Mandate, but efforts are not good enough for critics near and far. Municipal planning authorities have defended themselves against chronic charges of poor taste by citing a number of projects that it has rejected. "It could have been worse" is the theme of this campaign. Among the items mentioned are high-rise hotels, massive commercial buildings, and elaborate roadways, bridges, and tunnels offered for the area adjacent to the Old City; the replacement of the Russian Compound in the central business district of the new city with 22-story office towers; and modernistic plans for the reconstruction of the Hurva Synagogue in the heart of the Jewish Quarter.[31] The synagogue reconstruction was shelved in the interest of a simple arch to symbolize the profile of the synagogue that was destroyed by the Jordanians.

Mayor Teddy Kollek also defended the projects of his Jerusalem Foundation by noting the gifts that he has rejected. He told of one donor who would have built a large gold monument in the shape of the tablets of the law to be erected where the main road from the coast reaches Jerusalem.

The aesthetic good intentions of the Jerusalem Foundation with respect to the Old City ran afoul of communal suspicions. It paid for the paving of dirt streets with costly stone, as well as the provision of modern water, electric, and sewer lines. Then it tried to replace unsightly television antennae by offering free cable connections to a central antenna. It implemented the program by fiat in the Jewish Quarter and persuaded the Armenian Church (sole landlord in the Armenian Quarter) to go along. The foundation had limited success with householders in the Christian Quarter. Most residents of the Moslem Quarter resisted the foundation, and the project went on another of Jerusalem's back burners.

It is popular to criticize the Jewish neighborhoods and the Mt. Scopus campus of the Hebrew University begun soon after the 1967 war for what is called monumental or fortresslike architecture. Aesthetic failings may have been inevitable. Large projects were built in a period of great national pride and intense political pressure, out of fear that Jews would lose the land through threat of international sanctions if they did not occupy it quickly.

A concern for the city's beauty came up against the historic concern for water after the 1991 winter of inadequate rain. The minister of agriculture declared that no water could be used for parks and gardens. Then Teddy Kollek led a coalition of mayors and householders in behalf of city parks, private gardens, and indoor plants. He was willing to conserve in behalf of the national water shortage, but he would not order the city's gardeners to close the taps completely and see Jerusalem turn from green to brown.

CITY BOUNDARIES

Jerusalem's boundaries are more sensitive than those of other central cities surrounded by suburbs and satellite towns. In Jerusalem's case, the issue involves not so much the issue of where residents will pay taxes and send their children to school as the proportion of Jews and Palestinians who live in Jerusalem and the national aspirations of the two communities. In the late 1980s the municipality and the Jerusalem Development Authority commissioned a major study to assess several proposals for extending Jerusalem's municipal boundaries.[32] The report identified a number of key goals for the city's development and evaluated various proposals for annexing territory. The primary goals were a city that was made more secure with a larger Jewish majority and a viable economy. Desirable land annexations would include existing Jewish suburbs plus Jewish-owned land to the west of the present boundaries. This would allow the continued construction of Jewish neighborhoods with a minimum of Palestinian objections and provide industrial areas that would allow the broadening of the Jerusalem economy beyond service employment in government offices and other public institutions. The industrial jobs would dissuade productive young residents from leaving Jerusalem for more attractive opportunities on the coastal plain. A decreased out-migration would counter the recent increase in the city's proportion of elderly people who must be supported with social services. Annexation of existing Jewish settlements would provide for the efficient provision of services in one large municipality uninterrupted by autonomous suburbs.

In response to the report, the municipality took a posture in favor of expanding its borders westward to include an additional 30,000 dunams, or a 25–30 percent increase in the municipal area. Minister of Housing and Construction Ariel Sharon opposed the municipality's proposal and favored the extension of Jerusalem's boundaries eastward. His proposal was consistent with his policy to emphasize settlement in the occupied territories and seemed likely to arouse foreign critics of Israeli expansionism into what they see as Palestinian land. Right-wing members of the city council supported Sharon. They expressed the view that the city's expansion westward would drain development resources from building Jewish settlements among the Palestinian villages to the east of Jerusalem and bring about the de facto division of the Jerusalem area into Jewish and Palestinian sectors.[33] Secular Jewish activists said that the issue was not so much to assure the city a large Jewish majority as to assure it a majority of Jews who were not ultra-Orthodox.[34]

The prospect of Jerusalem's expansion also brought forth statements like those heard in other countries when cities contemplate annexations of surrounding territory. Members of agricultural settlements worried about the farmland that lay west of Jerusalem's present boundaries, and residents of a suburban town signed a petition against being gobbled up by the city they had chosen to leave.[35]

The Interior Ministry made its formal determination of annexations to Jerusalem's boundaries in February 1992. It added some 13 percent to the city's area, taking in Jewish areas to the south and west of the existing borders.[36] It was not until May 1993 that Interior Minister Ariyeh Deri finalized the extension of municipal boundaries. Teddy Kollek was prominent in the photographs of the signing ceremony and took advantage of the opportunity to express his warm thanks for Deri's cooperation with the municipality. Deri was under the cloud of a police investigation that would result in his indictment later in 1993.

At the same time that one set of discussions concerned changes in the municipal boundaries of Jerusalem another set of discussions was focusing on plans for a Jerusalem metropolitan area. By some conceptions, this would extend substantially outward from the city in all directions and include areas of dense Palestinian settlement. Palestinians were among the voices that spoke out about these plans, indicating that Israel could expect them to invoke pressure from international forums if there was unilateral action on Jerusalem or its hinterland without appropriate negotiations.[37]

WHO RULES JERUSALEM?

It is no simple task to identify the individuals and institutions that determine who gets what in Jerusalem or the operative definition of what urban researchers call the "local state." Individuals and organizations who seem to dominate some issues are disinterested or powerless in others. Instead of any clearly fixed or ranked power elite, it is most accurate to describe a list of personalities and functionaries who provide the basis of alliances that form around particular issues.[38] There may be no official or individual who can decide a major item alone, without recruiting support from other power holders.

The list should begin with the mayor and interior minister, plus other national government ministers who take an interest in Jerusalem and direct special resources to the city or use their legal authority to advance Jerusalem projects. Heads of quasi-governmental or nongovernmental bodies invoke the resources and prestige of their organizations on matters of special concern. Prominent religious leaders and individual Palestinians with an international following can call on local and foreign media, foreign governments and overseas religious bodies to support their demands or protests.

The fluidity of Jerusalem's ruling alliances appeared in the issue of expanding the Jewish presence in Arab neighborhoods and villages. During the period of Ariel Sharon's tenure as minister of housing and construction he was a major source of funding and governmental support in the cabinet dominated by the nationalist Likud bloc. Government-owned companies and the Israel Lands Authority, under the control of the Ministry of Housing and Construction, served as conduits for the transfer of land and buildings, some of them at subsidized rentals, to Jews willing to live in Arab neighborhoods. The religious academy Aterit Hacohanim provided settlers for individual site acquisitions. Against this combination Mayor Teddy Kollek proclaimed his dismay at the provocation that would assure continued hostility among Jews, Palestinians, and other Gentiles in his city. His international and national standing might have restrained the desires of Sharon and his allies for taking more land more prominently, but the mayor could not be assured of halting individual projects. At times departments of his own municipality provided formal approvals or other support for the projects of Sharon and his allies. Perhaps a younger Kollek would have proved more forceful. Or it may have been that Kollek's own desires for strengthening the Jewish presence in Jerusalem might have led him to object only to Sharon's style and not his goals.

The issue of expanding Jerusalem's boundaries produced at least temporary shifting in the alliances and antagonisms involving religious, secular, and nationalist politicians. The nationalist and secular Sharon pressed for expanding the city to the east in order to assert the Jewish presence in the areas of the occupied territories heavily settled by Palestinians. He was supported by local council members associated with the Zionist-Orthodox National Religious Party but not ultra-Orthodox politicians who tend to be more concerned with religious than nationalist issues. A crucial figure in the issue was Ariyeh Deri, the interior minister who actually had the formal power of determining Jerusalem's boundaries. Deri took a position alongside Teddy Kollek, in keeping with Deri's previous postures in behalf of being more sensitive with respect to Palestinian concerns. Deri decided that the city's boundaries would be expanded in southern and western directions likely to minimize conflicts with Palestinian claims. This earned Deri some limited praise from Israel's secular left wing, which otherwise was calling for his scalp on account of his using the Interior Ministry to funnel public resources to religious institutions.

The issue of Jewish residence in Arab neighborhoods changed with the coming to power of a Labor government after the 1992 elections. The new Minister of Housing and Construction took steps to halt the use of governmental institutions and funds to assist Jews to live in Arab neighborhoods. In the first weeks of the new government, however, nationalist Jews from Israel managed to raise funds from overseas donors to help them pursue the purchase of dwellings in Arab neighborhoods without governmental support.[39]

MAJOR THEMES OF JERUSALEM POLICY

The many authorities concerned with Jerusalem make it difficult to define policy in ways that are authoritative, simple, and unambiguous. Municipal and national officials, as well as quasi-governmental authorities, have their own priorities. What one body declares as policy may come up against the policy of another body or be altered as it is implemented by another body. Perhaps the only way of defining policy de facto is to infer it post hoc, by observing what actually happens in numerous circumstances, over the course of several years. The following themes emerge from episodes already reported, as well as from statements made by the mayor and other prominent figures. The phrasing and order of the items have been chosen with an eye to what has wide agreement among present authorities. It is in the nature of the city that numerous residents and observers are likely to quarrel with how they are defined and ranked.

1. *Maintain Jerusalem as a predominantly Jewish city and the capital of Israel.* The two elements to this statement are connected with one another. Should the Jewish percentage of the Jerusalem population fall below a certain level of dominance, then it may not be feasible to maintain the city as the national capital.

The concern for a large Jewish majority in Jerusalem appeared in the new boundaries drawn for the city after the 1967 war and expanded further in 1992–93. They left a number of Palestinian settlements outside the city and included large vacant areas that could be made into Jewish neighborhoods. Israeli authorities insist, against the formal postures taken by other governments, that the new neighborhoods are integrally part of Israel and Jerusalem and are not "occupied territories." They seek to attract Jewish immigrants to Jerusalem, and they have expanded the municipal boundaries westward in order to increase its Jewish proportion above the current 72 percent.

2. *Satisfy the essential demands of the major religious communities in the city, and keep the peace between them.* This policy objective is connected with the first. Israel's major competitors for title to the city are Moslems and Christians who claim that it is holy for them as well as for Jews and Palestinian nationalists who insist that it should be the capital of their state. Leaving Christian and Moslem holy sites in foreign hands is part of an overall strategy with respect to Jerusalem that seeks to minimize friction at the points of contact among the city's communities. Potential disputes between religious and secular Jews receive as much attention as those involving Jews, Moslems, and Christians. Preserving the status quo is the principle line of policy, but the details of the status quo are open to tendentious interpretation.

At times the conflicting claims put Jerusalem's policymakers in the most awkward of situations. A Jewish regime cannot accede to Moslem demands for exclusive control of Haram al-Sharif that would deny all Jewish rights with respect to the Temple Mount or all applications by archaeologists to excavate sites in its vicinity. Demands of Christian churchman to bar Jewish residents from the vicinity of the Church of the Holy Sepulcher sound too much like the Nazis' demand for a Europe that was *judenrein*, or free of Jews. Sometimes the Jewish regime asks Jews not to provoke non-Jewish sensitivities by insisting on the full realization of Jewish rights.

Housing and school segregation is one expression of municipal policy to minimize friction. The issue is complex and sensitive, especially against the background of international concerns for segregation as it has been defined in the United States and South Africa. Religious and secular Jews, Christians, and Moslems are not forbidden by law from moving into one another's neighborhoods. It appears that the overwhelming majority of Jews and Palestinians desire to live in their own neighborhoods. Few Jewish neighborhoods are entirely secular, and some apartment houses function well with a mixture of secular and religious Jews. Other areas bristle with tension over the proper observance of Sabbath, the attire worn by girls and women, and the publications to be sold at local kiosks. The mayor has spoken many times about the usefulness of separate neighborhoods in the mosaic of Jerusalem, even while he condemns demonstrations against individuals who are unconventional in their choice of a residence.

School segregation also seems to be a condition for the city's communities living together in peace. Jerusalem has separate systems of Arab and Jewish education, each with its own language of instruction and curriculum. Students in Jerusalem's Arab secondary schools can choose to study according to an Israeli or a Jordanian curriculum. Within the Jewish sector, there are state secular and state religious schools, which differ according to their treatment of Jewish history and religion. "Independent" Jewish schools are affiliated with ultra-Orthodox congregations. They offer a strict segregation of males and females. The curricula in some of these schools is almost exclusively religious, with minimal instruction in arithmetic and science and no attention to secular humanities or history. In some religious schools there is a de facto segregation of pupils from Ashkenazi and Sephardi backgrounds. This is not likely to be controversial where it is simply a reflection of the families' choice of a school on the basis of their congregation. There are occasions when Sephardi parents claim their children are being kept apart from Ashkenazi children, in a form of apartheid to benefit upper-status Ashkenazim.[40]

3. *Postpone the settlement of the Jerusalem issue.* National policymakers have said that the Jerusalem issue should be the last of the Israeli-Palestinian issues that is scheduled for resolution, after the

achievement of formal accords with the neighboring countries of Jordan, Syria, and Lebanon. They admit that Jerusalem's problems will be the most difficult to solve. They hope that goodwill and trust between Israelis, Palestinians, and other Arabs can grow as a result of other agreements that will come first. Israeli leaders do not want to make concessions on Jerusalem prior to settling the country's external borders, out of fear that further concessions on Jerusalem might be demanded as part of subsequent border negotiations. They also hope that the world's tolerance of Israel's control over Jerusalem will grow along with the continued development of the city and the Israelis' management of its affairs. Acceptance de facto of Israeli control over Jerusalem may be the most the regime can achieve, if it cannot solve formally the problems of national borders and other outstanding issues.

Teddy Kollek supported the postponement of the Jerusalem issue from the mayor's office. Since the election of 1993, Mayor Ehud Olmert has expressed his reservations with respect to the policy. He has said that the most difficult problem ought to be faced directly. For the time being, he does not seem to have led the prime minister or the foreign minister to question the established posture.

4. *Keep the city beautiful.* This goal touches religious and aesthetic concerns. It has appeal in its own right and serves to quiet a number of the local and international sources that can make trouble for the present regime. In some formulations, the beauty of the city also includes the richness of its cultural offerings. Beauty and culture together fit the sensitivities of Teddy Kollek and add to the success of the Jerusalem Foundation. In the Jerusalem context no less than elsewhere, however, beauty and culture are topics that invite condemnation as well as applause. The sacred and the profane do not mix well in the city, especially on the Sabbath, near a holy site or a religious neighborhood.

5. *Develop the city's economy.* It is not enough to build houses for Jews. It is also important to provide a livelihood for those willing to live in Jerusalem and to give the non-Jewish minority an economic reason for keeping the peace. Policymakers must take account of the economic disadvantages of Jerusalem, located thirty miles from the country's concentration of markets, sources of industrial supply, and international ports. Moreover, economic development cannot proceed at the cost of Jerusalem's sanctity or beauty. These constraints add to the appeal of plans that would develop additional Jewish settlements and industrial areas to the west of Jerusalem in

the direction of the coast and extend Jerusalem's municipal boundaries in the same direction.

6. *Satisfy the essential demands of the city's weaker residents.* This may be viewed as part of a larger policy to keep the city quiet or to seek the ideals of social justice articulated in Jerusalem by the prophets Isaiah and Jeremiah.[41] The "Black Panthers" emerged from Jerusalem slums in the 1970s to demand a greater share of resources for poor Sephardi Jews. The municipality and the Jerusalem Foundation have been concerned to put parks, playgrounds, and community centers in the poorest of the city's neighborhoods. Neighborhood associations and Project Renewal have sought to nurture neighborhood leaders and identify demands before they boil over into confrontations.

A degree of uncertainty is a universal problem that is endemic to policymaking and implementation. It reflects a lack of knowledge or lack of agreement about the problems that policymakers face or the actions that are appropriate, as well as gaming among politicians and bureaucratic infighting.[42] In Jerusalem, uncertainties have been heightened beyond their usual degree by ethnic and religious tension, domestic violence, international hostility, economic problems, and the possibility of regime change. Among the adjectives that may be used to describe Jerusalem are turbulence, threat, adversity, ambiguity, instability, and confusion.[43]

The neat ordering of policy themes that are pursued for Jerusalem, shown above, is a considered assessment of their relative importance, rather than any agreed-upon set of priorities among the governing elites. As is already apparent, different individuals among those elites interpret their missions in their own ways and sometime work to frustrate their rivals' interpretations. There may also be contradictions in their goals. Thus, efforts to maintain Jerusalem as a predominantly Jewish city can work against keeping the peace among the city's religious groups or postponing the discussion of Jerusalem in international forums. Teddy Kollek may have thought that he could manage all of these goals together. Some Moslem and Christian leaders, as well as Palestinian nationalists, had trouble distinguishing his moderate ways from the dramatic activities of Ariel Sharon to expand the Jewish presence in Jerusalem and its surroundings.[44] After the national election of 1992 Sharon ceased having ministerial responsibility for housing and construction in Jerusalem. After the municipal election of 1993, Kollek went into the retirement that he once seemed to wish, and then reneged in order to fight yet another election campaign. Insofar as both Sharon and Kollek had to work with many others in making policy for Jerusalem, the retirement of neither seemed likely to change in a major way the city's character.

CHAPTER 7

Again on the World's Agenda

One task of this book is to ask questions similar to those posed by political scientists about other cities. Another task is to recognize the special features of Jerusalem, which lessen the importance of questions developed for ordinary places. The most critical policy issue that focuses on Jerusalem is not "who gets what within the city?" but "whose city is it?" The question goes beyond who sits in the mayor's office or who controls the local bureaucracy. The story of this book is more than the governing of a city. Issues concerned with Jerusalem touch the most important goals of Israel's foreign policy. Jerusalem is associated with aspirations and anxiety for Israelis who want to preserve their country as a Jewish state at the same time that they aspire to reach an accommodation with Palestinians and other Arabs.

If a reader has perceived a lack of certainty in previous chapters, then the chapters have succeeded in conveying the feeling that prevails in the city. It is an uncertainty that extends over several dimensions. Israel's formal centralization of government and impressive array of regulations is often mocked by the failure of authorities to implement the rules as they are written. Issues of accommodation and domination are rendered uncertain by the pulling and tugging of right- and left-wing Israelis, as well as by the assertions of Palestinians and their supporters that all Israeli actions reflect a strategy of domination. It is also uncertain whether Israelis' proclamations about their continued rule of an undivided Jerusalem can withstand the pressures of Palestinian hostility and foreign concern for the Holy City.

The contending forces in the competition for Jerusalem are Jewish, Moslem, Christian, and Palestinian. The Christians are a distant last in this round, but they have important international support. Many Moslems and Christians would prefer to be labeled

Palestinians. Tensions arise from differences in culture as well as religious doctrine. Palestinian and oriental Jewish neighborhoods are Asiatic, sometimes assertively so, even though they may be only across the street from a neighborhood that is European.

The uncertainty sharpened as a result of two events that occurred in September and November 1993. Israel and the PLO departed from their long-standing enmity and signed an accord that committed them to reach a peaceful settlement of their disputes; and Ehud Olmert defeated Teddy Kollek in Jerusalem's mayoralty election. From one view, the two events would have no direct and immediate impact on the city. Israel and the PLO agreed not to consider the status of Jerusalem at this stage of their relationship, and Olmert campaigned as a candidate who would administer the city according to Kollek's style. Olmert began his campaign by criticizing the mayor gently, as a tired old man not capable of running the city for another term. The national government's control by the Kollek's Labor Party allies would appear to limit Olmert's capacity to embark on radically new policies. Despite the Israel-PLO accord, the city's Palestinians dithered about their participation in the municipal election and abstained for the most part. This abstention helped Olmert defeat Kollek and indicates once again that Palestinians will not easily accommodate themselves to Israeli officialdom in Jerusalem.

Looking beyond these details, however, there seem likely to be changes, sooner or later. Yet is unwise to predict what will happen. Better to portray a number of scenarios that are possible, identify the factors likely to influence which will occur, and let the play of local and international politics do their work. This chapter will offer some speculations about the future that are appropriately modest in their certainty, as well as offering a summary assessment about the governing of Jerusalem as it has occurred since Israel's assumed control of an expanded city in 1967. These two elements of the chapter are related to one another: what is said in praise or condemnation of Jerusalem's governance since 1967 reflects the stance that negotiators will assume with respect to the city's future and will affect the support that each side may garner from international allies.

JERUSALEM AS PART OF ISRAEL'S PROBLEM

One source of Jerusalem's importance is its contribution to Israel's disputes with Palestinians and Arab countries. Palestinian nationalists demand that some or all of Jerusalem be the capital of their own country. Surveys of Jerusalem Palestinians find that they have limited contacts with Israelis and express strong antagonism to the regime and its public services. Palestinian leaders have forgone benefits they might leverage out of the national and municipal governments by urging their followers to refuse Israeli citizenship and boycott municipal elections.

The position proclaimed by major Israeli political parties is that there will be no Palestinian state west of the Jordan River and that a Jewish-controlled, united Jerusalem will remain the capital of Israel. With the coming to power of a government headed by Yitzhak Rabin in 1992, the policy announced was to move expeditiously with Israeli-Palestinian negotiations on the subject of autonomy or home rule in the occupied territories but not to deal with the status of Jerusalem. An Israel-PLO accord dealt with the areas of Gaza and Jericho, and not Jerusalem. Since the accord, Israeli officials have spoken about a Palestinian authority headed by chairman Arafat, while Palestinians have talked about a Palestinian state headed by president Arafat.

As measured by indicators of population and construction, Jerusalem has thrived under Israeli rule since 1967. The population more than doubled by 1992. Resources have come to the city from Israeli taxpayers, overseas donors, and investors. There has been a surge of building homes and public facilities more impressive than anything since Herod or Solomon. Jerusalem's voters, almost all of them Jewish, indicated their support for the status quo by giving large majorities to Mayor Teddy Kollek in local elections until 1993, and by the greater support they have given to right-wing parties in Knesset elections than those parties receive elsewhere in Israel.

Modern Israel may be stronger than the ancient country of the Jews and more secure than the authorities who governed Jerusalem in the late Ottoman period. Despite the objective indicators of population growth and physical developments, the Israeli regime is anxious. It compromises its own laws in the administration of East Jerusalem in the hope of appeasing a hostile minority. Israeli authorities accepted the use of Jordanian currency, educational curriculum, professional licenses, and other governmental documents despite the lack of diplomatic relations with the Hashemite Kingdom. Israel follows a policy of leaving the administration of Moslem and Christian holy places in the hands of their own religious authorities and has set the Israeli Police against Jews who would build a Temple or simply pray on what Moslems call Haram al-Sharif.

Israel is not the first nominal sovereign to recognize the problematic nature of Jerusalem. Ancient Greeks and Romans sought to tread gently on the resident's sensitivities. They honored Jewish hostility to foreign cults, especially in the area around the Temple. Neither the Greeks nor the Romans were sensitive enough. Some governors provoked Jewish violence or responded to Jewish animosity by turning their troops against the Jews and adding Gentile features to Jerusalem.

One thousand years later, when the Jews were of minor consequence in Jerusalem, Moslem conquerors of the Crusaders sought to moderate their impact on Christian sensitivities and avoid another European onslaught. They preserved the Christian character of the Church of the Holy Sepulcher, even while they purified the Haram al-Sharif of Christian symbols and took other churches for Moslem purposes.

By the second half of the nineteenth century, Jerusalem was less and less subject to the control of its nominal rulers. Capitulations signed between weak Ottoman caliphs in Constantinople and European governments gave foreign consuls extraterritorial rights, influence on Jerusalem land use, and special status to those Jerusalemites who claimed foreign citizenship.

Israel's local and national governments have sought to justify their regime in Jerusalem by enhancing the city's beauty and the quality of its public services. Yet the resources that can be directed at Jerusalem's enhancement are lessened by competition with other towns having their own problems. There is a limit to the extent that democratically elected policymakers can make one city into the national showcase, even if it is Jerusalem. The tenuous security of Israel and Jerusalem requires that an inordinate percentage of resources be allocated to defense. There are frequent acts of Palestinian terror and occasional retaliations by Jewish civilians. Measures taken by the police are not always as temperate as they might be if the regime was unchallenged. Palestinian animosity receives reinforcement by mass detention of Palestinians at the site of a stabbing or bombing, the imposition of curfew on a neighborhood, and the wounding or killing of Palestinians by security forces.

EVALUATING JERUSALEM'S POLICYMAKING AND POLICIES

The evaluation of Jerusalem's accomplishments in the recent past is part of a look forward in a framework of negotiations about the future of the region and the city. This section makes an effort to judge Jerusalem's record in the period since 1967. It does so in recognition of the emotions that cloud judgment. Palestinian and Jewish residents divide in their fervent animosity or support for the Jewish regime. Expectations are inflated by the image of Jerusalem above. People the world over look to the city with spiritual aspirations and the feeling that the worldly city should be more ideal than others. There is no obvious list of measurements that could be used to judge those who control the city and that would find acceptance among their antagonists.[1]

Judging the recent past is an appropriate part of commentary about a dynamic present, even though it will not silence heated arguments about sacred rights and divine justice. The evaluation of policymaking for Jerusalem that is offered here is made within the Israeli perspective introduced in chapter 1. The work of present authorities is evaluated with respect to their own goals. The judgments reflect a pragmatic concern with what has been feasible, given extensive aspirations along with limited resources and other constraints. The focus continues on Jerusalem below, and not the Jerusalem above where all groups' aspirations are optimized. An evaluation in those terms must wait until we can meet in Paradise, where earthly considerations of limited resources and intense rivalries may not prevail.

Palestinian Jerusalemites are the least adequately served by Israeli ministries and municipalities. They also are those who most clearly have taken themselves out of the political process that determines who gets what in the city. Their abstentions cause them to forgo the opportunities to select perhaps one-quarter of the city council and three members of the national Knesset. Israeli policymakers take account of Palestinian sentiments out of a sense of what foreign observers in western democracies would expect to be offered a hostile minority or what it would take to minimize Palestinian disaffection. One can only guess about the results of full participation by Palestinian Jerusalemites in local and national politics. Depending on alliances shaped with established Israeli parties and non-Jerusalem Arab members of the Knesset, a bloc of Jerusalemite Palestinians would seem able to increase the resources allocated to their supporters. In the long or short run, such alliances might sharpen or blunt Palestinian nationalism, advance or retard the drive in behalf of a Palestinian state.

The lack of Palestinian participation in national or local politics adds to the technical problems in evaluating Israeli policies with respect to Jerusalem. Except for expressions of opposition to the current regime, there is no authoritative list of Palestinian demands that might serve as a standard of comparison for judging how well the municipality meets the aspirations of Palestinian individuals or neighborhoods for public services.

Other technical issues also make it difficult to judge how current policies serve local residents. Most Israeli polls lack samples of Jerusalem respondents. Ultra-Orthodox Jews as well as Palestinians are sizable elements in the Jerusalem population that are closed to outsiders and suspicious of conventional polling techniques. Even if questioned by Palestinians or religious Jews, with an additional concern that only male or female pollsters contact male or female informants, it is doubtful that the responses would be as candid as in western, secular communities where political issues are less emotional than in Jerusalem.

While remaining aware of the limitations, it is possible to evaluate certain features of public policy and other aspects of living conditions in Jerusalem. Some traits can be examined against standards widely used in political science: a comparison of Jerusalem with other localities; a comparison of Jerusalem with its own record over time; a comparison of the benefits received by different groups in the city's population; and a comparison of policymakers' intentions with their achievements.

But what localities can be compared with Jerusalem? Other cities that have been idealized, like Paris, London, New York, and Berlin, are the capitals or showpieces of countries much wealthier than Israel and have not been bitterly contested as cities that should belong to another nation. Troubled cities, like Belfast, Beirut, and Nicosia, lack the spiritual aura that leads those who love Jerusalem to invest in its improvement despite ethnic and religious tensions.

The most appropriate comparisons appear to be with other large cities in Israel or indicators for the whole of Israel. Israel provides most of the public resources used in Jerusalem. A comparison within Israel will show how Jerusalem fares in relation to communities that rely on the same economic base. And insofar as the city has changed hands violently on a number of occasions and currently has rival claimants for its control, it is appropriate to assess the stability of the current regime.

The following discussion is more suggestive than definitive. It identifies issues and measurements that are relevant to the evaluation of Jerusalem, without claiming to resolve issues that are beset with contrasting readings of historical and contemporary reality.

Table 7.1
Quality of Life Selected Indicators

	All Jerusalem	Jerusalem Jews	Jerusalem Non-Jews	All Israel	Tel Aviv	Haifa
Air quality (standard rating):						
Sulfur Dioxide	10				21	56
Nitrogen Oxide	20				37	na
Infant mortality rate (per 1,000 live births)	8.7	7.4	11.4	9.8		
Divorce rate (per 1,000 pop.)	1.3	1.5	0.7	1.4		
Standard of living						
Net inc/household	3,710				3,620	3,990
Percent households w/ at least 2 persons/rm.		13.1	14.2		7.3	6.0
Unemployment	10.9	9.2	na	10.6	11.0	13.9
Education:						
Schooling of household head (yrs.)	13.8				12.6	13.0
Primary school pupils/classroom		24–32	30	26		
Road accidents involving injuries (total no.)	1,385				3,728	806
Crime rates (per 1,000 residents):						
Against persons	.71			1.31		
Against property	.15			2.29		

Sources: Statistical Abstract of Israel, 1990 (Jerusalem: Central Bureau of Statistics, 1990), 31, 583, 618; *Statistical Yearbook of Jerusalem, 1988* (Jerusalem: Municipality of Jerusalem and Jerusalem Institute for Israel Studies, 1990), 205, 242; *Statistical Yearbook of Jerusalem, 1991* (Jerusalem: Municipality of Jerusalem and Jerusalem Institute for Israel Studies, 1993), 67, 70, 107, 116, 124–25, 222.

The most sensitive issues that focus on Jerusalem do not lend themselves to evaluation on the basis of standard statistics available for relevant cities or population groups. Indicators for the quality of life in Jerusalem quantify some aspects of "who gets what?" Data for a number of these for recent years are provided in table 7.1. Because of the mixture of national, municipal, and quasi-governmental inputs to policymaking for Jerusalem, none of the indicators reflect the work of the municipality or any other authority acting alone. Indeed, most of the measures reflect the influence of economic and social conditions on what occurs in Jerusalem, as well as the actions of public officials.

How do the benefits of the city's residents compare with those of other Israelis?

This is a standard question of political science that is properly asked about Jerusalem. It is limited, to be sure, in not addressing the concerns of those nonresidents who view the place as the world's city, or at least as the possession of all the world's Moslems, Christians, or Jews.

Jerusalem's air is better than that of other Israeli cities, thanks in part to policies that have kept heavy industry out of the city. The air quality also owes something to mountain winds, as well as economic conditions that discourage industrialists from investing in the city.

Jerusalem's crime rates are generally lower than those for all of Israel. The explanation may lie in the culture of a city that is heavily populated by religiously inclined Jews, Moslems, and Christians, as well as a high incidence of policing in a city troubled by terrorism. It is tempting to compare Jerusalem's crime rates with those of the United States, which also suffers from multicultural tensions. Insofar as Israel statistics report convictions, as opposed to crimes reported to the police, they do not correspond with the uniform crime statistics for the United States. Yet the image remains of a city that is less troubled by crime than American cities. Jerusalem's incidence of convictions during a recent year was .71 for crimes against property and .15 for crimes against persons per 1,000 inhabitants, compared with United States statistics that report 48.6 property crimes and 6.2 crimes against persons per 1,000 inhabitants.[2]

Jerusalem has substantially fewer traffic accidents involving injuries than Tel Aviv, although more than Haifa. This may reflect the lower incidence of motor vehicles in the city, which in turn reflects lower family incomes.

There seems to be a higher incidence of parks and cultural facilities in Jerusalem than other Israeli cities, although residents of Tel Aviv might quarrel about the merits of theater, orchestras, and museums in each city. Jerusalem's family heads are somewhat better educated than those of Tel Aviv or Haifa. A negative finding is that class sizes in Jerusalem's Jewish state primary schools are in the upper part of the 24–32 range, shown in table 7.1 (the city's Jewish religious schools have smaller classes) and are larger than the Israeli average.

How do various groups in the city's population benefit or suffer from existing policies?

This question can be answered in the positive and the negative for all groups concerned. Jews, Palestinians, Christians, and Moslems suffer and benefit from existing policies. All suffer from being denied sole control over their Holy City and sacred sites within it.

Rivalries among Christian sects, among Moslem religious authorities, and among secular and religious Jews are only marginally less intense than the more prominent disputes among Moslems, Christians, and Jews. Jerusalemites who are Palestinian nationalists are frustrated by having to live in Israel's capital. Jews are nervous about the world's respect for Palestinian claims. Jews must be alert to an abandoned package that may be a bomb or a Palestinian who shouts "God is great" and stabs Jews. After an act of Palestinian terror has succeeded, Palestinians must worry about Jews seeking revenge.

Housing congestion is more of a problem in the Palestinian sector than in the Jewish sector, and housing in Palestinian neighborhoods receives only a fraction of the public resources available in Jewish neighborhoods. Divorce rates may be seen as a general indicator of social stability. They are substantially lower among Palestinians than Jews in Jerusalem. In contrast, the health indicator of infant mortality is substantially lower (that is, more desirable) among Jerusalem Jews than among Palestinians. Some Israelis assert that the average local Palestinian is better off materially and politically than most residents in Arab countries. Few Palestinians would agree that such facts, if true, are sufficient to reduce their national aspirations.

Jerusalem's Palestinians appear to benefit from a wider variety and higher quality of educational and cultural opportunities than in other Palestinian communities in Israel or the occupied territories. Yet Jerusalem's Palestinians compare their services unfavorably to those received by the Jews. The city's Palestinians benefit from nongovernmental schools and cultural facilities that historically have made Jerusalem a center of Palestinian intellectual life.

A measure of each community's use of publicly funded schools demonstrates some of the extent to which Palestinians opt out of the Israeli service network. The incidence of non-Jewish Jerusalemites between the ages of five and nineteen who study in publicly supported schools is only 28 percent of the incidence of Jewish Jerusalemites in the same age group who study in publicly supported schools.[3] The municipality has tried on several occasions to attract Palestinians to its schools and away from the church-supported and other private options, but most Palestinians have rejected the offer of free schooling, presumably on account of its taint with an Israeli curriculum and an identification with the Israeli state.

One indication of Israeli response to Palestinian rejection might be found in the chapter of the *Statistical Yearbook of Jerusalem* that reports on education. In only three of the seventeen tables are there data about the Arab sector.[4] The implication is that official attention will concentrate on the Jewish sector if Palestinians do not want to affiliate.

How may Jerusalem's current condition be judged in the context of its periods of progress and decline over a long history?

This is an elementary question for policy analysts who are concerned that officials do not, at the very least, make things worse. It is also a question that would bring a more positive response from Jews than Palestinians. The conventional indicator of population size suggests a level of economic development that surpasses Jerusalem's record in any previous era. Jerusalem ranks as a modern city, with European or North American standards of housing, access to clean water, electricity, communications, transportation, and other public services. The comparison is stark with respect to travelers' reports from the nineteenth century under Ottoman rule and for the 1948–67 period in the Old City under Jordanian rule.

The overall picture of mutual respect and access to holy sites also appears to be at its historic high point. There has been no wholesale purging of Christian or Moslem sites under Israeli rule. In practice, each religious group has control over its holy sites, although there is friction among competing Christians, Moslems, and Jews about the control of some sites. Antagonists claim that Israelis desecrated the city's skyline, expropriated Palestinian homes for the Western Wall plaza, and took Palestinian land for the development of Jewish neighborhoods. These charges are countered with Jewish descriptions of Jordanian desecration of Jewish graves and synagogues and the denial of Jewish access to the Western Wall from 1948 to 1967. Most of the new Jewish neighborhoods have been built on vacant land not suitable for agriculture. Israelis do not respond gently to criticisms from United Nations bodies that have been one-sided in condemning Israel without reference to contrary evidence about distorted Arab propaganda and terrorist actions against Israelis.

How does policymaking for Jerusalem measure up to norms of assessing the city's problems and needs in a comprehensive and rational manner and implementing policies that are effective and efficient in dealing with those problems?

It may be no accident that Israel has produced one of the most prominent academicians devoted to criticizing government decision making for not being sufficiently professional. Yehezkel Dror has been tireless in citing the quixotic choice of policies under pressure and the failure to establish a professional cadre of policy analysts to make systematic studies of social problems and policy options.[5] Another Israeli political scientist, Gadi Wolfsfeld, shows that Israelis are given to more extreme forms of political expression than people in several other western democracies.[6]

The municipality's posture toward the Palestinian minority invites criticism from the perspective of comprehensive policymaking. It also invites understanding from the historical perspective that recognizes the intensity of competition over the city's control. The Israeli regime has been the closest in the city's history to the accommodation end of the spectrum shown in figure 1.2. However, it falls short on criteria of being perceived as an illegitimate occupier by the Palestinian minority, as well as because of the limited benefits and opportunities enjoyed by Palestinians. The Palestinians' avoidance of Israeli politics confounds any comparison of the Jerusalem regime with multicultural cities in North America. A policy strategy that is more thoroughgoing in its accommodation of Palestinians in Jerusalem might add to the regime's security. At least through the end of the Kollek era, however, neither Palestinians nor Israelis seemed willing to forgo their concern for nationalist goals against the prospect of lasting comity.

Jerusalem policymaking also invites criticism with respect to prosaic issues of municipal services. Previous chapters have shown that formal rules about local finances and planning are administered in a loose, somewhat chaotic fashion.

Coping, rather than finding solutions, has traditionally been the Jewish style of making do. Coping is likely to be inelegant as numerous demands and warnings are overlooked or shunted aside in the pursuit of solutions that are good enough. Yet coping does not preclude some movement or a resolution of issues in a way that keeps continued disputes on a low flame. In the context of Jewish history, coping allows survival at a minimum and may permit Israel to thrive as a Jewish state with a tolerable degree of independence and Jerusalem as its capital.

Have the national government and the municipality achieved their policy goals for Jerusalem?

This question lends itself to dispute between those who wish to credit policymakers with achievements and those who accuse them of falling short of aspirations.

Most of the policy goals listed in the previous chapter are not amenable to precise measurement. There is no clear answer as to whether the essential demands of the major religious communities or the weaker socioeconomic segments have been met and the economy developed to its maximum potential while preserving the city's beauty and environmental quality. Taking as an appropriate period the Kollek regime, which began shortly before the city's unification under the Israelis, it is possible to maintain that there are both positive and negative indicators with respect to the achievement of each policy goal. Things could have been much worse, and they could be made better.

The municipal and national governments have been successful in postponing the settlement of the Jerusalem issue. It is not yet clear if this will contribute to the more basic goal of assuring continued Israeli rule over the whole of Jerusalem.

The goal of maintaining Jerusalem as a predominantly Jewish city and the capital of Israel can be examined in several ways. From a simple perspective, it seems to have been achieved. As of 1992, the municipality had a sizable Jewish majority of some 72 percent. This represents a decline of one percent since 1967 but an increase of 11 percent over 1948. The continued development of Jewish neighborhoods, along with immigration from the Soviet Union, may add to the Jewish majority. There has been no formal achievement of the wide international recognition for Jerusalem as the capital of Israel. Almost all countries maintain their embassies in Tel Aviv, but ambassadors and visiting heads of state come to Jerusalem to meet with Israeli officials. Thus, there appears to be success in making Jerusalem the national capital de facto.

The issue of the city's Jewish majority is clouded by the artificial nature of its boundaries. In the operative metropolitan area, defined by patterns of commuting, the proportions are not known with any certainty. There has been no census in the occupied territories since 1967. The failure of the Israeli authorities to update Palestinian population records is owing to the animosity toward the regime that casts a shadow on all efforts to assess the success of its policy goals for Jerusalem. Estimates range from 58 percent Jews in the metropolitan area to only 50 percent Jews or even less.

Critics of the Israeli regime emphasize the artificiality not only of Jerusalem's borders but of the city's unity. The borders serve to put a demographic wall around a city that is predominantly Jewish only because substantial Palestinian settlements have been kept outside. The borders are effective only because the Israeli regime remains strong and insistent on the lines it has drawn. A recent book composed from conversations with Israeli Arabs makes the point that while Jews view themselves as a majority within Israel, Arabs view themselves as a much larger majority in the Middle East and can bide their time until a change in regime.[7]

Within Jerusalem's borders, the minimal intercourse between Jewish and Palestinian sectors mocks the Israeli claim of a united city. Frequent police inspections of Palestinians' documents keep Palestinians out of Jewish areas. Palestinians work in Jewish areas but do little shopping and no visiting there. Jews ceased shopping in Palestinian areas with the onset of *Intifada* and altered their travel routes to avoid the stoning of cars that could be identified as Jewish. Cars registered to Israeli citizens (whether they are Jews or not) carry yellow license tags, while those registered by non-Jewish residents of the occupied territories carry blue tags. Stone throwers generally identify the car of a Jewish Israeli, as opposed to a Palestinian Israeli, by the nature of the car or the appearance of the occupants. Sometimes they err.

Is Jerusalem secure?

The city is a potential flash point of national and international conflict, but it has only simmered since 1967. Pessimists see the future as something like Belfast prior to British-IRA negotiations with frequent exchanges of gunfire and bombings.[8] Optimists should not deny the possibility of this scenario but assert that it has not occurred. The city is not peaceful, but neither has it exploded. Public opinion polls indicate that the majority of Jerusalem's Palestinians feel severe hostility toward the Israeli regime but prefer to cope with unresolved issues peacefully.[9] Since the *Intifada* began in December 1987 Jerusalem has been less violent than the West Bank or the Gaza Strip. Israel's security forces succeed more often than not in frustrating the plans of terrorists. Car burning and other acts of communal vandalism enrage the victims. Successful acts of terror produce individual tragedies. The Israeli establishment is anxious, but it appears secure.

There is superficial evidence for the proposition that a policy of accommodation has been more successful in helping a regime maintain control of Jerusalem. The Crusader and Jordanian regimes most clearly followed a strategy of domination, and they were the most short-lived in the city's history. The historical record is not sufficiently detailed or reliable to assess policy strategies for their contribution to regime continuity. The most recent regimes of the late Ottoman, British, Jordanians, and Israelis have been affected by numerous concerns. Some of the weightiest have dealt not so much with policies of accommodation or domination in Jerusalem per se as with issues of larger regional significance, economic resources, and military power.

There are inherent moral attractions to a strategy of accommodation over one of domination that stand apart from any claim that one has been more successful than another. In Jerusalem's case, regime continuity is a problematic standard of success. If history offers any lesson about this city, it is that no regime has had a certainty of control to compare with those over cities that are located in countries that are larger, more homogeneous, or stronger economically. It is also the case that no regime has given a chance to a thoroughgoing policy of accommodation. Perhaps because of the intense emotions attached to Jerusalem, no regime has shared power fully with all the city's communities.

DOES JERUSALEM GOVERN ITSELF?

The first chapter introduced a problem that troubles observers of local government in many countries: To what extent do local officials actually govern their cities? On the one side are a long list of factors that limit the capacity of elected officials and municipal civil servants to determine the course of their community's economic development, the taxes paid and the services received by its residents. These include the powers exercised by national or regional authorities; the weight of economic decisions pursued by industrial, commercial, financial institutions, and property developers; and the impacts on the locality of economic cycles that respond to national or international causes.

Jerusalem may experience more than the average outside interference in its policymaking. The formal procedures give national ministries a commanding voice in activities carried out by municipal authorities. The spiritual and political importance of Jerusalem heightens the concern of national and international actors for what occurs in the city.

It is not possible to define with certainty the autonomous actions of Jerusalem's municipal officials. However, the city qualifies the thesis that urban governance has slipped from the hands of local authorities. The entrepreneurial Teddy Kollek and his aides influenced prominent developments in social and cultural programming and physical growth. They did this partly with quasi-governmental organizations that evade the formal procedures of the municipality and rely on the cooperation of foreign donors and investors. The city's sensitivity that invites the scrutiny of national policymakers also provided the mayor some room for maneuver by means of the financial and political support he received from outsiders. As noted in previous chapters, Israel is a country with a major role for public officials in economic management. The big powers in Jerusalem issues are likely to be public officials as opposed to the managers of private firms. Some of those labeled foreign "investors" may actually be "donors," who will more clearly succeed in leaving a piece of their fortune in the Holy City than in profiting from its meager economic opportunities.[10]

Jerusalem's long and contentious history requires a note of caution with respect to the mayor's influence via quasi-governmental organizations. What is described here is the current moment in the city's history of four thousand years. The municipality's capacity to shape the city and its programs occurred with organizations in their initial period, when the mayor who founded them was still in office. With a change from a Kollek to an Olmert administration the quasi-governmental organizations may acquire a life of their own, become loyal to the new mayor, or become dormant. The Jerusalem Foundation, in particular, was created as a nongovernmental body but acted as quasi-governmental insofar as Teddy Kollek was its president. After a period that allows for a transition and perhaps a cooling of political tempers, it will be appropriate to inquire how Ehud Olmert works with the personnel of the foundation and its donors and whether the foundation retains significant leverage on the city's economic development and cultural and social programming.

The city's historic location on several cultural boundaries (east and west; Arab and European; Islam, Christianity, and Judaism) render it especially vulnerable to the vicissitudes of international politics. Jerusalem is in the same place as when the prophets Isaiah and Jeremiah, each in his own circumstances, warned the current regime against relying on foreign alliances. The Jewish municipality has been successful during the most recent decades while the Israeli national government has managed to survive and even thrive amidst the temptations and constraints of changing circumstances. Should international conditions change against Israel's interests or national leaders prove unable to maneuver amidst its opportunities and dangers, then the actions of the municipality may prove to be insignificant and futile.

ARE THERE SOLUTIONS FOR THE PROBLEMS OF JERUSALEM?

There is no end of proposals for the problems of Jerusalem and Israel. Artful and well-meaning individuals from Israel and overseas suggest putting borders here or there. Some would depart from conventional ideas to allow shared sovereignty or administration of the city or its holy places.[11] Jerusalem might serve as the capitals of both Israel and Palestine. Teddy Kollek expressed his support for creating boroughs along lines of ethnicity, religion, ultra-Orthodox, or secular population, but was not successful in convincing other Jewish politicians that this would not be a first step toward the redivision of the city.

The empirical approach of this book has put the emphasis on describing and explaining key features of Jerusalem's politics and public policies. It would be out of keeping to depart quickly to a set of favorite solutions. Indeed, a number of the traits identified for Jerusalem and Israel suggest a continuation of tension rather than imminent peace. Despite numerous proposals, so far there is insufficient political will to make any of them acceptable. No amount of creative mapping or nomenclature will satisfy politicians who are distrustful or disinterested.

One theme in the literature about policymaking also cautions against any facile offer of proposals in this final chapter. There is much that is quixotic in the process by which ideas reach the agenda for discussion by the public and policymakers or move from the agenda to formal decision. Proposals developed in a reasoned, systematic fashion must compete in a political marketplace affected by the personalities of key figures, shifting alliances among individuals and groups, as well as public opinion.[12]

With all this, it is fair to ask if the actions or inaction of Israeli policymakers with respect to Jerusalem advance or hinder the achievement of agreement on the outstanding disputes about the city. As in so many controversies that touch upon Jerusalem, there is no simple response.

First is the problem of defining clearly Israel's policies. Should the efforts of former Mayor Teddy Kollek to moderate conflict be taken as the central theme, or the actions of former Likud Minister of Housing and Construction Ariel Sharon and his supporters who would put Jewish residents and institutions in areas that are predominantly Palestinian? Some prestigious Israelis are willing to accept Palestinian demands for an independent state with its capital located in Jerusalem and for Palestinian control over parts of the city. As noted in chapter 5, Teddy Kollek took administrative responsibilities away from a city council member who went beyond the idea of boroughs and proposed the creation of separate Jewish and Palestinian cities within the present territory of Jerusalem. The new mayor, Ehud Olmert, comes out of a nationalist political tradition. Yet he campaigned at least partly on the theme of continuing Teddy Kollek's policy of tending to the concerns of all the city's communities. Moreover, Olmert came to office during the tenure of a national government committed to making peace with the Palestinians. As noted in several connections, the mayor may be prominent in the city, but he is not able to govern Jerusalem by himself.

The very presence of conflicting statements and actions that emanate from the Israeli establishment may add to the problems. The messy pluralism that is characteristic of Israel and Jewish culture can be read as indications of healthy democracy or as the inability of key institutions to reach decisions and then stick to them. Hostile or friendly observers can focus on the comments or actions that fit their image of Israel and assert that they are the essential features of Israeli policy. The chronic lack of order at the peak of Israeli institutions may be especially problematic in the context of the Israeli-Arab dispute. Whereas Jewish culture tolerates conflict and ambiguity and is inclined to nonviolent resolution of internal disputes, Arab culture emphasizes unity and discipline and does not shy away from violent resolution of internal disputes. Leaders of each culture have trouble understanding the other.[13]

Previous chapters reveal the chronically intense competition for control over the city, which extended far backward in time from the onset of the current regime. Whether its rulers have been Romans, Crusaders, Moslems, or Israelis there has been a lack of willingness to be moderate or compromising with respect to issues of formal authority. No regime in Jerusalem has been so thoroughgoing in a strategy of accommodation as to create an egalitarian pluralism, where all groups are genuinely equal in their access to political power. Yet pragmatic arrangements have granted effective autonomy over certain issues or locales to groups not formally in control of the entire city. Under this heading of pragmatic arrangements should be put Israeli concessions of autonomy for issues of education, the regulation of professions, currency in Palestinian sections of Jerusalem, and the control of Christian and Moslem holy places. Perhaps such a mixture of rigidity on the unity of formal rule in the city along with practical concessions is the most that can be expected for Jerusalem below. It works even if it is not ideal.

The Israeli regime formally pursues a policy of accommodation with respect to non-Jews, but within the context of a policy that Jerusalem have a substantial Jewish majority and serve as the capital of a Jewish state. Most Jerusalem Moslems and Christians live peacefully under the Israeli regime but may be biding their time until there is another upheaval in the city's history. It can take a year, a decade, or a millennium, but they or their descendants will be in Jerusalem to enjoy it. Policy strategy in the city may not become more fully accommodating, to the point of being egalitarian, until its contending parties can agree on the spiritual goals they are pursuing.

A BRIEFING FOR NEGOTIATIONS THAT HAVE BEGUN AND MAY CONTINUE

Jerusalem is at another of the dramatic points in its history. Since formal negotiations began in 1991, accords have been signed by Israeli authorities with Palestinians and Jordan. Further talks are under way with Syria and Lebanon. The agreement with the Palestinians is explicitly an interim stage, with issues concerning Jerusalem likely to arise again sooner or later.

The materials in this book are inherently relevant to this period of drama. Even if no agreement were to touch upon Jerusalem explicitly, its subsequent character will reflect changes that occur in the tiny country of which it is the capital. In order to make explicit what has been implicit until now, this section identifies the major actors with an interest in Jerusalem; principal items on their agendas; pressures on various sides of each issue; and alternative scenarios of local, national, regional and global factors that might affect the outcomes. And insofar as even a best case assessment of what emerges is not likely to be free of all the frictions inherent in the city, it is appropriate to conclude this briefing with a listing of some problems likely to remain into the next century.

The evaluation of Jerusalem's governance offered earlier in this chapter is part of the briefing. It is offered as a tentative assessment of a city whose governance may be up for review. It pointedly identifies the city's Palestinians as remaining outside the arenas of Jerusalem's municipal politics or Israeli national politics. Palestinians see themselves as part of a struggle over control of the city and for the sake of that struggle have given up much potential influence over the distribution of benefits in the municipality that is governed by Israel.

A number of cumbersome issues are likely to be involved in negotiating Jerusalem's future. Even if the parties adhere to a timetable that postpones the resolution of Jerusalem's status, the borders and status of a Palestinian entity (independent state, autonomous region, or part of a Jordanian federation) are likely to influence Jerusalem. There will be Palestinian demands for a capital in Jerusalem, as well as Moslem and Christian demands for formal autonomy over their holy places, along with the sticky issues of defining the boundaries of holy sites, and apportioning rights for those sites claimed by more than one Christian or Moslem entity. There are as yet no indications that Jerusalem's character as one of the world's principal centers of religious faith will facilitate compromise. A certainty of conviction more than a flexibility of posture is the central element of the faiths that are concerned with Jerusalem. Assuming that negotiators will come from the most flexible of their communities, they will wrestle with numerous issues that might seem trivial to secular readers who are distant from the conflict but that are important to those who are more involved.

Other issues involve how city residents should be designated: Jews and Palestinians (or Arabs)? or Jews, Christians, and Moslems? The fundamental question of the city's borders will have to take account of Jewish and Palestinian neighborhoods and satellite communities. Developments since 1967 will influence the agenda. If there is a continuing commitment to avoiding a redivision of the city as in 1948–67, then negotiators may have to work out a scheme for assigning different functions to what may become culturally distinct governmental entities, with borders that can be crossed freely. The issues of taxation and the provision of education, health, and other social services, as well as public safety, will determine how the urban entity works for its residents. Should these functions be assigned to a citywide body, divided among authorities having responsibility for different sectors and cultural pockets, or divided among authorities with responsibility for Jews or Palestinians wherever they reside?

The explicit opposition of Palestinians and some Christian churchmen to having Jews move into "their" areas may produce demands to formalize the emotional issue of residential segregation and perhaps move existing residents in order to create homogeneous neighborhoods. The control of new construction within Jerusalem and its environs will arise against the background of Palestinian charges that Israelis have taken land that is rightfully theirs and discriminated against them in the granting of building permits. Against these claims are Jewish charges that Palestinian homes spread wastefully across the land, without planning for the orderly development of roads, sewers, drainage, and other public needs. The prospect of peace in the holy city may spur foreign bodies to another round of creating monumental structures. This may involve overseas Moslem, Christian, and Jewish entities in the negotiations, as well as local Israelis and Palestinians concerned about the allocation of land that is precious economically as well as spiritually.

A Palestinian entity seems likely to acquire status in the area that is close to Jerusalem, including the locales of Ramallah, Bethlehem, and Beit Jallah. At the least there will be pressures for settling issues of utility connections, as well as procedures for Palestinians who wish to continue working, shopping, praying, visiting, or residing in Jerusalem and elsewhere in Israel, and for Jews who want to visit or shop in the Palestinian area or maintain their homes in the settlements created for Israeli Jews since 1967.

There is no certainty as to how the various parties will play their roles with respect to Jerusalem. Creativity and pragmatism may prevail over zealotry. When the prime minister of Jordan, Dr. Abd-al-Salam al-Majali, was interviewed in November 1993, he demonstrated a facility with language and political concepts that offer the ingredients of compromise: "human brains that create problems can create solutions, too. . . . The word Jerusalem is derived from sanctity or places of worship. . . . Political Jerusalem is different from the religious Jerusalem that is sacred to the three religions. Thus, a political solution is possible."[14] There is no obvious meaning to al-Majali's words. By an optimistic interpretation they do not depart greatly from the de facto Moslem and Christian control of holy places that Israel has already put into practice. If a Palestinian entity would be satisfied with a symbolic capitol building somewhere in Jerusalem, it may only be a matter of choosing the site, calling in the architects, and ordering the flags.

By one scenario, the new relationship between Israel and the PLO may bring Jerusalem's Palestinian politics more clearly above ground and out of the realm where fluidity and the obscurity of being partly illegal and underground gets in the way of a systematic description and analysis. This had not happened as of the municipal election of November 1993. As noted in chapter 5, one reason for Kollek's defeat was Palestinian dithering about supporting him and widespread Palestinian abstention from voting. The next book on governing Jerusalem might be able to include a well-informed discussion of Palestinian politics in the city. It is not yet possible to write that book.

A mixture of grand gestures with pedestrian actions appeared in the second week of the government headed by Yitzhak Rabin following the elections of 1992. Israeli newspapers featured the prime minister's meetings with the president of Egypt and the United States secretary of state. Israeli ministers of finance and housing announced their decisions to stop the construction of numerous units of public housing and roads in the occupied territories, which added to the image of a new government seeking progress in international negotiations. At the same time, officials of the Jerusalem and Bethlehem municipalities agreed to join the sewer lines of the two cities.[15] A newspaper reader could only wonder if integrated sewage would aid the peace process or retard the eventual separation of national communities.

The view from late 1994 is that Yitzhak Rabin is by no means assured of victory in the next national elections, which must occur no later than 1996. A Likud government would be likely to deal differently with the issue of Jerusalem. And it is not certain that Rabin and his Labor Party colleagues are inclined to be generous with the Palestinians on the issue of Jerusalem.

Regional accords among Israel, Egypt, Jordan, and perhaps Syria and Lebanon may affect postures with respect to Jerusalem. They may render Israeli officials more secure about national security and thereby more willing to make concessions involving Jerusalem. Events further afield have played a crucial role in the peace process to date. The collapse of the Soviet Union and the 1991 Gulf War weakened the Arab front that refused to deal with Israel and led the United States to prod Israel and its neighbors to make peace. Other changes on the world scene may reduce the pressures on the countries of the Middle East to reach accords with one another or even provoke another round of violence. Islamic fundamentalism is widely seen as a danger. Chaos emerging from the former orbit of the Soviet Union is yet another. Related to these is the prospect of free-floating nuclear weapons, traded from stockpiles of the former Soviet Union to Islamic fundamentalists or other groups opposed to Israeli-Arab accords.

Peace in its ultimate sense of quiet, routine coexistence does not seem possible. Religious and ethnic sensitivities seem unlikely to submerge themselves to political agreements. Jordanian and Saudi monarchies and Palestinian authorities will quarrel about the management of Moslem holy sites. Roman Catholics, Greek Catholics, Orthodox, and Coptic Churches will argue about the Church of the Holy Sepulcher. Religious and secular Jews will not halt their squabbles. A Jewish butcher who sells pork, the source of funds to repair a mosque or a church, or the fate of bones uncovered at a construction site will exercise Jerusalemites into the future. Optimists say that the problems will occur mostly at the "seams" between Jerusalem's communities. Realists remind us that Jerusalem is small, with seams between communities covering the map at intervals of a few hundred meters.

WHAT DOES JERUSALEM TELL US ABOUT GOVERNING POLITIES WITH VEXATIOUS PROBLEMS?

Jerusalem provides an archetype of severe urban problems. Social tensions between communities defined by religion, religiosity, and ethnicity are especially prominent. The economics of Jerusalem are by no means enviable, even while grand efforts by national authorities and overseas friends have financed impressive growth without fiscal crisis. Basic issues of sovereignty and regime legitimacy hang over the city as in few other urban areas, mixed with heavy ingredients of spiritual motivation that seem to get in the way of making decisions by more conventional economic or political criteria.

Can the discipline of political science or the craft of governance learn anything from this book? Or can the city of the present Jewish regime be a light unto the Gentiles?

Admittedly, the lessons are modest. There is only so much that can be learned from one city, even it if it Jerusalem.

The governing of Jerusalem offers its lessons in coping, or how to succeed partially in policymaking and program implementation. Israeli authorities, as typified by Mayor Teddy Kollek, have made their mark by choosing *not* to pursue a clear and final resolution of basic conflicts. Israeli efforts to assure their control of Jerusalem appear to fit within the category of engagement coping, as presented in chapter 1. Ranking Israeli policymakers recognize their problems in maintaining possession of Jerusalem. They have assigned it high priority above other goals, decided that a delay in facing the issue is more favorable than head-on confrontation, compromised conventional elements of sovereignty in order to bolster their control, and sought domestic as well as international support for their position.

Palestinians, in contrast, have chosen to deal with their stresses by avoidance coping, as shown in community leaders' calls to boycott Israeli political opportunities and in frequent acts of violence. Numerous attacks on civilians by Palestinians express rage in the minority community but may have served the Israeli cause more than their own. Palestinian violence helps the Israeli government recruit international support among states opposed to terrorism, reduces the legitimacy of the Palestinian cause among Israelis, and may further limit the benefits provided to Palestinians.[16]

For Israel, the appeals of coping are bolstered by the small size and population of the country, the weakness of its economy, and its dependence on great powers. These conditions were also present during the Jews' ancient tenure in the Promised Land. Now they are combined with the great powers' desire to placate Moslems and Christians who wish to constrain the Israelis. They keep the Israeli regime from insisting on the straightforward implementation of its law on all the territory that it controls and having that implementation recognized throughout the world.

Jewish morality and tradition may contribute to the coping that has occurred. Jewish religious law and Jews' knowledge of what it is like to suffer oppression from Moslems or Christians have tempered the passions of Jewish rulers. The unprovoked killing of civilians as well as rape and looting have been minor elements in Israeli activities and have been condemned by the society's leaders when they have occurred.

Events from September through November 1993 provided mixed clues as to Palestinian coping with respect to Jerusalem. In September, Israel and the PLO departed from their long-standing enmity and signed an accord that committed them to reach a peaceful settlement of disputes. A crucial feature of the agreement that helped the Israelis cede control over sections of the occupied territories (Gaza and Jericho) was the PLO's willingness to postpone the resolution of Jerusalem. As the date approached for November elections in Israeli municipalities, Palestinians in Jerusalem dithered between participating in the election in a way to oppose the more nationalist Olmert and being unwilling to endorse the Israeli regime in Jerusalem with their votes for Kollek. Some 7 percent of the eligible Palestinians voted. This was a higher incidence than voted in the early *Intifada* election of 1989 but a lower incidence than voted in the elections of 1969, 1978, and 1985.

The long run may demonstrate that avoidance coping by the Palestinians of Jerusalem will have enabled them to maintain their distance from the Israeli regime and preserve their community in readiness for the day when they will create their own polity in Jerusalem. Until now, however, avoidance coping has been associated with lost opportunities. They have given up the possibility of translating 25–30 percent of the city's population into a significant voting bloc. With the power they could achieve in the city council and the Knesset, they might enhance the economic and social conditions of their community. With skillful politicking, Palestinian leaders might multiply their weight by joining Jewish political parties in permanent coalitions or floating alliances.

Even after the beginning of negotiations between the PLO and the Israeli government and the implementation of agreements between them, some Palestinian organizations and individuals not formally associated with organizations expressed their hostility to the Israeli regime by means of violence directed against Jewish civilians and security personnel in Jerusalem. Prior to the onset of negotiations, terror was a more frequent occurrence and was conducted by mainstream as well as fringe elements of the PLO.

Violence in Jerusalem, as elsewhere, is difficult to evaluate in conjunction with the coping categories of engagement and avoidance. From one perspective, terror appears to be a quintessential manifestation of avoidance coping, reflecting the frustration and rage of those who employ it. Terror may have stiffened the resolve of Israeli victims, and added to their support among western democracies.[17] Yet terror is among the power elements that may bring adversaries to bargain. Whether the *Intifada* was terror or was successful will be an issue for historians to debate. On the one hand, it did not bring Israel to its knees. It produced some ten times the number of casualties among Palestinians as among Israelis, with between 30 and 50 percent of the Palestinian casualties attributed to violence within the Palestinian community.[18] On the other hand, the *Intifada* persuaded many Israelis that they could not resolve their conflict with the Palestinians by force alone. Perhaps the violence contributed to sentiments of both Palestinians and Israelis in support of engagement coping via negotiation.

In a setting that is so affected by fluidity and strong emotions there will be conflicting analyses as well as behaviors. Some observers may conclude that the Israeli regime has practiced avoidance coping with respect to Jerusalem by refusing to deal with Palestinian demands about the city, while the Palestinians have practiced engagement coping by preserving communal unity and resistance against the day when there can be a Palestinian regime in the city. For the Palestinians to engage the Israeli regime on its own terms might entail some gains with respect to the issue of "who gets what in Jerusalem?" but a total loss with respect to "whose city is Jerusalem?"

Jerusalem also illustrates the importance of ambiguous power relations in coping behaviors. Israelis have power locally and are well-connected with the United States. Until recently, Palestinians seemed to have played almost exclusively to their power bases in the Middle East, among third world countries, the former eastern bloc, and western leftists. Their inaccurate assessment of the drift in international power put them outside the inner circle and contributed to the assessment that their coping fit the model of avoidance. Yet they preserved and even strengthened their community. Once they began engaging the power bloc of Israel and the United States, they achieved in a short time more formal autonomy than ever before, and additional Israeli concessions appear to be in the offing.

The task of Israeli policymakers appears to have been served by their pursuit of engagement coping. However, it is not clear what this choice of coping strategy has contributed to Israeli maintenance of control over Jerusalem for a quarter-century, as opposed to less subtle factors like a preponderance of the Jewish population in the city, economic weight, and military force. Moreover, Israel's coping may be successful only with respect to a temporary advantage. Regime supporters point to twenty-five years of a united city under Israeli rule, where the record of majority-minority relations may not fall below that in other cities with hostile minorities. Less sanguine observers note that the city is divided de facto between Jewish and Palestinian sections. They assert that Israelis do not know whether they have acquired an operative title to the city or have only been lucky in postponing a deluge. The test of Israeli and Palestinian coping may be determined only when representatives of the two communities reach a formal agreement on the boundaries of Jerusalem and its affiliation with Israeli and/or Palestinian entitles, or even later when such an agreement has survived the test of implementation over a number of years. The City of Peace is not peaceful. Its description and analysis must end on a note of ambiguity. No one who knows the city's history dares write a finish to its story.

Notes

CHAPTER 1

1. Teddy Kollek, "Introduction: Jerusalem—Today and Tomorrow," in *Jerusalem: Problems and Prospects,* edited by Joel L. Kraemer (New York: Praeger, 1980), 1–16. David captured the city from the Jebusites about 3,000 years ago. Some observers add another 1,000 years for a previous history.

2. Meron Benvenisti, *Jerusalem: The Torn City* (Minneapolis: University of Minnesota Press, 1976), vii.

3. For general surveys of urban social problems, politics, and public policy, with an emphasis on the scene in the United States, see Lawrence J. R. Herson and John M. Bolland, *The Urban Web: Politics, Policy, and Theory* (Chicago: Nelson-Hall, 1990); Dennis R. Judd, *The Politics of American Cities: Private Power and Public Policy* (Glenview, Ill.: Scott, Foresman and Company, 1988); and Robert L. Lineberry and Ira Sharkansky, *Urban Politics and Public Policy* (New York: Harper & Row, 1978). For more specialized treatments of discrete urban issues, see for example, David Harvey, *Social Justice and the City* (London: Edward Arnold, 1973); Blair Badcock, *Unfairly Structured Cities* (Oxford: Basil Blackwell, 1984); Ivan Light, *Cities in World Perspective* (New York: Macmillan, 1983); Michael P. Conzen, ed., *World Patterns of Modern Urban Change* (Chicago: University of Chicago Department of Geography, 1986); Jean Gottmann and Robert A. Harper, eds., *Since Megalopolis: The Urban Writings of Jean Gottmann* (Baltimore: Johns Hopkins University Press, 1990); Thomas L. Blair, *The International Urban Crisis* (New York: Hill and Wang, 1974); Ted Robert Gurr and Desmond S. King, *The State and the City* (Chicago: University of Chicago Press, 1987); Paul E. Peterson, *City Limits* (Chicago: University of Chicago Press, 1981); Douglas Yates, *The Ungovernable City: The Politics of Urban Problems and Policy Making* (Cambridge, Mass.: MIT Press, 1977); and M. Gottdiener, *The Decline of Urban Politics: Political Theory and the Crisis of the Local State* (Newbury Park, Calif.: Sage Publications, 1987); William Julius Wilson, *The Truly Disadvantaged: The Inner City, the Underclass, and Public Policy* (Chicago: University of Chicago Press, 1987); and J. Anthony Lukas, *Common Ground: A Turbulent Decade in the Lives of Three American Families* (New York: Vintage Books, 1986). For Israeli local government, see Daniel Elazar and Chaim Kalchheim, eds., *Local Government in Israel* (Lanham, Md.: University Press of America, 1988).

4. Yehezkel Dror, *Policymaking under Adversity* (New Brunswick, N.J.: Transaction Books, 1986); Murray Edelman, *The Symbolic Uses of Politics* (Urbana: University of Illinois Press, 1964).

5. John Matzer, Jr., "Local Control of Fiscal Stress"; Irene S. Rubin and Herbert J. Rubin, "Structural Theories and Urban Fiscal Stress"; and Alberta M. Sbragia, "Financial Capital and the City"; all in *Cities in Stress: A New Look at the Urban Crisis,* edited by M. Gottdiener (Newbury Park, Calif.: Sage Publications, 1986), 63–80, 177–98, 199–220.

6. Peterson, *City Limits.*

7. On the differences between the political science of American and European cities, see Gurr and King, *State and the City;* Peterson, *City Limits;* Yates, *Ungovernable City;* Gottdiener, *Decline of Urban Politics;* C. G. Pickvance, "The Crisis of Local Government in Great Britain: An Interpretation." in Gottdiener, *Cities in Stress,* 247–76; and John R. Logan and Todd Swanstrom, eds., *Beyond the City Limits: Urban Policy and Economic Restructuring in Comparative Perspective* (Philadelphia: Temple University Press, 1990).

8. See, for example, John Friedmann and Goetz Wolff, "World City Formation: An Agenda for Research and Action," *International Journal of Urban and Regional Research* 6, no. 3 (September 1982): 309–44; Joe R. Feagin and Michael Peter Smith, "Cities and the New International Division of Labor: An Overview," in *The Capitalist City: Global Restructuring and Community Politics,* edited by Smith and Feagin (Oxford: Basil Blackwell, 1991), 3–36; Michael Timberlake, "World-System Theory and the Study of Comparative Urbanization," in Smith and Feagin, *Capitalist City,* 37–65; Michael Peter Smith and Richard Tardanico, "Urban Theory Reconsidered: Production, Reproduction and Collective Action," in Smith and Feagin, *Capitalist City,* 87–112; Saskia Sassen, *The Global City: New York, London, Tokyo* (Princeton: Princeton University Press, 1991); Liam O'Dowd, "Policy, Politics and Urban Restructuring," *International Journal of Urban and Regional Research* 12, no. 4 (December 1988): 645–50; Stefan Kraetke and Fritz Schmoll, "The Local State and Social Restructuring," *International Journal of Urban and Regional Research* 15, no. 4 (December 1991): 542–52; and Sidney Plotkin, "Property, Policy and Politics: Towards a Theory of Urban Land-Use Conflict," *International Journal of Urban and Regional Research* 11, no. 3 (September 1987): 382–404.

9. This book will follow the Jewish convention in dating, with B.C.E. (Before the Common Era) and C.E. (Common Era) being equivalent to the Christian notations of B.C. and A.D., respectively.

10. Ezra 4.

11. Sidney Plotkin, *Keep Out: The Struggle for Land Use Control* (Berkeley and Los Angeles: University of California, 1987). With the exceptions of some neighborhoods, secular Jews would be unwelcome as residents in most neighborhoods that are almost exclusively ultra-Orthodox, and Jews and Palestinians would be unwelcome as residents in most neighborhoods identified with the other ethnic group.

12. *Ha'aretz,* January 21, 1993. Hebrew.

13. Yossi Feintuch, *United States Policy on Jerusalem* (New York: Green-

wood Press, 1987); and W. Thomas Mallison and Sally V. Mallison, *The Palestine Problem in International Law and World Order* (Essex, England: Longman, 1986).

14. Dion Geldenhuys, *Isolated States* (Johannesburg: Jonathan Ball, 1990).

15. *Statistical Abstract of Israel, 1990* (Jerusalem: Central Bureau of Statistics, 1990), chap. 1; and *Statistical Yearbook of Jerusalem, 1988* (Jerusalem: Municipality of Jerusalem, 1990), chap. 1.

16. In 1987 conviction rates per 1,000 population for Jerusalem as compared to all of Israel were .03 and .12 for offenses against national security; 1.01 and 2.09 against public order; .01 and .01 against human life; .70 and 1.28 causing bodily harm; .06 and .13 sexual offenses; .07 and .86 moral offenses; .15 and 2.29 against property; .23 and .69 fraud; and .16 and .44 for other offenses. These categories and measurements of convictions, as opposed to incidents of crime, do not correspond with the uniform crime statistics for the United States. U.S. crime rates for a recent year were 6.2 violent crimes against persons per 1,000 inhabitants, and 48.6 property crimes per 1,000 inhabitants. Details appear in *Statistical Yearbook of Jerusalem, 1988*, 242; *Statistical Abstract of Israel, 1990*, 583; and *Statistical Abstract of the United States, 1988* (Washington: U.S. Government Printing Office, 1988).

17. Kathleen M. Kenyon, *Jerusalem: Excavating 3000 Years of History* (London: Thames and Hudson, 1967).

18. U. O. Schmelz, *Modern Jerusalem's Demographic Evolution* (Jerusalem: Hebrew University Institute of Contemporary Jewry, 1987), 67.

19. Islamic Council of Europe, *Jerusalem, The Key to World Peace* (London: Islamic Council of Europe,1980), vii.

20. M. A. Aamiry, *Jerusalem: Arab Origin and Heritage* (London: Longman, 1978). The quotations come from the preface and pp. 1–12.

21. Terrence Prittie, *Whose Jerusalem?* (London: Frederick Muller, 1981), 1.

22. Quoted from Henry Near, ed., *The Seventh Day* (London: Andre Deutsch, 1970), by Ronald Segal, *Whose Jerusalem? The Conflicts of Israel* (London: Jonathan Cape, 1973), 135.

23. Saul B. Cohen, *Jerusalem: Bridging the Four Walls: A Geopolitical Perspective* (New York: Herzl Press, 1977), 23.

24. Quoted from Near by Segal, 136.

25. See my *The Political Economy of Israel* (New Brunswick, N.J.: Transaction Books, 1987). As will be documented in chapter 4, Israel ranked highest among a group of forty-three highly and moderately developed countries in 1990 with respect to the percentage of Gross Domestic Product represented by government consumption expenditures. See *International Financial Statistics* (Washington: International Monetary Fund, 1992).

26. Gurr and King, *State and the City;* Peterson, *City Limits;* Yates, *Ungovernable City;* and Gottdiener, *Decline of Urban Politics.*

27. Susan Clarke and Andrew Kirby, "In Search of the Corpse: The

Mysterious Case of Local Politics," *Urban Affairs Quarterly* 25, no. 3 (March 1990): 389–412.

28. Matzer, "Local Control of Fiscal Stress"; and Sbragia, "Financial Capital and the City."

29. Robert A. Caro, *The Power Broker: Robert Moses and the Fall of New York* (New York: Knopf, 1974); Robert Dahl, *Who Governs?* (New Haven: Yale University Press, 1961); Dennis R. Judd, "Electoral Coalitions, Minority Mayors, and the Contradictions in the Municipal Policy Agenda," in Gottdiener, *Cities in Stress,* 145–70; Annmarie Hauck Walsh, *The Public's Business: The Politics and Practices of Government Corporations* (Cambridge, Mass.: MIT Press, 1978).

30. Pickvance, "Crisis of Local Government in Great Britain"; Logan and Swanstrom, *Beyond the City Limits.*

31. Ira Sharkansky, "Governing a City That Some Would Internationalize: The Case of Jerusalem," *Jerusalem Journal of International Relations* 14, no. 1 (March 1992): 16–32.

32. On public sector entrepreneurialism see Peter Marris and Anthony Somerset, *African Businessmen: A Study of Entrepreneurship and Development in Kenya* (London: Routledge & Kegan Paul, 1971); Dennis Dresang, "Public Sector Entrepreurialism," *Administrative Science Quarterly* 18 (March 1973): 76–85; and my *Political Economy of Israel,* chap. 9.

33. Anatol Rapoport, *Strategy and Conscience* (New York: Harper & Row, 1964); Ken Booth, *Strategy and Ethnocentricism* (London: Croom Helm, 1979); Edward N. Luttwak, *Strategy and Politics: Collected Essays* (New Brunswick, N.J.: Transaction Books, 1980); and Morton A. Kaplan, ed., *Strategic Thinking and Its Moral Implications* (Chicago: University of Chicago Center for Policy Study, 1973).

34. Charles E. Lindblom, *The Policy-Making Process* (Englewood Cliffs, N.J.: Prentice-Hall, 1968); Yehezkel Dror, *Public Policymaking Reexamined* (San Francisco: Chandler Publishing, 1968); Dror, *Policymaking under Adversity;* and E. S. Quade and Grace M. Carter, *Analysis for Public Decisions* (New York: North-Holland, 1989).

35. Naomi Caiden and Aaron Wildavsky, *Planning and Budgeting in Poor Countries* (New York: John Wiley & Sons, 1974).

36. For example, Barbara W. Tuchman, *The March of Folly: From Troy to Vietnam* (New York: Ballantine Books, 1984); Amnon Cohen, *Jewish Life under Islam: Jerusalem in the Sixteenth Century* (Cambridge: Harvard University Press, 1984); and Bernard Wasserstein, *The British in Palestine: The Mandatory Government and the Arab-Jewish Conflict, 1917–29* (Oxford: Basil Blackwell, 1991).

37. See, for example, Charles H. McIlwain, *Constitutionalism, Ancient and Modern* (Ithaca, N.Y.: Cornell University Press, 1947); J. Ronald Pennock and John W. Chapman, eds., *Constitutionalism* (New York: New York University Press, 1977); John Patrick Kirscht, *Dimensions of Authoritarianism: A Review of Research and Theory* (Lexington: University of Kentucky Press, 1967);

and Amos Permutter, *Modern Authoritarianism: A Comparative Institutional Analysis* (New Haven: Yale University Press, 1981).

38. Expressions of Jewish and Palestinian perceptions of one another in the Israeli context appears in David Grossman, *The Yellow Wind*, translated by Haim Watzman (London: J. Cape, 1988).

39. Graham H. Stuart, *The International City of Tangier* (Stanford: Stanford University Press, 1955), 183.

40. George V. Coelho, David A. Hamburg, and John E. Adams, eds., *Coping and Adaptation*, (New York: Basic Books, 1974).

41. Herbert Simon, *Administrative Behavior* (New York: Free Press, 1976).

42. Jack T. Tapp, "Multisystems Holistic Model of Health, Stress and Coping," in *Stress and Coping*, edited by Tiffany M. Field, Philip M. McCabe, and Neil Schneiderman (Hillsdale, N.J.: Lawrence Erlbaum Associates, 1985), 285–304. Some writers perceive engagement coping as leading to more effective adaptations to situations of crisis. See Rudolf H. Moos and Jeanne A. Schaefer, "Life Transitions and Crises: A Conceptual Overview," in *Coping with Life Crises: An Integrated Approach*, edited by Rudolf H. Moos, in collaboration with Jeanne A. Schaefer (New York: Plenum Press, 1986), 3–28. Other researchers make the point that the literature has yet to confirm any strong linkage between types of coping and the outcomes of stressful situations. See Susan Folkman, "Personal Control and Stress and Coping Processes: A Theoretical Analysis," *Journal of Personality and Social Psychology* 46 (1984): 839–52.

43. Michael Walzer, *Exodus and Revolution* (New York: Basic Books, 1985).

44. David Biale, *Power and Powerlessness in Jewish History* (New York: Schocken Books, 1987).

45. Lineberry and Sharkansky, *Urban Politics and Public Policy*, chap. 1.

46. Theda Skocpol, *States and Social Revolutions* (New York: Cambridge University Press, 1979).

CHAPTER 2

1. See, for example, Baruch Halpern, *The First Historians: The Hebrew Bible and History* (San Francisco: Harper & Row, 1988); Joel Rosenberg, *King and Kin: Political Allegory in the Hebrew Bible* (Bloomington: Indiana University Press, 1986). For a skeptical view of the history that can be found in the Bible, see Northrop Frye, *The Great Code: The Bible and Literature* (San Diego: Harcourt Brace Jovanovich, 1983).

2. A. D. H. Hayes, "The Period of the Judges and the Rise of the Monarchy," in *Israelite and Judaean History*, edited by John H. Hayes and J. Maxwell Miller (London: SCM Press, 1977), 285–331. By another view, Saul controlled an area reaching to about 10 kilometers south of modern Arad,

even though he did not control Jerusalem. See Yohanan Aharoni, *Carta Atlas of the Biblical Period* (Jerusalem: Carta, 1974), Map 90. Hebrew.

3. 1 Samuel 22:2. Biblical quotations in this book come from a variety of translations, including my own.

4. 2 Samuel 5:8.

5. 2 Samuel 24:17–25; and 1 Chronicles 22:1.

6. Larry Collins and Dominique Lapierre, *O Jerusalem* (New York: Simon and Schuster, 1972).

7. For insight into the extensive and controversial literature that deals with biblical authorship, a reader may begin with Richard Elliott Friedman, *Who Wrote the Bible?* (New York: Harper & Row, 1987).

8. 1 Kings 4.

9. 1 Kings 10.

10. 1 Kings 9.

11. 1 Kings 11.

12. Siegfried Herrmann, *A History of Israel in Old Testament Times* (London: SCM Press, 1975), 148.

13. 2 Kings 21:16.

14. Numbers 13:17–29.

15. William G. Dever and W. Malcolm Clark, "The Patriarchal Traditions," in *Israelite and Judaean History,* edited by John H. Hayes and J. Maxwell Miller (London: SCM Press, 1977), 70–148.

16. Yohanan Aharoni, *The Land of the Bible: A Historical Geography,* translated by A. F. Rainey (Philadelphia: Westminister Press, 1979), 6.

17. A. Leo Oppenheim, *Ancient Mesopotamia: Portrait of a Dead Civilization* (Chicago: University of Chicago Press, 1977), 163.

18. Samuel Sandmel, *Judaism and Christian Beginnings* (New York: Oxford University Press, 1978), 3.

19. Isaiah 1:7–8; 2:2–4.

20. Revelation 21:2.

21. John Bright, *Jeremiah* (Garden City, N.Y.: Doubleday, 1965), xlvi.

22. Professor Israel Ephal, appearing on "Lamentations," Israel Television, July 30, 1990 (9th of Av).

23. Jeremiah 9:10.

24. Jeremiah 19:8–9.

25. Lamentations 1:1.

26. Ezra, 5, 6.

27. Aharoni, *Carta Atlas,* Map 171.

28. Howard F. Vos, *Ezra, Nehemiah, and Esther* (Grand Rapids, Mich.: Zondervan Publishing House, 1987), 127. John Bright reports population estimates of 250,000 Judeans before the exile, 20,000 after the first wave of returning exiles, and 50,000 by the time of Nehemiah. Bright, *A History of Israel,* (London: SCM Press, 1980), 376–77.

29. Nehemiah 2:20. Those looking for examples of Jewish universalism, can look to the Books of Ruth and Jonah. They were written at about

the same time as the Books of Ezra and Nehemiah and express quite different attitudes toward non-Jews.

30. Haggai 2:3.

31. Zechariah 1:17.

32. Victor Tcherikover, *Hellenistic Civilization and the Jews,* translated by S. Applebaum (New York: Atheneum, 1959); and D. S. Russell, *The Jews from Alexander to Herod* (Oxford: Oxford University Press, 1967).

33. Tcherikover, *Hellenistic Civilization and the Jews,* part 2, chap. 6.

34. *The Apocrypha: An American Translation,* translated by Edgard J. Goodspeed (New York: Vintage Books, 1959), 1 Maccabees 1:13–15.

35. 1 Maccabees 2:24–25.

36. Eliezer Don-Yehiya, "Hanukkah and the Myth of the Maccabees in Zionist Ideology and In Israeli Society," *Jewish Journal of Sociology* 34, no. 1 (June 1992): 5–23.

37. A. R. C. Leaney and Jacob Neusner, "The Roman Era," in Hayes and Miller, *Israelite and Judaean History,* 605–77.

38. Gerd Theissen, *Sociology of Early Palestinian Christianity* (Philadelphia: Fortress Press, 1978).

39. See G. A. Williamson, introduction to his translation of Josephus's *The Jewish War* (New York: Penguin Books, 1970). The New Testament is problematic by virtue of being less concerned to report social conditions accurately than to justify a new faith that was in competition with conventional Judaism. See Anthony J. Saldarini, "Reconstructions of Rabbinic Judaism," and John G. Gager "Judaism as Seen by Outsiders," in *Early Judaism and Its Modern Interpreters,* edited by Robert A. Kraft and George W. E. Nickelsburg (Philadelphia: Fortress Press, 1986).

40. Paul Johnson, *A History of the Jews* (New York: Harper, 1987), 110–18.

41. Gerd Theissen, *Sociology of Early Palestinian Christianity* (Philadelphia: Fortress Press, 1978), 74–75.

42. Joachim Jeremias, *Jerusalem in the Time of Jesus* (London: SCM Press, 1969), chap. 1.

43. Ibid.

44. Josephus, *The Jewish War,* translated by G. A. Williamson (New York: Penguin Books, 1970), 24.

45. Ibid., 263–65, 380f.

46. William Reuben Farmer, *Maccabees, Zealots, and Josephus: An Inquiry into Jewish Nationalism in the Greco-Roman Period* (New York: Columbia University Press, 1956).

47. Jacob Neusner, *A History of the Jews in Babylonia,* vol. 1 (Leiden: E.J. Brill, 1969); and Neusner, *From Politics to Piety: The Emergence of Pharisaic Judaism* (Englewood Cliffs, N.J.: Prentice-Hall, 1973), chap. 3.

48. G. A. Williamson, introduction to his translation of Josephus, *Jewish War.*

49. See his *The Bar Kokhba Syndrome: Risk and Realism in International*

Relations, translated by Max D. Ticktin, edited by David Altshuler (Chappaqua, N.Y.: Rossel Books, 1983). Harkabi updated his views after the Lebanon War and the early period of intifada in *Israel's Fateful Hour,* translated by Lenn Schramm (New York: Harper & Row, 1988).

50. This section relies on my *Ancient and Modern Israel: An Exploration of Political Parallels* (Albany: State University of New York Press, 1991).

51. Aharoni, *Land of the Bible,* 42.

52. Harry Orlinsky, *Ancient Israel* (Ithaca, N.Y.: Cornell University Press, 1954), chap. 7.

53. 6:6.

54. D. S. Russell, *The Jews from Alexander to Herod* (Oxford: Oxford University Press, 1967), chap. 2.

55. Joshua 23:9–13; Judges 2:20–21.

56. 2 Samuel 24 records 800,000 Jewish warriors among the people of Israel and 500,000 among those of Judah during the time of David. 2 Chronicles 2 reports that Solomon used a similar mode of recording and found 153,600 strangers in his kingdom. These proportions—overlooking the time differences between the two censuses—show 89 percent Jews, compared with 83 percent of Jews within contemporary Israel.

57. Max I. Dimont, *Jews, God and History* (New York: Signet Books, 1964), chap. 3.

58. On the problematic issue of "geographic determinism," see Alan D. Burnett and Peter J. Taylor, eds., *Political Studies from Spatial Perspectives: Anglo American Essays on Political Geography* (New York: John Wiley & Sons, 1981).

59. Quoted in Neil Asher Silberman, *Digging for God and Country: Exploration, Archeology, and the Secret Struggle for the Holy Land, 1799–1917* (New York: Anchor Books, 1990), 86.

60. Paul Johnson, *A History of Christianity* (New York: Atheneum, 1976), 11.

61. Robert Davidson, *The Courage to Doubt: Exploring An Old Testament Theme* (London: SCM Press, 1983), 213. Here Davidson is quoting A. M. Greeley, *Journeys,* edited by G. Baum (New York, 1975), 202.

CHAPTER 3

1. See my *The Routines of Politics* (New York: Van Nostrand, 1970).

2. For a comparative view of urban development, in particular the various influences on urban development policies in the United States, see Eric H. Monkkonen, *America Becomes Urban: The Development of U.S. Cities and Towns, 1780–1980* (Berkeley: University of California Press, 1988).

3. P. W. L. Walker, *Holy City, Holy Places? Christian Attitudes to Jerusalem and the Holy Land in the Fourth Century* (Oxford: Clarendon Press, 1990).

4. F. E. Peters, *Jerusalem: The Holy City in the Eyes of Chroniclers, Visitors, Pilgrims, and Prophets from the Days of Abraham to the Beginnings of Modern Times* (Princeton: Princeton University Press, 1985), 145, 155.

5. John Wilkinson, *Jerusalem Pilgrims: Before the Crusades* (Jerusalem: Ariel Publishing House, 1977), introduction.

6. For an example of an influential Israeli who compares the Romans to the present world power, and draws explicit lessons for contemporary Israeli policymakers, see Yehoshafat Harkabi, *The Bar Kokhba Syndrome: Risk and Realism in International Relations*, translated by Max D. Ticktin, edited by David Altshuler (Chappaqua, N.Y.: Rossel Books, 1983).

7. M. Avi-Yonah, *The Jews under Roman and Byzantine Rule* (Jerusalem: Magnes Press, 1984), chaps. 10, 12.

8. Peters, *Jerusalem*, 173.

9. Ibid., 253 ff.

10. Aharon Ben-Ami, *Social Change in a Hostile Environment: The Crusader's Kingdom of Jerusalem* (Princeton: Princeton University Press, 1969). For a history that puts the emphasis on the sanctity of holy places, see Jean Richard, *The Latin Kingdom of Jerusalem*, translated by Janet Shirly (Amsterdam: North Holland Publishing Company, 1979).

11. Meron Benvenisti, *The Crusaders in the Holy Land* (Jerusalem: Israel Universities Press, 1970), 36.

12. Peters, *Jerusalem*, 285–86.

13. Terrence Prittie, *Whose Jerusalem?* (London: Frederick Muller, 1981).

14. The Christians also had nominal control of Jerusalem during 1229–39 and 1241–44.

15. Karl R. Schaefer, "Jerusalem in the Ayyubid and Mamluk Eras." Ph.D. dissertation, Department of Near Eastern Languages and Literatures, New York University, 1985, chap. 4.

16. Ibid., chap. 5.

17. Ibid., chap. 7.

18. Haim Z'ew Hirschberg, Walter Pinhas Pick, and Joshua Kaniel, "Under Ottoman Rule (1517–1917)," in *Jerusalem* (Jerusalem: Keter, 1973), 77–142.

19. Schaefer, "Jerusalem in the Ayyubid and Mamluk Eras," chap. 6.

20. Peters, *Jerusalem*, 493.

21. Amnon Cohen, *Jewish Life under Islam: Jerusalem in the Sixteenth Century* (Cambridge: Harvard University Press, 1984), chap. 3.

22. Ibid., chaps. 5, 7.

23. Yehoshua Ben-Arieh, *Jerusalem in the Nineteenth Century: The Old City* (New York: St. Martin's Press, 1984), 319.

24. Cohen, *Jewish Life under Islam*, chap. 6.

25. Peters, *Jerusalem*, 521.

26. Norman Rich, *Why the Crimean War? A Cautionary Tale* (Hanover, N.H.: University Press of New England, 1985); Brison D. Gooch, ed., *The Origins of the Crimean War* (Lexington, Mass.: D.C. Heath, 1969).

27. *Kal Ha'ir* February 7, 1992. Hebrew.

28. Ben-Arieh, *Old City*, 14.

29. Mark Twain, *The Innocents Abroad* (London, 1869), 295; quoted in Ben-Arieh, *Old City*, 57.

30. Quoted in D. H. K. Amiran, "The Development of Jerusalem, 1860–1979," in *Urban Geography of Jerusalem: A Companion Volume to the Atlas of Jerusalem*, edited by David H. K. Amiran, Arie Shachar, and Israel Kimhi (Jerusalem: Massada Press, 1973), 26.

31. Ben-Arieh, *Old City*, 94.

32. Ibid., 136.

33. Peters, *Jerusalem*, 551–52.

34. Hirschberg, Pick, and Kaniel, "Under Ottoman Rule."

35. Quoted by Ben-Arieh, *Old City*, 53.

36. Yehoshua Ben-Arieh, *Jerusalem in the Nineteenth Century: Emergence of the New City* (New York: St. Martin's Press, 1986), 95.

37. Ben-Arieh, *Old City*, 37.

38. Peters, *Jerusalem*, 583.

39. Ben-Arieh, *New City*, 323.

40. Alfred E. Lieber, "An Economic History of Jerusalem," in *Jerusalem*, edited by Msgr. John M. Oesterreicher and Anne Sinai (New York: John Day, 1974), 31–52.

41. Ben-Arieh, *Old City*, 136, 194, 263–64; Ben-Arieh, *New City*, 455; and U. O. Schmelz, *Modern Jerusalem's Demographic Evolution* (Jerusalem: Hebrew University Institute of Contemporary Jewry, 1987), 28.

42. Ben-Arieh, *Old City*, 359.

43. Ben-Arieh, *New City*, 359.

44. Ben-Arieh, *New City*, part 5.

45. Erik Cohen, "The City in The Zionist Ideology" (Jerusalem: Hebrew University Institute of Urban and Regional Studies, 1970).

46. Quoted in Jeff Halper, *Between Redemption and Revival: The Jewish Yishuv of Jerusalem in the Nineteenth Century* (Boulder, Colorado: Westview Press, 1991), 198.

47. Ibid.

48. Ben-Arieh, *New City*, 77–79, 112.

49. Ben-Arieh, *New City*, 239, 388, 461–62.

50. Bernard Wasserstein, *The British in Palestine: The Mandatory Government and the Arab-Jewish Conflict, 1917–29* (Oxford: Basil Blackwell, 1991), 48, 52.

51. Ronald Storrs, *Orientations* (London: Ivor Nicholson & Watson, 1939), chaps. 13–17.

52. *Statistical Yearbook of Jerusalem, 1988* (Jerusalem: Jerusalem Municipality and Jerusalem Institute for Israel Studies, 1990), 26.

53. Sarah Markovitz, "The Development of Modern Jerusalem: An Evaluation of Planning Decisions and the Effectiveness of the Planning Process." Senior thesis, Princeton University School of Architecture and the Woodrow Wilson School for Public and International Affairs, 1982, chap. 2.

54. Semah Cecil Hyman, "Under British Rule (1917–1948)," in *Jerusalem*, 143–67.

55. Saul B. Cohen, *Jerusalem: Bridging the Four Walls: A Geopolitical Perspective* (New York: Herzl Press, 1977), 43; see also Larry Collins and Dominique Lapieere, *O Jerusalem* (New York: Simon and Schuster, 1972).

56. Ian Lustick, *Arabs in the Jewish State: Israel's Control of a National Minority* (Austin: University of Texas Press, 1980), 49.

57. Quoted in Uri Bialer, "The Road to the Capital—The Establishment of Jerusalem as the Official Seat of the Israeli Government in 1949," *Studies in Zionism: An International Journal of Social, Political, and Intellectual History* 5, no. 2 (1984): 273–96.

58. Ibid.

59. Meron Benvenisti, *Jerusalem: The Torn City* (Minneapolis: University of Minnesota Press, 1976), chap. 4.

60. For an account of Jordanian-Palestinian animosity in a book that is generally warmly supportive of the Jordanian monarchy, see James Hunt, *Hussein of Jordan: A Political Biography* (London: Macmillan, 1989), chap. 8; for a dispassionate account, see Clinton Bailey, *The Participation of the Palestinians in the Politics of Jordan* (Ann Arbor: University Microfilms, 1969).

61. Avi Shlaim, *Collusion Across the Jordan: King Abdullah, the Zionist Movement, and the Partition of Palestine* (New York: Columbia University Press, 1988); and Uri Bar-Joseph, *The Best of Enemies: Israel and Transjordan in the War of 1948* (London: Rank Cass, 1987).

62. Table 5.1 in chapter 5 shows a Jewish population growth of 97 percent, against a growth rate for Moslems of 45 percent and all non-Jews of only 18 percent, owing to the Christian decline. Changing boundaries and different methods of estimating population preclude a precise comparison of population changes in Jordanian and Israeli Jerusalem during the period 1948–67. See *Statistical Yearbook of Jerusalem, 1988* (Jerusalem: Municipality of Jerusalem and Jerusalem Institute for Israel Studies, 1990), 22.

63. *Kal Ha'ir*, July 5, 1991. Hebrew.

64. Joseph Schweid, "The Planning of Jerusalem before and after 1967: Attitudes toward Uncertainty," in *Planning in Turbulence*, edited by David Morley and Arie Shachar (Jerusalem: Magnes Press, 1986), 107–13.

65. Shlaim, *Collusion Across the Jordan;* and Bar-Joseph, *Best of Enemies.*

66. Yael Yishai, "Israeli Annexation of East Jerusalem and the Golan Heights: Factors and Processes," *Middle East Studies* 21 (January 1985): 45–60.

67. Shlomo Slonim, "The United States and the Status of Jerusalem, 1947–1984," *Israel Law Review* 19, no. 2 (Spring 1984): 179–252.

68. Teddy Kollek, with Amos Kollek, *For Jerusalem: A Life* (New York: Random House, 1978), chap. 14.

69. See, for example, Avner Yaniv, ed., *National Security and Democracy in Israel* (Boulder: Lynne Rienner Publishers, 1993); Michael Shalev, *Labour and the Political Economy in Israel* (New York: Oxford University Press,

1992); and Baruch Kimmerling, ed., *The Israeli State and Society: Boundaries and Frontiers* (Albany: State University of New York Press, 1989).

70. Shabtai Teveth, *Moshe Dayan,* translated by Leah and David Zinder (Boston: Houghton Mifflin, 1973).

71. *Jerusalem Statistical Data* (Jerusalem: Jerusalem Municipality and Jerusalem Institute for Israel Studies, 1983), 26–27; *Statistical Yearbook of Jerusalem, 1988,* 31.

72. Yishai, "Israeli Annexation."

73. Moshe Amirav, "East Jerusalem is Palestinian," *Ha'Aretz,* July 31, 1991, Hebrew; see also Benvenisti, *Jerusalem;* and Gerald Caplan with Ruth B. Caplan, *Arab and Jew in Jerusalem: Explorations in Community Mental Health* (Cambridge: Harvard University Press, 1980), chap. 5.

74. Schweid, "Planning of Jerusalem."

75. U. O. Schmelz, "Jerusalem's Arab Population since the Mandatory Period (1918–1990)," in *The Arabs in Jerusalem: From the Late Ottoman Period to the Beginning of the 1990s—Religious, Social and Cultural Distinctiveness,* edited by Aharon Layish (Jerusalem: Magnes Press, 1992), 6–42. Hebrew.

CHAPTER 4

1. Israel ranked highest among a group of forty-three highly and moderately developed countries in 1990 with respect to the percentage of gross domestic product represented by government consumption expenditures. Selected percentages are Israel, 30.3; Sweden, 27.2; Denmark, 25.2; United States, 21.7; and Japan, 9.1. See *International Financial Statistics* (Washington: International Monetary Fund, 1992). See also Ira Sharkansky, *The Political Economy of Israel* (New Brunswick, N.J.: Transaction Books, 1987).

2. For a view that sees a growth of regionalism in Israel, see Y. Gradus, "The Emergence of Regionalism in a Centralized System: The Case of Israel," *Environment and Planning D: Society and Space* 2 (1984): 87–100.

3. A series of "Basic Laws" require extraordinary majorities to change them. To date, no basic law has been enacted to provide a "bill of rights" for Israel's local governments.

4. Chaim Kalchheim, "The Division of Functions and the Interrelationships between Local and State Authorities," in *Local Government in Israel,* edited by Daniel Elazar and Chaim Kalchheim (Lanham, Md.: University Press of America, 1988), 41–82.

5. On the character and techniques of Israel's civil service, see Ya'acov Reuveni, *Public Administration in Israel: The Government System in Israel and Its Development During the Years 1948–73* (Ramat Gan: Massada, 1974), Hebrew. The incidence of appointments open to political considerations, noted here as between 20 and 40 percent, varies with the indicators and the time periods employed. Details appear in my "Israeli Civil Service Positions Open to Political Appointments," *International Journal of Public Administration* 12, no. 5 (1989): 731–48. For further implications of the politicization of

Israel's public service, see David Deri, *Political Appointments in Israel* (Jerusalem: Israel Democracy Institute, 1993). Hebrew.

6. See Benjamin Geist, ed., *State Audit: Developments in Public Accountability* (London: Macmillan, 1981); and Asher Friedberg, Benjamin Geist, Nissim Mizrahi, and Ira Sharkansky, eds., *Accountability and State Audit: A Reader* (Jerusalem: State Comptroller, 1991).

7. *Audit Report on the Support Given to Institutions By Local Authorities* (Jerusalem: State Comptroller, 1991).

8. *Kal Ha'ir*, November 8, 1991, Hebrew.

9. Dan Caspi, *Media Decentralization: The Case of Israel's Local Newspapers* (New Brunswick, N.J.: Transaction Books, 1986).

10. Israel Peled, "Legal Structure of the Local Authority," in Elazar and Kalchheim, *Local Government in Israel*, 165–98.

11. Insofar as the Hebrew calendar is lunar, this date varies from year to year in its correspondence with the international calendar. The municipal elections of 1993 occurred on November 2.

12. On the potential significance of the single, citywide district, see Susan Welch and Timothy Bledsoe, *Urban Reform and Its Consequences: A Study in Representation* (Chicago: University of Chicago Press, 1988).

13. Peled, "Legal Structure of the Local Authority."

14. A summary of the council's political style since the election of 1989 appears in *Kal Ha'ir*, August 9, 1991, Hebrew.

15. Jacob Reuveni, "Administrative Issues in Local Government," in Elazar and Kalchheim, *Local Government in Israel*, 199–260.

16. *Statistical Yearbook of Jerusalem, 1991* (Jerusalem: Jerusalem Municipality and Jerusalem Institute for Israel Studies, 1993), 316, 320.

17. *Reports on the Audit of Local Governments*, 5.

18. Kalchheim, "Division of Functions."

19. Ibid.

20. Elazar and Kalchheim, *Local Government in Israel.*

21. Arye Hecht, "The Financial of Local Authorities," in Elazar and Kalchheim, *Local Government in Israel*, 263–372.

22. *Kal Ha'ir*, October 4, 1991, Hebrew.

23. Ibid., November 1, 1991, Hebrew.

24. Ira Sharkansky, *What Makes Israel Tick? How Domestic Policy-Makers Cope with Constraints* (Chicago: Nelson Hall, 1985).

25. Kalchheim, "Division of Functions"; and Frederick A. Lazin, *Policy Implementation and Social Welfare: Israel and the United States* (New Brunswick, N.J.: Transaction Books, 1986).

26. The ratios of accumulated debt in relation to population at the beginning of the 1980s was Tel Aviv, .82; Haifa, .58; Beer Sheva, .38; and Jerusalem, .02. The source of the data is *Local Authorities Financial Data, 1981/82* (Jerusalem: Central Bureau of Statistics and Ministry of Interior, 1983). See my *Political Economy of Israel*, chap. 5.

27. *Kal Ha'ir*, November 1, 1991, Hebrew.

28. John R. Logan and Harvey L. Molotch, *Urban Fortunes: The Political Economy of Place* (Berkeley and Los Angeles: University of California Press, 1987), especially chap. 5.

29. For a survey of planning issues and controversies since 1967, see Israel Kimhi, "Lines of Jerusalem's Development, 1988–1993," and David Kroyanker, "Faces of the City," both in *Urban Geography in Jerusalem, 1967–1992* (Jerusalem: Jerusalem Institute for Israel Studies, 1992), 17–32; 33–78. Hebrew.

30. Sarah Markovitz, "The Development of Modern Jerusalem: An Evaluation of Planning Decisions and the Effectiveness of the Planning Process." Senior thesis, Princeton University School of Architecture and the Woodrow Wilson School for Public and International Affairs, 1982, chap. 2.

31. Neil Smith and Peter Williams, eds., *Gentrification of the City* (Boston: Allen and Unwin, 1986); Sidney Plotkin, *Keep Out: The Struggle for Land Use Control* (Berkeley and Los Angeles: University of California, 1987); and Peter Marris, *Community Planning and Conceptions of Change* (London: Routledge and Kegan Paul, 1982).

32. Nimrod Salamon, "Landmark Preservation in Jerusalem" (Jerusalem Municipality: Town Planning Department, 1984); David Kroyanker, *Jerusalem: Planning and Development, 1982–1985: New Trends* (Jerusalem: Jerusalem Committee and Jerusalem Institute for Israeli Studies, 1985).

33. Markovitz, "Development of Modern Jerusalem," chap. 2.

34. Ibid.

35. *Kal Ha'ir*, May 24, 1991, Hebrew.

36. Kroyanker, "Faces of the City."

37. By way of comparison, see Charles T. Goodsell, *The Social Meaning of Civic Space: Studying Political Authority through Architecture* (Lawrence: University Press of Kansas, 1988).

38. Shlomo Slonim, "The United States and the Status of Jerusalem, 1947–1984," *Israel Law Review* 19, no. 2 (Spring 1984): 179–252.

39. On the general issue, see Daniel A. Mazmanian and Paul A. Sabatier, *Implementation and Public Policy* (Glenview, Ill.: Scott, Foresman and Company, 1983).

40. *Kal Ha'ir*, September 13, 1991, Hebrew.

41. Ibid., June 28, 1991, Hebrew.

42. Ibid., July 31, 1992, Hebrew.

43. Ibid., October 18, 1991, Hebrew.

44. Markovitz, "Development of Modern Jerusalem," chap. 3.

45. *Kal Ha'ir*, December 6, 1991, Hebrew.

46. Moshe Amirav, "Toward Coexisting in the Capital," *Jerusalem Post*, October 18, 1990.

47. *Ha'aretz*, August 4, 1992, Hebrew.

48. *Kal Ha'ir*, July 9, 1993, Hebrew.

49. Ibid., January 17, 1992, Hebrew.

50. Israel Radio, August 3, 1992.

51. See my *Wither the State? Politics and Public Enterprise in Three Countries* (Chatham, N.J.: Chatham House, 1979).

52. Ronald Storrs, *Orientations* (London: Ivor Nicholson & Watson, 1939), 456.

53. Jameson W. Doig, "If I See a Murderous Fellow Sharpening a Knife Cleverly . . . The Wilsonian Dichotomy and the Public Authority Tradition," *Public Administration Review* 43, no. 4 (July/August 1983): 292–304.

54. Details in this section come from the author's "Mayor Teddy Kollek and the Jerusalem Foundation: Governing the Holy City," *Public Administration Review*, vol. 44 (July/August 1984): 299–304; *Kal Ha'ir*, May 17, 1991, Hebrew; and Supplement for the 25th Anniversary of the Jerusalem Foundation, *Kal Ha'ir*, May 24, 1991, Hebrew.

55. *Kal Ha'ir*, February 28, 1992, Hebrew.

56. An extensive interview with Wechsler appeared in *Kal Ha'ir*, April 26, 1991, Hebrew.

57. Mount Moriah is one of the Hebrew terms for the site of the Temple.

58. *Kal Ha'ir*, January 17, 1992, Hebrew.

59. Jerusalem Institute of Israel Studies, "Extension of Metropolitan Jerusalem: Alternative Municipal Frameworks." Report commissioned from the Jerusalem Institute of Israel Studies by Jerusalem Municipality and Jerusalem Development Authority, Jerusalem, 1990, Hebrew.

60. *Kal Ha'ir*, January 24, 1992, Hebrew.

61. Ibid., July 10, 1993, Hebrew.

62. Ibid., May 24, 1991, Hebrew.

63. Ibid., May 28, 1993. Hebrew.

64. The proportions vary depending on indicators of national government income or expenditures or the larger indicator of expenditures of "government, national institutions, and local authorities." *Statistical Abstract of Israel, 1990* (Jerusalem: Central Bureau of Statistics, 1990), 228, 557, 559; *Statistical Abstract of Israel, 1992* (Jerusalem: Central Bureau of Statistics 1993), 236.

65. For a comparative perspective, see Michael Peter Smith, *City, State, and Market: The Political Economy of Urban Society* (New York: Basil Blackwell, 1988); Paul E. Peterson, *City Limits* (Chicago: University of Chicago Press, 1981); and Douglas Yates, *The Ungovernable City: The Politics of Urban Problems and Policy Making* (Cambridge: M.I.T. Press, 1977).

66. *Kal Ha'ir*, August 23, 1991, Hebrew.

67. As reported in Kroyanker, "Faces of the City."

68. *Kal Ha'ir*, January 3, 1992, Hebrew; and Amir Cheshin, "East Jerusalem—Policy vs. Reality," in *The Arabs in Jerusalem: From the Late Ottoman Period to the Beginning of the 1990s—Religious, Social and Cultural Distinctiveness*, edited by Aharon Layish (Jerusalem: Magnes Press, 1992), 178–92. Hebrew.

69. *Statistical Yearbook of Jerusalem, 1988* (Jerusalem: Municipality of

Jerusalem and Jerusalem Institute for Israel Studies, 1990), 278; *Statistical Yearbook of Jerusalem, 1991* (Jerusalem: Municipality of Jerusalem and Jerusalem Institute for Israel Studies, 1993), 357. For a guardedly optimistic review of the neighborhood associations, see Shlomo Chosen, "Urban Democracy in Jerusalem," in *Urban Geography in Jerusalem, 1967–1992* (Jerusalem: Jerusalem Institute for Israel Studies, 1992), 171–202. Hebrew.

70. *Ha'Aretz,* November 27, 1992, Hebrew.

71. *Kal Ha'ir,* January 3, 1992, Hebrew.

72. For comparative experience on citizen involvement in local policy issues and administration, see Douglas Yates, *Neighborhood Democracy: The Politics and Impacts of Decentralization* (Lexington, Mass.: D. C. Heath, 1973); Jack DeSario and Stuart Langton, eds., *Citizen Participation in Public Decision Making* (Westport, Connecticut: Greenwood, 1987); Philip B. Coulter, *Political Voice: Citizen Demand for Urban Public Services* (Tuscaloosa: University of Alabama Press, 1988); and Michael Lipsky, *Street-Level Bureaucracy: Dilemmas of the Individual in Public Services* (New York: Russell Sage Foundation, 1980).

73. *Kal Ha'ir* July 26, 1991, Hebrew.

74. Ibid., January 24, 1992, Hebrew.

75. *Ma'ariv,* May 27, 1992, Hebrew.

CHAPTER 5

1. Saul B. Cohen, *Jerusalem: Bridging the Four Walls: A Geopolitical Perspective* (New York: Herzl Press, 1977).

2. Daphne Tsimhoni, "Continuity and Change in Communal Autonomy: The Christian Communal Organizations in Jerusalem, 1948–1980," *Middle East Studies* 22 (July 1986): 398–417.

3. *Ha'aretz,* August 9, 1992, Hebrew.

4. For various views on the Palestinian-Jewish conflict as it applies to Jerusalem, see Henry Near, ed., *The Seventh Day* (London: Andre Deutsch, 1970); Ronald Segal, *Whose Jerusalem? The Conflicts of Israel* (London: Jonathan Cape, 1973); Cohen, *Jerusalem;* Meron Benvenisti, *The Shepherds' War: Collected Essays (1981–1989)* (Jerusalem: Jerusalem Post, 1989); Benvenisti, *The West Bank Data Project: A Survey of Israel's Policies* (Washington: American Enterprise Institute, 1984); Benvenisti, *The Sling and the Club* (Jerusalem: Keter, 1988), Hebrew; Avner Yaniv, ed., *National Security and Democracy in Israel,* (Boulder: Lynne Rienner Publishers, 1993); Michael Shalev, *Labour and the Political Economy in Israel* (New York: Oxford University Press, 1992); Baruch Kimmerling, ed., *The Israeli State and Society: Boundaries and Frontiers* (Albany: State University of New York Press, 1989); Michael Romann and Alex Weingrod, *Living Together Separately: Arabs and Jews in Contemporary Jerusalem* (Princeton: Princeton University Press, 1991); M. A. Aamiry, *Jerusalem: Arab Origin and Heritage* (London: Longman, 1978); Islamic Council of Europe, *Jerusalem: The Key to World Peace* (London: Islamic Council of Europe, 1980); Walid Khalidi, *From Haven to Conquest: Readings in Zionism*

and the Palestine Problem until 1948 (Beirut: Institute for Palestine Studies, 1971); George T. Abed, "The Economic Viability of a Palestinian State," *Journal of Palestine Studies* 19, no. 2 (Winter 1990): 3–28; Edward W. Said, "Reflections on Twenty Years of Palestinian History," *Journal of Palestine Studies* 20, no. 4 (Summer 1991): 5–22; Elia Zureik, "Prospects of the Palestinians in Israel: I," *Journal of Palestine Studies* 22, no. 2 (Winter 1993): 90–109.

5. For the estimate associated with the Interior Ministry, see *Kal Ha'ir,* January 17, 1992, Hebrew. The lower estimate was provided by a senior official of the municipality.

6. Israeli statisticians admitted to difficulties in updating their surveys of the occupied territories since the beginning of *Intifada.* See *Statistical Abstract of Israel, 1990* (Jerusalem: Central Bureau of Statistics, 1990), 705, 730.

7. Israel Kimhi, Shalom Reichman, and Joseph Schweid, "Arab Settlement in the Metropolitan Area of Jerusalem" (Jerusalem: Jerusalem Institute for Israel Studies, 1986), Hebrew; and "The Metropolitan Area of Jerusalem" (Jerusalem: Jerusalem Institute for Israel Studies, 1984).

8. *Ha'aretz,* July 18, 1992, Hebrew.

9. Abraham Ashkenasi, "Israeli Policies and Palestinian Fragmentation: Political and Social Impacts in Israel and Jerusalem" (Jerusalem: Hebrew University Leonard Davis Institute, 1988); and Ashkenasi, "Opinion Trends Among Jerusalem Palestinians" (Jerusalem: Hebrew University Leonard Davis Institute, 1990).

10. Romann and Weingrod, *Living Together Separately.*

11. For a description of politics in the Palestinian sector based on research prior to the onset of *Intifada,* see Romann and Weingrod, *Living Together Separately,* chap. 8.

12. Moshe Amirav, "Jerusalem: The Open-City Solution," *Jerusalem Post,* February 4, 1990; and Amirav, "Toward Coexisting in the Capital," *Jerusalem Post,* October 18, 1990.

13. Sidney Plotkin, *Keep Out: The Struggle for Land Use Control* (Berkeley and Los Angeles: University of California, 1987).

14. Michael Romann, "Inter-Relationship between the Jewish and Arab Sectors in Jerusalem" (Jerusalem: Jerusalem Institute for Israel Studies, 1984), 135. Hebrew.

15. Moshe Amirav, "Jerusalem: The Open-City Solution," *Jerusalem Post,* February 4, 1990.

16. Joseph Savitzky and Tzvi Frank, "A Comparative Study of Ethnically-Mixed Cities: Socio-political Aspects, Public Policies and Programs." Typescript. Institute of Urban and Regional Studies, Hebrew University of Jerusalem, March 1976, 43–49.

17. U. O. Schmelz, *Modern Jerusalem's Demographic Evolution* (Jerusalem: Jerusalem Institute for Israel Studies, 1987), 84–85.

18. See, for example, S. N. Eisenstadt, *Israeli Society* (New York: Basic Books, 1967); Jeffrey Halper, "Ethnicity and Education: The Schooling of

Afro-Asian Jewish Children in a Jerusalem Locality." Ph.D. dissertation in Anthropology, University of Wisconsin-Milwaukee, 1977; Avraham Shama and Mark Iris, *Immigration Without Integration: Third World Jews in Israel* (Cambridge, Mass.: Schenkman Publishing, 1977).

19. Schmelz, *Modern Jerusalem's Demographic Evolution,* 111.

20. The concept of "independent" refers to the relative lack of state pedagogical interference in ultra-Orthodox schools. Their curriculum is heavily weighted with religious subjects, with a minimum of mathematics and science, plus little if any secular humanities.

21. The religious schools also have smaller class sizes than prevail in the Jewish secular sector. *Statistical Yearbook of Jerusalem, 1988* (Jerusalem: Municipality of Jerusalem and Jerusalem Institute for Israel Studies, 1990), 202, 205. Average class sizes for primary school grades in state elementary schools were thirty-two during 1988/89. They were twenty-eight in the state religious schools, thirty-one in independent schools, and twenty-four in Talmud Torah.

22. *Kal Ha'ir,* May 17, 1991, Hebrew.

23. *Statistical Yearbook of Jerusalem, 1991,* 66, 67, 70.

24. *Statistical Abstract of the United States, 1988* (Washington: U.S. Government Printing Office, 1988).

25. *Statistical Yearbook of Jerusalem, 1988,* 89.

26. Ibid., 183.

27. Ibid., 75, 167.

28. Ibid., 167, 176; *Statistical Abstract of the United States, 1988,* 524, 582.

29. *Statistical Yearbook for Jerusalem, 1988,* 58. See also Maya Cheshen and Israel Kimhi, "Outlook on Migration To and From Jerusalem," in *Urban Geography in Jerusalem, 1967–1992* (Jerusalem: Jerusalem Institute for Israel Studies, 1992), 203–7. Hebrew.

30. Romann and Weingrod, *Living Together Separately.*

31. For Meron Benvenisti's description of segregated living in Abu Tor, see his *Shepherds' War,* 87–100.

32. Yehoshua Cohen, "Attachment to Place and Social Networks in Times of Change," in David Morley and Arie Shachar, eds., *Planning in Turbulence* (Jerusalem: Magnes Press, 1986), 114–26.

33. Menachem Friedman, *The Haredi (Ultra-Orthodox) Society—Sources, Trends and Processes* (Jerusalem: Jerusalem Institute for Israel Studies, 1991). Hebrew.

34. Some residents of the Christian Quarter are not Palestinians but clerics assigned to Jerusalem by overseas churches.

35. Romann and Weingrod, *Living Together Separately,* chap. 9.

36. Detailed results show 39 percent of Beit Safafa's votes cast for the Labour Party, 12 percent for the Citizens' Rights Party, 31 percent for the Arab Democratic Party, and 8 percent for the Progressive List for Peace.

Maya Choshen, "The Elections to the Knesset in Jerusalem: Statistical Outlook" (Jerusalem: Jerusalem Institute for Israel Studies, 1990). Hebrew.

37. The estimates appear in Romann and Weingrod, *Living Together Separately*, 207; Terrence Prittie, *Whose Jerusalem?* (London: Frederick Muller, 1981); and Ashkenasi, "Israeli Policies and Palestinian Fragmentation."

38. The National Religious Party, but not the ultra-Orthodox religious parties, is counted among the Zionist parties of Israel by virtue of its explicit support of State of Israel institutions, its male members' tendency to serve in the military, and its female members' tendency to do national service in a social service institution in lieu of military service. Ultra-Orthodox parties developed in a tradition that elevates piety above commitment to the State of Israel. Their members are less likely to celebrate state holidays and more likely to take advantage of provisions that exempt from military or national service religious women and male students in religious academies.

39. On the political behavior of the ultra-Orthodox, see Menachem Friedman, "Religious Zealotry in Israeli Society," in Solomon Poll and Ernest Krausz, eds., *On Ethnic and Religious Diversity in Israel* (Ramat Gan: Bar Ilan University Institute for the Study of Ethnic and Religious Groups, 1975), 91–112; and Yosef Shilhav, "Religious Influence on the Cultural Front: The Haredim in Jerusalem," in *Urban Geography in Jerusalem, 1967–1992* (Jerusalem: Jerusalem Institute for Israel Studies, 1992), 102–26. Hebrew.

40. Choshen, "Elections to the Knesset in Jerusalem."

41. Asher Arian, *Politics in Israel: The Second Generation* (Chathem, NJ.: Chatham House Publishers, 1985).

42. Yael Yishai, *Interest Groups in Israel* (Tel Aviv: Am Oved Publishers, 1987), Hebrew; and Marcia Drezon-Tepler, *Interest Groups and Political Change in Israel* (Albany: State University of New York Press, 1990).

43. The classic statement of the theme appears in Murray Edelman, *The Symbolic Uses of Politics* (Urbana: University of Illinois Press, 1964).

44. *Kal Ha'ir*, June 7, 1991, Hebrew.

45. *Statistical Yearbook of Jerusalem, 1988*, 286, 288.

46. Teddy Kollek, with Amos Kollek, *For Jerusalem: A Life* (New York: Random House, 1978).

47. Ibid., chaps. 14, 15.

48. *Kal Ha'ir*, February 24, 1992, Hebrew.

49. Ashkenasi, "Israeli Policies and Palestinian Fragmentation," 41.

50. *Ha'aretz*, December 14, 1992, Hebrew.

51. *Kal Ha'ir*, July 9, 1993, and *Ha'aretz*, July 9 and 12, 1993, Hebrew.

52. Supplement for the 25th Anniversary of the Jerusalem Foundation, *Kal Ha'ir*, May 24, 1991, Hebrew.

53. *Kal Ha'ir* May 24, 1991, Hebrew.

54. Supplement for the 25th Anniversary of the Jerusalem Foundation, *Kal Ha'ir*, May 24, 1991, Hebrew.

55. Teddy Kollek, foreword to *Jerusalem: Planning and Development*,

1982–1985: New Trends, by David Kroyanker (Jerusalem: Jerusalem Committee and Jerusalem Institute for Israeli Studies, 1985).

56. Ashkenasi, "Israeli Policies and Palestinian Fragmentation," 15.

57. Romann and Weingrod, *Living Together Separately,* chap. 8.

58. Abraham Rabinovich, *Jerusalem on Earth: People Passions and Politics in the Holy City* (New York: Free Press, 1988), 17.

59. Yael Yishai, "Israeli Annexation of East Jerusalem and the Golan Heights: Factors and Processes," *Middle East Studies* 21 (January 1985): 45–60.

60. Supplement for the 25th Anniversary of the Jerusalem Foundation, *Kal Ha'ir,* May 24, 1991, Hebrew.

61. *Kal Ha'ir,* June 14, 1991, Hebrew.

62. Benvenisti, *Shepherd's War,* 96.

63. Nadav Shargai, "Kollek's Twilight Period," *Ha'aretz,* December 16, 1992, Hebrew.

64. *Kal Ha'ir,* July 30, 1993, Hebrew.

65. *Ha'aretz,* June 2, 1993, and June 3, 1993, Hebrew.

66. Ibid., 80 percent of Israeli Jewish voters typically participate in national elections.

67. *Kal Ha'ir,* December 4, 1994, Hebrew.

68. Sammy Smooha, *Arabs and Jews in Israel: Conflicting and Shared Attitudes in a Divided Society* (Boulder: Westview Press, 1989).

69. Mina Zemach, "Through Israeli Eyes: Attitudes Toward Judaism, American Jewry, Zionism and the Arab-Israeli Conflict" (New York: Institute on American Jewish-Israeli Relations, American Jewish Committee, 1987).

70. Asher Arian, Ilan Talmud, and Tamar Hermann, *National Security and Public Opinion in Israel* (Boulder: Westview Press, 1988), 89–92.

71. *Ma'ariv,* May 6, 1991, Hebrew.

72. Steven M. Cohen, "Ties and Tensions: The 1986 Survey of American Jewish Attitudes Toward Israel and Israelis" (New York: Institute on American Jewish-Israeli Relations, American Jewish Committee, 1987).

73. Fouad Moughraba and Pat El-Nazer, "What Do Palestinian Americans Think? Results of a Public Opinion Survey," *Journal of Palestine Studies* 18, no. 4 (Summer 1989): 91–101.

74. Andrea Barron, "Referenda on the Palestinian Question in Four U.S. Cities," *Journal of Palestine Studies* 18, no. 4 (Summer 1989): 71–83.

75. For example, Prittie, *Whose Jerusalem?*; and Cohen, *Jerusalem.*

76. Ashkenasi, "Israeli Policies and Palestinian Fragmentation"; and Ian Lustick, *Arabs in the Jewish State: Israel's Control of a National Minority* (Austin: University of Texas Press, 1980). Also see Romann and Weingrod, *Living Together Separately,* especially chap. 9.

77. Michael Romann, "The Impact of the *Intifada* on Jewish-Arab Relations in Jerusalem," in Aharon Layish, ed., *The Arabs in Jerusalem: From the*

Late Ottoman Period to the Beginning of the 1990s—Religious, Social and Cultural Distinctiveness (Jerusalem: Magnes Press, 1992), 162–77. Hebrew.

78. This section relies on Ashkenasi, "Opinion Trends Among Jerusalem Palestinians."

79. Giora Goldberg, Gad Barzilai, and Efraim Inbar, "The Impact of Intercommunal Conflict: The Intifada and Israeli Public Opinion" (Jerusalem: Hebrew University Leonard Davis Institute, 1991).

CHAPTER 6

1. *Kal Ha'ir,* October 25, 1991, Hebrew.
2. On earlier social protests in Jerusalem, see Shlomo Hasson, *Urban Social Movements in Jerusalem: The Protest of the Second Generation* (Albany: State University of New York Press, 1993).
3. Charles Piller, *The Fail-Safe Society: Community Defiance and the End of Technological Optimism* (New York: Basic Books, 1991).
4. *Kal Ha'ir,* May 17, 1991, Hebrew.
5. Ibid., May 31, 1991, Hebrew.
6. Ibid., June 7, 1991, Hebrew.
7. Ibid., September 20, 1991, Hebrew.
8. Ibid., August 30, 1991, Hebrew.
9. Ibid., September 20, 1991, Hebrew.
10. Ibid., April 19, 1991, Hebrew.
11. Ibid., October 11, 1991, Hebrew.
12. David Kroyanker, *Jerusalem: Planning and Development, 1982–1985: New Trends* (Jerusalem: Jerusalem Committee and Jerusalem Institute for Israeli Studies, 1985).
13. In violation of Sabbath prohibitions involving the use of electrical appliances.
14. Uri Huppert, *Back to the Ghetto: Zionism in Retreat* (Buffalo, N.Y.: Prometheus Books, 1988).
15. *Kal Ha'ir,* April 26, 1991, Hebrew.
16. Ibid., May 10, 1991, Hebrew.
17. Ibid., May 24, 1991, Hebrew.
18. Ibid., June 14, 1991, Hebrew.
19. Ibid., June 7, 1991, Hebrew.
20. Ibid., November 1, 1991, Hebrew.
21. Sarah Markovitz, "The Development of Modern Jerusalem: An Evaluation of Planning Decisions and the Effectiveness of the Planning Process." Senior thesis, Princeton University School of Architecture and the Woodrow Wilson School for Public and International Affairs, 1982, chap. 3.
22. *Kal Ha'ir,* September 6, 1991, Hebrew.
23. Ibid., June 7, 1991, Hebrew.
24. Ibid., July 5, 1991, Hebrew.
25. Ibid., April 26, 1991, Hebrew.
26. *Ma'ariv,* October 10–11, 1991; *Kal Ha'ir,* October 11, 1991, Hebrew.

27. *Ma'ariv,* March 29, 1992, Hebrew.
28. Ibid., April 8, 1992, Hebrew.
29. *Kal Ha'ir,* April 17, 1992, Hebrew.
30. Ibid., May 15, 1992, Hebrew.
31. Kroyanker, *Jerusalem.*
32. Jerusalem Institute of Israel Studies, "Extension of Metropolitan Jerusalem: Alternative Municipal Frameworks." Report commissioned from the Jerusalem Institute of Israel Studies by Jerusalem Municipality and Jerusalem Development Authority, Jerusalem, 1990, Hebrew.
33. *Kal Ha'ir,* June 14, 1991, Hebrew.
34. Ibid., May 17, 1991, Hebrew.
35. Ibid., July 26, 1991, Hebrew.
36. *Ma'ariv,* February 14, 1992, Hebrew.
37. *Kal Ha'ir,* December 27, 1991, Hebrew.
38. There are obvious parallels between this section and Robert A. Dahl's classic, *Who Governs? Democracy and Power in an American City* (New Haven: Yale University Press, 1961).
39. *Ha'aretz,* August 12, 1992, Hebrew.
40. *Kal Ha'ir,* September 20, 1991, Hebrew.
41. See, for example, Isaiah 3:12, and Jeremiah 5:1, 22:3, 13–14.
42. David Dery, *Problem Definition in Policy Analysis* (Lawrence: University of Kansas Press, 1984).
43. Yehezkel Dror, *Policymaking under Adversity* (New Brunswick, N.J.: Transaction Press, 1986).
44. Joost R. Hiltermann, "Settling for War: Soviet Immigration and Israel's Settlement Policy in East Jerusalem," *Journal of Palestine Studies* 20, no. 2 (Winter 1991): 71–85.

CHAPTER 7

1. On the variety of standards that are appropriate to the evaluation of public policies and their implementation, see Terry Busson and Philip Coulter, eds., *Policy Evaluation for Local Government* (Westport, Conn.: Greenwood, 1987); Aaron Wildavsky, *Speaking Truth to Power: The Art and Craft of Policy Analysis* (Boston: Little, Brown, 1979); and Eleanor Chelimsky, *Program Evaluation: Patterns and Directions* (Washington: American Society for Public Administration, 1985).
2. *Statistical Abstract of the United States, 1988* (Washington: U.S. Government Printing Office, 1988).
3. *Statistical Yearbook of Jerusalem, 1991* (Jerusalem: Municipality of Jerusalem and Jerusalem Institute for Israel Studies, 1993), chap. 13.
4. *Statistical Yearbook of Jerusalem, 1992* (Jerusalem: Municipality of Jerusalem and Jerusalem Institute for Israel Studies, 1994), chap. 13.
5. Yehezkel Dror, *Policymaking under Adversity* (New Brunswick, N.J.: Transaction Press, 1986).

6. Gadi Wolfsfeld, *The Politics of Provocation* (Albany: State University of New York Press, 1988).

7. David Grossman, *Present Absentees* (Tel Aviv: Kibbutz Meuchad, 1992), esp. 111. Hebrew.

8. Meron Benvenisti, *The Shepherds' War: Collected Essays (1981–1989)* (Jerusalem: Jerusalem Post, 1989).

9. Abraham Ashkenasi, "Israeli Policies and Palestinian Fragmentation: Political and Social Impacts in Israel and Jerusalem" (Jerusalem: Hebrew University Leonard Davis Institute, 1988); and Ashkenasi, "Opinion Trends Among Jerusalem Palestinians" (Jerusalem: Hebrew University Leonard Davis Institute, 1990).

10. For the economic and governmental significance of this point, see John R. Logan and Harvey L. Molotch, *Urban Fortunes: The Political Economy of Place* (Berkeley and Los Angeles: University of California Press, 1987).

11. For example, Daniel J. Elazar, *From Autonomy to Shared Rule: Options for Judea, Samaria, and Gaza* (Jerusalem: Jerusalem Center for Public Affairs, 1983); for a newspaper article that reviewed some of what were counted as fifty-six separate proposals, see *Kal Ha'ir*, August 6, 1993, Hebrew.

12. Charles E. Lindblom and David K. Cohen, *Usable Knowledge: Social Science and Social Problem Solving* (New Haven: Yale University Press, 1979); David Dery, *Data and Policy Change* (Boston: Kluwer Academic Publishers, 1990); and John W. Kingdon, *Agendas, Alternatives, and Public Policies* (Boston: Little, Brown, 1984).

13. Grossman makes this point in his *Present Absentees*, chapter 16.

14. *Foreign Broadcast Information Service*, FBIS-NES-93–217, 47.

15. *Kal Ha'ir*, July 24, 1992, Hebrew.

16. Martha Crenshaw, introduction to *Terrorism, Legitimacy, and Power: The Consequences of Political Violence*, edited by Crenshaw (Middletown, Conn.: Wesleyan University Press, 1983).

17. Crenshaw, *Terrorism, Legitimacy, and Power;* and Brian Crozier, *A Theory of Conflict* (London: Hamish Hamilton, 1974).

18. Robert F.Hunter, *The Palestinian Uprising: A War by Other Means* (Berkeley and Los Angeles: University of California Press, 1993).

Bibliography

Aamiry, M. A. *Jerusalem: Arab Origin and Heritage*. London: Longman, 1978.

Abed, George T. "The Economic Viability of a Palestinian State." *Journal of Palestine Studies* 19, no. 2 (Winter 1990): 3–28.

Aharoni, Yohanan. *Carta Atlas of the Biblical Period*. Jerusalem: Carta, 1974. Hebrew.

———. *The Land of the Bible: A Historical Geography*. Translated by A. F. Rainey. Philadelphia: Westminister Press, 1979.

Amiran, David H. K., Arie Shachar, and Israel Kimhi, eds. *Urban Geography of Jerusalem: A Companion Volume to the Atlas of Jerusalem*. Jerusalem: Massada Press, 1973.

Arian, Asher. *Politics in Israel: The Second Generation*. Chatham, N.J.: Chatham House, 1985.

Arian, Asher, Ilan Talmud, and Tamar Hermann. *National Security and Public Opinion in Israel*. Boulder: Westview Press, 1988.

Ashkenasi, Abraham. "Israeli Policies and Palestinian Fragmentation: Political and Social Impacts in Israel and Jerusalem." Jerusalem: Hebrew University Leonard Davis Institute, 1988.

———. "Opinion Trends among Jerusalem Palestinians." Jerusalem: Hebrew University Leonard Davis Institute, 1990.

Avi-Yonah, M. *The Jews Under Roman and Byzantine Rule*. Jerusalem: Magnes Press, 1984.

Badcock, Blair. *Unfairly Structured Cities*. Oxford: Basil Blackwell, 1984.

Bailey, Clinton. *The Participation of the Palestinians in the Politics of Jordan*. Ann Arbor: University Microfilms, 1969.

Bar-Joseph, Uri. *The Best of Enemies: Israel and Transjordan in the War of 1948*. London: Rank Cass, 1987.

Barron, Andrea. "Referenda on the Palestinian Question in Four U.S. Cities." *Journal of Palestine Studies* 18, no. 4 (Summer 1989): 71–83.

Ben-Ami, Aharon. *Social Change in a Hostile Environment: The Crusader's Kingdom of Jerusalem*. Princeton: Princeton University Press, 1969.

Ben-Arieh, Yehoshua. *Jerusalem in the Nineteenth Century: Emergence of the New City*. New York: St. Martin's Press, 1986.

———. *Jerusalem in the Nineteenth Century: The Old City*. New York: St. Martin's Press, 1984.

Benvenisti, Meron. *The Crusaders in the Holy Land*. Jerusalem: Israel Universities Press, 1970.

———. *Jerusalem: The Torn City*. Minneapolis: University of Minnesota Press, 1976.

———. *The Shepherds' War: Collected Essays (1981–1989).* Jerusalem: Jerusalem Post, 1989.

———. *The Sling and the Club.* Jerusalem: Keter, 1988. Hebrew.

———. *The West Bank Data Project: A Survey of Israel's Policies.* Washington: American Enterprise Institute, 1984.

Biale, David. *Power and Powerlessness in Jewish History.* New York: Schocken Books, 1987.

Bialer, Uri. "The Road to the Capital—The Establishment of Jerusalem as the Official Seat of the Israeli Government in 1949." *Studies in Zionism: An International Journal of Social, Political, and Intellectual History* 5, no. 2 (1984): 273–96.

Blair, Thomas L. *The International Urban Crisis.* New York: Hill and Wang, 1974.

Booth, Ken. *Strategy and Ethnocentricism.* London: Croom Helm, 1979.

Bright, John. *Jeremiah.* Garden City, N.Y.: Doubleday, 1965.

———. *A History of Israel.* London: SCM Press, 1980.

Burnett, Alan D., and Peter J. Taylor, eds. *Political Studies from Spatial Perspectives: Anglo American Essays on Political Geography.* New York: John Wiley and Sons, 1981.

Busson, Terry, and Philip Coulter, eds. *Policy Evaluation for Local Government.* Westport, Conn.: Greenwood, 1987.

Caiden, Naomi, and Aaron Wildavsky. *Planning and Budgeting in Poor Countries.* New York: John Wiley and Sons, 1974.

Caplan, Gerald, with Ruth B. Caplan. *Arab and Jew in Jerusalem: Explorations in Community Mental Health.* Cambridge: Harvard University Press, 1980.

Caro, Robert A. *The Power Broker: Robert Moses and the Fall of New York.* New York: Knopf, 1974.

Caspi, Dan. *Media Decentralization: The Case of Israel's Local Newspapers.* New Brunswick, N.J.: Transaction Books, 1986.

Chelimsky, Eleanor. *Program Evaluation: Patterns and Directions.* Washington: American Society for Public Administration, 1985.

Cheshen, Maya, and Israel Kimhi. "Outlook on Migration to and from Jerusalem." In *Urban Geography in Jerusalem, 1967–1992.* Jerusalem: Jerusalem Institute for Israel Studies, 1992. Hebrew.

Chosen, Shlomo. "Urban Democracy in Jerusalem." In *Urban Geography in Jerusalem, 1967–1992.* Jerusalem: Jerusalem Institute for Israel Studies, 1992. Hebrew.

Clarke, Susan, and Andrew Kirby. "In Search of the Corpse: The Mysterious Case of Local Politics." *Urban Affairs Quarterly* 25, no. 3 (March 1990): 389–412.

Coelho, George V., David A. Hamburg, and John E. Adams, eds. *Coping and Adaptation.* New York: Basic Books, 1974.

Cohen, Amnon. *Jewish Life under Islam: Jerusalem in the Sixteenth Century.* Cambridge: Harvard University Press, 1984.

Cohen, Erik. "The City in The Zionist Ideology." Jerusalem: Hebrew University Institute of Urban and Regional Studies, 1970.
Cohen, Saul B. *Jerusalem: Bridging the Four Walls: A Geopolitical Perspective.* New York: Herzl Press, 1977.
Cohen, Steven M. "Ties and Tensions: The 1986 Survey of American Jewish Attitudes Toward Israel and Israelis." New York: Institute on American Jewish-Israeli Relations, American Jewish Committee, 1987.
Collins, Larry, and Dominique Lapierre. *O Jerusalem.* New York: Simon and Schuster, 1972.
Conzen, Michael P., ed. *World Patterns of Modern Urban Change.* Chicago: University of Chicago Department of Geography, 1986.
Coulter, Philip B. *Political Voice: Citizen Demand for Urban Public Services.* Tuscaloosa: University of Alabama Press, 1988.
Crenshaw, Martha, ed. *Terrorism, Legitimacy, and Power: The Consequences of Political Violence.* Middletown, Conn.: Wesleyan University Press, 1983.
Crozier, Brian. *A Theory of Conflict.* London: Hamish Hamilton, 1974.
Dahl, Robert A. *Who Governs? Democracy and Power in an American City.* New Haven: Yale University Press, 1961.
Davidson, Robert. *The Courage to Doubt: Exploring An Old Testament Theme.* London: SCM Press, 1983.
Dery, David. *Data and Policy Change.* Boston: Kluwer Academic Publishers, 1990.
———. *Political Appointments in Israel.* Jerusalem: Israel Democracy Institute: 1993. Hebrew.
———. *Problem Definition in Policy Analysis.* Lawrence: University of Kansas Press, 1984.
DeSario, Jack, and Stuart Langton, eds. *Citizen Participation in Public Decision Making.* Westport, Conn.: Greenwood, 1987.
Dimont, Max I. *Jews, God and History.* New York: Signet Books, 1964.
Doig, Jameson W. "If I See a Murderous Fellow Sharpening a Knife Cleverly . . . The Wilsonian Dichotomy and the Public Authority Tradition." *Public Administration Review* 43, no. 4 (July/August 1983): 292–304.
Don-Yehiya, Eliezer. "Hanukkah and the Myth of the Maccabees in Zionist Ideology and In Israeli Society." *Jewish Journal of Sociology* 34, no. 1 (June 1992): 5–23.
Dresang, Dennis. "Public Sector Entrepreurialism." *Administrative Science Quarterly* 18 (March 1973): 76–85.
Drezon-Tepler, Marcia. *Interest Groups and Political Change in Israel.* Albany: State University of New York Press, 1990.
Dror, Yehezkel. *Policymaking under Adversity.* New Brunswick, N.J.: Transaction Books, 1986.
———. *Public Policymaking Reexamined* San Francisco: Chandler, 1968.
Edelman, Murray. *The Symbolic Uses of Politics.* Urbana: University of Illinois Press, 1964.

Eisenstadt, S. N. *Israeli Society*. New York: Basic Books, 1967.

Elazar, Daniel J. *From Autonomy to Shared Rule: Options for Judea, Samaria, and Gaza*. Jerusalem: Jerusalem Center for Public Affairs, 1983.

Elazar, Daniel, and Chaim Kalchheim, eds. *Local Government in Israel*. Lanham, Md.: University Press of America, 1988.

Farmer, William Reuben. *Maccabees, Zealots, and Josephus: An Inquiry into Jewish Nationalism in the Greco-Roman Period*. New York: Columbia University Press, 1956.

Feintuch, Yossi. *United States Policy on Jerusalem*. New York: Greenwood Press, 1987.

Field, Tiffany M., Philip M. McCabe, and Neil Schneiderman, eds. *Stress and Coping*. Hillsdale, N.J.: Lawrence Erlbaum Associates, 1985.

Folkman, Susan. "Personal Control and Stress and Coping Processes: A Theoretical Analysis." *Journal of Personality and Social Psychology* 46 (1984): 839–52.

Friedberg, Asher, Benjamin Geist, Nissim Mizrahi, and Ira Sharkansky, eds. *Accountability and State Audit: A Reader*. Jerusalem: State Comptroller, 1991.

Friedman, Richard Elliott. *Who Wrote the Bible?* New York: Harper & Row, 1987.

Friedman, Menachem. *The Haredi (Ultra-Orthodox) Society—Sources, Trends and Processes*. Jerusalem: The Jerusalem Institute for Israel Studies, 1991. Hebrew.

Friedmann, John, and Goetz Wolff. "World City Formation: An Agenda for Research and Action." *International Journal of Urban and Regional Research* 6, no. 3 (September 1982): 309–44.

Frye, Northrop. *The Great Code: The Bible and Literature*. San Diego: Harcourt Brace Jovanovich, 1983.

Geist, Benjamin, ed. *State Audit: Developments in Public Accountability*. London: Macmillan, 1981.

Geldenhuys, Dion. *Isolated States*. Johannesburg: Jonathan Ball, 1990.

Goldberg, Giora, Gad Barzilai, and Efraim Inbar. "The Impact of Intercommunal Conflict: The Intifada and Israeli Public Opinion." Jerusalem: Hebrew University Leonard Davis Institute, 1991.

Gooch, Brison D., ed. *The Origins of the Crimean War*. (Lexington, Mass: D.C. Heath, 1969.

Goodsell, Charles T. *The Social Meaning of Civic Space: Studying Political Authority through Architecture*. Lawrence: University Press of Kansas, 1988.

Gottdiener, M. *The Decline of Urban Politics: Political Theory and the Crisis of the Local State*. Newbury Park, Calif.: Sage Publications, 1987.

Gottdiener, M., ed. *Cities in Stress: A New Look at the Urban Crisis*. Newbury Park, Calif.: Sage Publications, 1986.

Gottmann, Jean, and Robert A. Harper, eds. *Since Megalopolis: The Urban*

Writings of Jean Gottmann. Baltimore: Johns Hopkins University Press, 1990.

Gradus, Y. "The Emergence of Regionalism in a Centralized System: The Case of Israel." *Environment and Planning D: Society and Space* 2 (1984): 87–100.

Grossman, David. *Present Absentees*. Tel Aviv: Kibbutz Meuchad, 1992. Hebrew.

Grossman, David. *The Yellow Wind*. Translated by Haim Watzman. London: J. Cape, 1988.

Gurr, Ted Robert, and Desmond S. King. *The State and the City*. Chicago: University of Chicago Press, 1987.

Halper, Jeff. *Between Redemption and Revival: The Jewish Yishuv of Jerusalem in the Nineteenth Century*. Boulder: Westview Press, 1991.

Halper, Jeffrey. "Ethnicity and Education: The Schooling of Afro-Asian Jewish Children in a Jerusalem Locality." Ph.D. dissertation in anthropology, University of Wisconsin-Milwaukee, 1977.

Halpern, Baruch. *The First Historians: The Hebrew Bible and History*. San Francisco: Harper & Row, 1988.

Harkabi, Yehoshafat. *The Bar Kokhba Syndrome: Risk and Realism in International Relations*. Translated by Max D. Ticktin. Edited by David Altshuler. Chappaqua, N.Y.: Rossel Books, 1983.

———. *Fateful Hour*. Translated by Lenn Schramm. New York: Harper & Row, 1988.

Harvey, David. *Social Justice and the City*. London: Edward Arnold, 1973.

Hasson, Shlomo. *Urban Social Movements in Jerusalem: The Protest of the Second Generation*. Albany: State University of New York Press, 1993.

Hayes, John H., and J. Maxwell Miller, eds. *Israelite and Judaean History*. London: SCM Press, 1977.

Herrmann, Siegfried. *A History of Israel in Old Testament Times*. London: SCM Press, 1975.

Herson, Lawrence J. R., and John M. Bolland. *The Urban Web: Politics, Policy, and Theory*. Chicago: Nelson-Hall, 1990.

Hiltermann, Joost R. "Settling for War: Soviet Immigration and Israel's Settlement Policy in East Jerusalem." *Journal of Palestine Studies* 20, no. 2 (Winter 1991): 71–85.

Hunt, James. *Hussein of Jordan: A Political Biography*. London: Macmillan, 1989.

Hunter, Robert F. *The Palestinian Uprising: A War by Other Means*, Berkeley and Los Angeles: University of California Press, 1993.

Huppert, Uri. *Back to the Ghetto: Zionism in Retreat*. Buffalo, N.Y.: Prometheus Books, 1988.

Islamic Council of Europe. *Jerusalem: The Key to World Peace*. London: Islamic Council of Europe, 1980.

Jeremias, Joachim. *Jerusalem in the Time of Jesus*. London: SCM Press, 1969.

Jerusalem Institute for Israel Studies. *Urban Geography in Jerusalem, 1967–1992.* Jerusalem: Jerusalem Institute for Israel Studies, 1992. Hebrew.

Johnson, Paul. *A History of the Jews.* New York: Harper, 1987.

———. *A History of Christianity.* New York: Atheneum, 1976.

Josephus. *The Jewish War.* New York: Penguin Books, 1970.

Judd, Dennis R. *The Politics of American Cities: Private Power and Public Policy.* Glenview, Ill.: Scott, Foresman and Company, 1988.

Kaplan, Morton A., ed. *Strategic Thinking and Its Moral Implications.* Chicago: University of Chicago Center for Policy Study, 1973.

Kenyon, Kathleen M. *Jerusalem: Excavating 3000 Years of History.* London: Thames and Hudson, 1967.

Khalidi, Walid. *From Haven to Conquest: Readings in Zionism and the Palestine Problem until 1948.* Beirut: Institute for Palestine Studies, 1971.

Kimhi, Israel, Shalom Reichman, and Joseph Schweid. "Arab Settlement in the Metropolitan Area of Jerusalem." Jerusalem: Jerusalem Institute for Israel Studies, 1986. Hebrew.

Kimmerling, Baruch, ed. *The Israeli State and Society: Boundaries and Frontiers.* Albany: State University of New York Press, 1989.

Kingdon, John W. *Agendas, Alternatives, and Public Policies.* Boston: Little, Brown, 1984.

Kirscht, John Patrick. *Dimensions of Authoritarianism: A Review of Research and Theory.* Lexington: University of Kentucky Press, 1967.

Kollek, Teddy, with Amos Kollek. *For Jerusalem: A Life.* New York: Random House, 1978.

Kraemer, Joel L., ed. *Jerusalem: Problems and Prospects.* New York: Praeger, 1980.

Kraetke, Stefan, and Fritz Schmoll. "The Local State and Social Restructuring." *International Journal of Urban and Regional Research* 15, no. 4 (December 1991): 542–52.

Kraft, Robert A., and George W. E. Nickelsburg, eds. *Early Judaism and Its Modern Interpreters.* Philadelphia: Fortress Press, 1986.

Kroyanker, David. *Jerusalem: Planning and Development 1982–1985: New Trends.* Jerusalem: Jerusalem Committee and Jerusalem Institute for Israeli Studies, 1985.

Layish, Aharon, ed. *The Arabs in Jerusalem: From the Late Ottoman Period to the Beginning of the 1990s—Religious, Social and Cultural Distinctiveness.* Jerusalem: Magnes Press, 1992. Hebrew.

Lazin, Frederick A. *Policy Implementation and Social Welfare: Israel and the United States.* New Brunswick, N.J.: Transaction Books, 1986.

Light, Ivan. *Cities in World Perspective.* New York: Macmillan, 1983.

Lindblom, Charles E. *The Policy-Making Process.* Englewood Cliffs, N.J.: Prentice-Hall, 1968.

Lindblom, Charles E., and David K. Cohen. *Usable Knowledge: Social Science and Social Problem Solving.* New Haven: Yale University Press, 1979.

Lineberry, Robert L., and Ira Sharkansky. *Urban Politics and Public Policy.* New York: Harper & Row, 1978.
Lipsky, Michael, *Street-Level Bureaucracy: Dilemmas of the Individual in Public Services.* New York: Russell Sage Foundation, 1980.
Logan, John R., and Todd Swanstrom, eds. *Beyond the City Limits: Urban Policy and Economic Restructuring in Comparative Perspective.* Philadelphia: Temple University Press, 1990.
Logan, John R., and Harvey L. Molotch. *Urban Fortunes: The Political Economy of Place.* Berkeley and Los Angeles: University of California Press, 1987.
Lukas, J. Anthony. *Common Ground: A Turbulent Decade in the Lives of Three American Families.* New York: Vintage Books, 1986.
Lustick, Ian. *Arabs in the Jewish State: Israel's Control of a National Minority.* Austin: University of Texas Press, 1980.
Luttwak, Edward N. *Strategy and Politics: Collected Essays.* New Brunswick, N.J.: Transaction Books, 1980.
Mallison, W. Thomas, and Sally V. Mallison. *The Palestine Problem in International Law and World Order.* Essex, England: Longman, 1986.
Markovitz, Sarah. "The Development of Modern Jerusalem: An Evaluation of Planning Decisions and the Effectiveness of the Planning Process." Undergraduate thesis, Princeton University School of Architecture and the Woodrow Wilson School for Public and International Affairs, 1982.
Marris, Peter. *Community Planning and Conceptions of Change.* London: Routledge and Kegan Paul, 1982.
Marris, Peter, and Anthony Somerset. *African Businessmen: A Study of Entrepreneurship and Development in Kenya.* London: Routledge & Kegan Paul, 1971.
Mazmanian, Daniel A., and Paul A. Sabatier. *Implementation and Public Policy.* Glenview, Ill.: Scott Foresman, 1983.
McIlwain, Charles H. *Constitutionalism, Ancient and Modern.* Ithaca, N.Y.: Cornell University Press, 1947.
Monkkonen, Eric H. *America Becomes Urban: The Development of U.S. Cities and Towns, 1780–1980.* Berkeley and Los Angeles: University of California Press, 1988.
Moos, Rudolf H., with Jeanne A. Schaefer, eds. *Coping with Life Crises: An Integrated Approach.* New York: Plenum Press, 1986.
Morley, David, and Arie Shachar, eds. *Planning in Turbulence.* Jerusalem: Magnes Press, 1986.
Moughraba, Fouad, and Pat El-Nazer. "What Do Palestinian Americans Think? Results of a Public Opinion Survey." *Journal of Palestine Studies* 18, no. 4 (Summer 1989): 91–101.
Near, Henry, ed. *The Seventh Day.* London: Andre Deutsch, 1970.
Neusner, Jacob. *A History of the Jews in Babylonia,* vol. 1. Leiden: E.J. Brill, 1969.

———. *From Politics to Piety: The Emergence of Pharisaic Judaism.* Englewood Cliffs, N.J.: Prentice-Hall, 1973.

O'Dowd, Liam. "Policy, Politics and Urban Restructuring." *International Journal of Urban and Regional Research* 12, no. 4 (December 1988): 645–50.

Oesterreicher, Msgr. John M., and Anne Sinai, eds. *Jerusalem.* New York: John Day Company, 1974.

Oppenheim, A. Leo. *Ancient Mesopotamia: Portrait of a Dead Civilization.* Chicago: University of Chicago Press, 1977.

Orlinsky, Harry. *Ancient Israel.* Ithaca, N.Y.: Cornell University Press, 1954.

Pennock, J. Ronald, and John W. Chapman, eds. *Constitutionalism.* New York: New York University Press, 1977.

Permutter, Amos. *Modern Authoritarianism: A Comparative Institutional Analysis.* New Haven: Yale University Press, 1981.

Peters, F. E. *Jerusalem: The Holy City in the Eyes of Chroniclers, Visitors, Pilgrims, and Prophets from the Days of Abraham to the Beginnings of Modern Times.* Princeton: Princeton University Press, 1985.

Peterson, Paul E. *City Limits.* Chicago: University of Chicago Press, 1981.

Piller, Charles. *The Fail-Safe Society: Community Defiance and the End of Technological Optimism.* New York: Basic Books, 1991.

Plotkin, Sidney. *Keep Out: The Struggle for Land Use Control.* Berkeley and Los Angeles: University of California, 1987.

———. "Property, Policy and Politics: Towards a Theory of Urban Land-Use Conflict." *International Journal of Urban and Regional Research* 11, no. 3 (September 1987): 382–404.

Poll, Solomon, and Ernest Krausz, eds. *On Ethnic and Religious Diversity in Israel.* Ramat Gan: Bar Ilan University Institute for the Study of Ethnic and Religious Groups, 1975.

Prittie, Terrence. *Whose Jerusalem?* London: Frederick Muller, 1981.

Quade, E. S., and Grace M. Carter. *Analysis for Public Decisions.* New York: North-Holland, 1989.

Rabinovich, Abraham. *Jerusalem on Earth: People Passions and Politics in the Holy City.* New York: Free Press, 1988.

Rapoport, Anatol. *Strategy and Conscience.* New York: Harper & Row, 1964.

Reuveni, Ya'acov. *Public Administration in Israel: The Government System in Israel and Its Development During the Years 1948–73.* Ramat Gan: Massada, 1974. Hebrew.

Rich, Norman. *Why the Crimean War? A Cautionary Tale.* Hanover, N.H.: University Press of New England, 1985.

Richard, Jean. *The Latin Kingdom of Jerusalem.* Translated by Janet Shirly. Amsterdam: North Holland Publishing, 1979.

Romann, Michael. "Inter-Relationship between the Jewish and Arab Sectors in Jerusalem." Jerusalem: Jerusalem Institute for Israel Studies, 1984. Hebrew.

Romann, Michael, and Alex Weingrod. *Living Together Separately: Arabs and*

Jews in Contemporary Jerusalem. Princeton: Princeton University Press, 1991.

Rosenberg, Joel. *King and Kin: Political Allegory in the Hebrew Bible.* Bloomington: Indiana University Press, 1986.

Russell, D. S. *The Jews from Alexander to Herod.* Oxford: Oxford University Press, 1967.

Said, Edward W. "Reflections on Twenty Years of Palestinian History." *Journal of Palestine Studies* 20, no. 4 (Summer 1991): 5–22.

Salamon, Nimrod. "Landmark Preservation in Jerusalem." Jerusalem Municipality: Town Planning Department, 1984.

Sandmel, Samuel. *Judaism and Christian Beginnings.* New York: Oxford University Press, 1978.

Sassen, Saskia. *The Global City: New York, London, Tokyo.* Princeton: Princeton University Press, 1991.

Savitzky, Joseph, and Tzvi Frank. "A Comparative Study of Ethnically-Mixed Cities: Socio-political Aspects, Public Policies and Programs." Typescript. Institute of Urban and Regional Studies, Hebrew University of Jerusalem, March 1976.

Schaefer, Karl R. "Jerusalem in the Ayyubid and Mamluk Eras." Ph.D. dissertation, Department of Near Eastern Languages and Literatures, New York University, 1985.

Schmelz, U. O. *Modern Jerusalem's Demographic Evolution.* Jerusalem: Hebrew University Institute of Contemporary Jewry, 1987.

Segal, Ronald. *Whose Jerusalem? The Conflicts of Israel.* London: Jonathan Cape, 1973.

Shalev, Michael. *Labour and the Political Economy in Israel.* New York: Oxford University Press, 1992.

Shama, Avraham, and Mark Iris. *Immigration Without Integration: Third World Jews in Israel.* Cambridge, Mass.: Schenkman Publishing, 1977.

Sharkansky, Ira. *Ancient and Modern Israel: An Exploration of Political Parallels.* Albany: State University of New York Press, 1991.

———. *The Political Economy of Israel.* New Brunswick, N.J.: Transaction Books, 1987.

———. *The Routines of Politics.* New York: Van Nostrand, 1970.

———. *What Makes Israel Tick? How Domestic Policy-Makers Cope with Constraints.* Chicago: Nelson Hall, 1985.

———. *Wither the State? Politics and Public Enterprise in Three Countries.* Chatham, N.J.: Chatham House, 1979.

Shlaim, Avi. *Collusion Across the Jordan: King Abdullah, The Zionist Movement, and the Partition of Palestine.* New York: Columbia University Press, 1988.

Silberman, Neil Asher. *Digging for God and Country: Exploration, Archeology, and the Secret Struggle for the Holy Land 1799–1917.* New York: Anchor Books, 1990.

Simon, Herbert. *Administrative Behavior.* New York: Free Press, 1976.

Skocpol, Theda. *States and Social Revolutions.* New York: Cambridge University Press, 1979.

Slonim, Shlomo. "The United States and the Status of Jerusalem, 1947–1984." *Israel Law Review* 19, no. 2 (Spring 1984): 179–252.

Smith, Michael Peter. *City, State, and Market: The Political Economy of Urban Society.* New York: Basil Blackwell, 1988.

Smith, Michael Peter, and Joe R. Feagin, eds. *The Capitalist City: Global Restructuring and Community Politics.* Oxford: Basil Blackwell, 1991.

Smith, Neil, and Peter Williams, eds. *Gentrification of the City.* Boston: Allen and Unwin, 1986.

Smooha, Sammy. *Arabs and Jews in Israel: Conflicting and Shared Attitudes in a Divided Society.* Boulder: Westview Press, 1989.

Storrs, Ronald. *Orientations.* London: Ivor Nicholson & Watson, 1939.

Stuart, Graham H. *The International City of Tangier.* Stanford: Stanford University Press, 1955.

Tcherikover, Victor. *Hellenistic Civilization and the Jews.* Translated by S. Applebaum. New York: Atheneum, 1959.

Teveth, Shabtai. *Moshe Dayan.* Translated by Leah and David Zinder. Boston: Houghton Mifflin, 1973.

Theissen, Gerd. *Sociology of Early Palestinian Christianity.* Philadelphia: Fortress Press, 1978.

Tsimhoni, Daphne. "Continuity and Change in Communal Autonomy: The Christian Communal Organizations in Jerusalem, 1948–1980." *Middle East Studies* 22 (July 1986): 398–417.

Tuchman, Barbara W. *The March of Folly: From Troy to Vietnam.* New York: Ballantine Books, 1984.

Twain, Mark. *The Innocents Abroad.* London, 1869.

Vos, Howard F. *Ezra, Nehemiah, and Esther.* Grand Rapids, Mich.: Zondervan Publishing House, 1987.

Walker, P. W. L. *Holy City, Holy Places? Christian Attitudes to Jerusalem and the Holy Land in the Fourth Century.* Oxford: Clarendon Press, 1990.

Walsh, Annmarie Hauck. *The Public's Business: The Politics and Practices of Government Corporations.* Cambridge, Mass.: MIT Press, 1978.

Walzer, Michael. *Exodus and Revolution.* New York: Basic Books, 1985.

Wasserstein, Bernard. *The British in Palestine: The Mandatory Government and the Arab-Jewish Conflict 1917–29.* Oxford: Basil Blackwell, 1991.

Welch, Susan, and Timothy Bledsoe. *Urban Reform and Its Consequences: A Study in Representation.* Chicago: University of Chicago Press, 1988.

Wildavsky, Aaron. *Speaking Truth to Power: The Art and Craft of Policy Analysis.* Boston: Little, Brown, 1979.

Wilkinson, John. *Jerusalem Pilgrims: Before the Crusades.* Jerusalem: Ariel Publishing House, 1977.

Wilson, William Julius. *The Truly Disadvantaged: The Inner City, the Underclass, and Public Policy.* Chicago: University of Chicago Press, 1987.

Wolfsfeld, Gadi. *The Politics of Provocation.* Albany: State University of New York Press, 1988.

Yaniv, Avner, ed. *National Security and Democracy in Israel.* Boulder: Lynne Rienner Publishers, 1993.

Yates, Douglas. *Neighborhood Democracy: The Politics and Impacts of Decentralization.* Lexington, Mass.: D. C. Heath, 1973.

———. *The Ungovernable City: The Politics of Urban Problems and Policy Making.* Cambridge: M.I.T. Press, 1977.

Yishai, Yael. *Interest Groups in Israel.* Tel Aviv: Am Oved Publishers, 1987. Hebrew.

———. "Israeli Annexation of East Jerusalem and the Golan Heights: Factors and Processes." *Middle East Studies* 21: (January 1985): 45–60.

Zemach, Mina. "Through Israeli Eyes: Attitudes Toward Judaism, American Jewry, Zionism and the Arab-Israeli Conflict." New York: Institute on American Jewish-Israeli Relations, American Jewish Committee, 1987.

Zureik, Elia. "Prospects of the Palestinians in Israel: I." *Journal of Palestine Studies* 22, no. 2 (Winter 1993): 90–109.

Index